MznLnx

Missing Links Exam Preps

Exam Prep for

Macroeconomics Theories and Policies

Froyen, 8th Edition

The MznLnx Exam Prep is your link from the texbook and lecture to your exams.
The MznLnx Exam Preps are unauthorized and comprehensive reviews of your textbooks.

All material provided by MznLnx and Rico Publications (c) 2010
Textbook publishers and textbook authors do not particpate in or contribute to these reviews.

MznLnx

Rico
Publications

Exam Prep for Macroeconomics Theories and Policies
8th Edition
Froyen

Publisher: Raymond Houge
Assistant Editor: Michael Rouger
Text and Cover Designer: Lisa Buckner
Marketing Manager: Sara Swagger
Project Manager, Editorial Production: Jerry Emerson
Art Director: Vernon Lowerui

Product Manager: Dave Mason
Editorial Assitant: Rachel Guzmanji
Pedagogy: Debra Long
Cover Image: Jim Reed/Getty Images
Text and Cover Printer: City Printing, Inc.
Compositor: Media Mix, Inc.

(c) 2010 Rico Publications
ALL RIGHTS RESERVED. No part of this work covered by the copyright may be reproduced or used in any form or by an means--graphic, electronic, or mechanical, including photocopying, recording, taping, Web distribution, information storage, and retrieval systems, or in any other manner--without the written permission of the publisher.

Printed in the United States
ISBN:

For more information about our products, contact us at:
Dave.Mason@RicoPublications.com

For permission to use material from this text or product, submit a request online to:
Dave.Mason@RicoPublications.com

Contents

CHAPTER 1
Introduction — 1

CHAPTER 2
Measurement of Macroeconomic Variables — 9

CHAPTER 3
Classical Macroeconomics (I): Equilibrium Output and Employment — 21

CHAPTER 4
Classical Macroeconomics (II): Money, Prices, and Interest — 32

CHAPTER 5
Long-Run Economic Growth: Origins of the Wealth of Nations — 43

CHAPTER 6
The Keynesian System (I): The Role of Aggregate Demand — 49

CHAPTER 7
The Keynesian System (II): Money, Interest, and Income — 60

CHAPTER 8
The Keynesian System (III): Policy Effects in the IS-LM Model — 68

CHAPTER 9
The Keynesian System (IV): Aggregate Supply and Demand — 73

CHAPTER 10
The Monetarist Counterrevolution — 83

CHAPTER 11
Output, Inflation, and Unemployment: Alternative Views — 91

CHAPTER 12
New Classical Economics — 97

CHAPTER 13
Real Business Cycles and New Keynesian Economics — 103

CHAPTER 14
Macroeconomic Models: A Summary — 109

CHAPTER 15
Exchange Rates and the International Monetary System — 115

CHAPTER 16
Monetary and Fiscal Policy in the Open Economy — 127

CHAPTER 17
The Money Supply and the Banking System — 133

CHAPTER 18
Monetary Policy — 143

CHAPTER 19
Fiscal Stabilization Policy — 151

CHAPTER 20
Policies to Promote Economic Growth — 160

Contents (Cont.)

CHAPTER 21
   Consumption and Investment   169

CHAPTER 22
   Money Demand   178

ANSWER KEY   184

TO THE STUDENT

COMPREHENSIVE

The *MznLnx* Exam Prep series is designed to help you pass your exams. Editors at MznLnx review your textbooks and then prepare these practice exams to help you master the textbook material. Unlike study guides, workbooks, and practice tests provided by the texbook publisher and textbook authors, *MznLnx* gives you **all** of the material in each chapter in exam form, not just samples, so you can be sure to nail your exam.

MECHANICAL

The MznLnx Exam Prep series creates exams that will help you learn the subject matter as well as test you on your understanding. Each question is designed to help you master the concept. Just working through the exams, you gain an understanding of the subject--its a simple mechanical process that produces success.

INTEGRATED STUDY GUIDE AND REVIEW

MznLnx is not just a set of exams designed to test you, its also a comprehensive review of the subject content. Each exam question is also a review of the concept, making sure that you will get the answer correct without having to go to other sources of material. You learn as you go! Its the easiest way to pass an exam.

HUMOR

Studying can be tedious and dry. MznLnx's instructional design includes moderate humor within the exam questions on occassion, to break the tedium and revitalize the brain

Chapter 1. Introduction

1. In economics, _____ is a rise in the general level of prices of goods and services in an economy over a period of time. When the general price level rises, each unit of currency buys fewer goods and services; consequently, _____ is also a decline in the real value of money--a loss of purchasing power in the medium of exchange which is also the monetary unit of account in the economy. A chief measure of general price-level _____ is the general _____ rate, which is the percentage change in a general price index (normally the Consumer Price Index) over time.
    a. Energy economics
    b. Opportunity cost
    c. Economic
    d. Inflation

2. _____ is the price at which an asset would trade in a competitive Walrasian auction setting. _____ is often used interchangeably with open _____, fair value or fair _____, although these terms have distinct definitions in different standards, and may differ in some circumstances.

    International Valuation Standards defines _____ as 'the estimated amount for which a property should exchange on the date of valuation between a willing buyer and a willing seller in an arm's-length transaction after proper marketing wherein the parties had each acted knowledgeably, prudently, and without compulsion.'

    _____ is a concept distinct from market price, which is 'the price at which one can transact', while _____ is 'the true underlying value' according to theoretical standards.

    a. Market value
    b. Personal financial management
    c. Netting
    d. Secured loan

3. _____ refers to the economic policies promoted by United States President Ronald Reagan during the 1980s. The four pillars of Reagan's economic policy were to:

    1. reduce the growth of government spending,
    2. reduce income and capital gains marginal tax rates,
    3. reduce government regulation of the economy,
    4. control the money supply to reduce inflation.

    In attempting to cut back on domestic spending while lowering taxes, Reagan's approach was a departure from his immediate predecessors.

    Reagan became president during a period of high inflation and unemployment (commonly referred to as stagflation), which had largely abated by the time he left office eight years later.

    Prior to the Reagan Administration was a roughly ten year period of economic stagnation and inflation, known as stagflation.

    a. Social savings
    b. Reaganomics
    c. Happiness economics
    d. Business sector

4. In finance, the _____s between two currencies specifies how much one currency is worth in terms of the other. It is the value of a foreign natione;s currency in terms of the home natione;s currency. For example an _____ of 102 Japanese yen to the United States dollar means that JPY 102 is worth the same as USD 1.

a. Exchange rate
b. Interbank market
c. ACCRA Cost of Living Index
d. ACEA agreement

5. _____ is a branch of economics that deals with the performance, structure, and behavior of a national or regional economy as a whole. Along with microeconomics, _____ is one of the two most general fields in economics. It is the study of the behavior and decision-making of entire economies.
   a. New Trade Theory
   b. Tobit model
   c. Nominal value
   d. Macroeconomics

6. _____ is the a method of technical and economic research of the systems for purpose to optimize a parity between system's consumer functions or properties and expenses to achieve those functions or properties.

This methodology for continuous perfection of production, industrial technologies, organizational structures was developed by Juryj Sobolev in 1948 at the 'Perm telephone factory'

- 1948 Juryj Sobolev - the first success in application of a method analysis at the 'Perm telephone factory' .
- 1949 - the first application for the invention as result of use of the new method.

Today in economically developed countries practically each enterprise or the company use methodology of the kind of functional-cost analysis as a practice of the quality management, most full satisfying to principles of standards of series ISO 9000.

- Interest of consumer not in products itself, but the advantage which it will receive from its usage.
- The consumer aspires to reduce his expenses
- Functions needed by consumer can be executed in the various ways, and, hence, with various efficiency and expenses. Among possible alternatives of realization of functions exist such in which the parity of quality and the price is the optimal for the consumer.

The goal of _____ is achievement of the highest consumer satisfaction of production at simultaneous decrease in all kinds of industrial expenses Classical _____ has three English synonyms - Value Engineering, Value Management, Value Analysis.

   a. Willingness to pay
   b. Staple financing
   c. Monopoly wage
   d. Function cost analysis

7. _____ is widely regarded as the first modern school of economic thought. It is the idea that free markets can regulate themselves.Its major developers include Adam Smith, David Ricardo, Thomas Malthus and John Stuart Mill. Sometimes the definition of _____ is expanded to include William Petty, Johann Heinrich von Thünen.
   a. Marginalism
   b. Classical economics
   c. Schools of economic thought
   d. Tendency of the rate of profit to fall

8. The _____ or gross domestic income (GDI), a basic measure of an economy's economic performance, is the market value of all final goods and services produced within the borders of a nation in a year. _____ can be defined in three ways, all of which are conceptually identical. First, it is equal to the total expenditures for all final goods and services produced within the country in a stipulated period of time (usually a 365-day year.)

a. Gross domestic product
c. Market structure
b. Countercyclical
d. Monopolistic competition

9. _____ and Keynesian Theory) is a macroeconomic theory based on the ideas of 20th-century British economist John Maynard Keynes. _____ argues that private sector decisions sometimes lead to inefficient macroeconomic outcomes and therefore advocates active policy responses by the public sector, including monetary policy actions by the central bank and fiscal policy actions by the government to stabilize output over the business cycle.

The theories forming the basis of _____ were first presented in The General Theory of Employment, Interest and Money, published in 1936.

a. Rational choice theory
c. Deflation
b. Market failure
d. Keynesian economics

10. _____ is the view within monetary economics that variation in the money supply has major influences on national output in the short run and the price level over longer periods and that objectives of monetary policy are best met by targeting the growth rate of the money supply.

_____ today is mainly associated with the work of Milton Friedman, who was among the generation of economists to accept Keynesian economics and then criticize it on his own terms. Friedman and Anna Schwartz wrote an influential book, Monetary History of the United States 1867-1960, and argued that 'inflation is always and everywhere a monetary phenomenon.' Friedman advocated a central bank policy aimed at keeping the supply and demand for money at equilibrium, as measured by growth in productivity and demand.

a. Complexity economics
c. Historical school of economics
b. Monetarism
d. Marginal revenue productivity theory of wages

11. _____ is a school of contemporary macroeconomics that strives to provide microeconomic foundations for Keynesian economics. It developed partly as a response to criticisms of Keynesian macroeconomics by adherents of New Classical macroeconomics.

a. Keynesian theory
c. Mainstream economics
b. Law of demand
d. New Keynesian economics

12. _____ Theory (or _____ Theory) is a class of macroeconomic models in which business cycle fluctuations to a large extent can be accounted for by real (in contrast to nominal) shocks. (The four primary economic fluctuations are secular (trend), business cycle, seasonal, and random.) Unlike other leading theories of the business cycle, it sees recessions and periods of economic growth as the efficient response to exogenous changes in the real economic environment.

a. SIMIC
c. Balanced-growth equilibrium
b. Real business cycle
d. Monetary policy reaction function

13. _____ was a global military conflict which involved a majority of the world's nations, including all of the great powers, organized into two opposing military alliances: the Allies and the Axis. The war involved the mobilization of over 100 million military personnel, making it the most widespread war in history. In a state of 'total war', the major participants placed their entire economic, industrial, and scientific capabilities at the service of the war effort, erasing the distinction between civilian and military resources.

a. 1921 recession
b. World War II
c. 100-year flood
d. 130-30 fund

14. The term _____ refers to economy-wide fluctuations in production or economic activity over several months or years. These fluctuations occur around a long-term growth trend, and typically involve shifts over time between periods of relatively rapid economic growth (expansion or boom), and periods of relative stagnation or decline (contraction or recession.)

These fluctuations are often measured using the growth rate of real gross domestic product.

a. Nominal value
b. Business cycle
c. Consumer theory
d. Tobit model

15. _____s is the social science that studies the production, distribution, and consumption of goods and services. The term _____s comes from the Ancient Greek oá¼°κονομῐα from oá¼¶κος (oikos, 'house') + νĺŒμος (nomos, 'custom' or 'law'), hence 'rules of the house(hold)'. Current _____ models developed out of the broader field of political economy in the late 19th century, owing to a desire to use an empirical approach more akin to the physical sciences.

a. Energy economics
b. Opportunity cost
c. Inflation
d. Economic

16. An _____, in economics, is the amount by which the real Gross domestic product exceeds potential GDP. The real GDP is also known as GDP 'adjusted for inflation', 'constant prices' GDP or 'constant dollar' GDP, because it measures the aggregate output in a country's income accounts in a given year, expressed in base-year prices. On the other hand, the potential GDP is the quantity of real GDP when a country's economy is at full-employment.

a. ACCRA Cost of Living Index
b. ACEA agreement
c. AD-IA Model
d. Inflationary gap

17. _____ is a broad label that refers to any individuals or households that use goods and services generated within the economy. The concept of a _____ is used in different contexts, so that the usage and significance of the term may vary.

Typically when business people and economists talk of _____s they are talking about person as _____, an aggregated commodity item with little individuality other than that expressed in the buy/not-buy decision.

a. 130-30 fund
b. 1921 recession
c. 100-year flood
d. Consumer

18. A _____ is a measure of the average price of consumer goods and services purchased by households. A _____ measures a price change for a constant market basket of goods and services from one period to the next within the same area (city, region, or nation.) It is a price index determined by measuring the price of a standard group of goods meant to represent the typical market basket of a typical urban consumer.

a. Lipstick index
b. CPI
c. Consumer price index
d. Cost-of-living index

19. _____ is a decrease in the rate of inflation. This phase of the business cycle, in which retailers can no longer pass on higher prices to their customers, often occurs during a recession. In contrast, deflation occurs when prices are actually dropping.
- a. Reflation
- b. Stealth inflation
- c. Mundell-Tobin effect
- d. Disinflation

20. _____ in economics and business is the result of an exchange and from that trade we assign a numerical monetary value to a good, service or asset. If Alice trades Bob 4 apples for an orange, the _____ of an orange is 4 apples. Inversely, the _____ of an apple is 1/4 oranges.
- a. Price war
- b. Price
- c. Premium pricing
- d. Price book

21. A _____ is a normalized average (typically a weighted average) of prices for a given class of goods or services in a given region, during a given interval of time. It is a statistic designed to help to compare how these prices, taken as a whole, differ between time periods or geographical locations.

Price indices have several potential uses.

- a. Product sabotage
- b. Price index
- c. Two-part tariff
- d. Transactional Net Margin Method

22. In economics, the _____ is a historical inverse relation between the rate of unemployment and the rate of inflation in an economy. Stated simply, the lower the unemployment in an economy, the higher the rate of increase in nominal wages in the economy. Rate of Change of Wages against Unemployment, United Kingdom 1913-1948 from Phillips (1958)

William Phillips, a New Zealand born economist, wrote a paper in 1958 titled The Relationship between Unemployment and the Rate of Change of Money Wages in the United Kingdom 1861-1957, which was published in the quarterly journal Economica.

- a. Phillips curve
- b. Cost curve
- c. Lorenz curve
- d. Demand curve

23. A _____ occurs when an entity spends more money than it takes in. The opposite of a _____ is a budget surplus. Debt is essentially an accumulated flow of deficits.
- a. Funding body
- b. Lump-sum tax
- c. Public Financial Management
- d. Budget Deficit

24. The balance of trade (or net exports, sometimes symbolized as NX) is the difference between the monetary value of exports and imports in an economy over a certain period of time. It is the relationship between a nation's imports and exports. A favorable balance of trade is known as a trade surplus and consists of exporting more than is imported; an unfavorable balance of trade is known as a _____ or, informally, a trade gap.
- a. Demographics of India
- b. Computational economic
- c. Trade deficit
- d. Complementary asset

Chapter 1. Introduction

25. _____ or government expenditure is classified by economists into three main types. Government purchases of goods and services for current use are classed as government consumption. Government purchases of goods and services intended to create future benefits, such as infrastructure investment or research spending, are classed as government investment.
   a. 1921 recession
   b. 100-year flood
   c. 130-30 fund
   d. Government spending

26. In economics, a _____ is a general slowdown in economic activity over a sustained period of time, or a business cycle contraction. During _____s, many macroeconomic indicators vary in a similar way. Production as measured by Gross Domestic Product (GDP), employment, investment spending, capacity utilization, household incomes and business profits all fall during _____s.
   a. Monetary economics
   b. Leading indicators
   c. Recession
   d. Treasury View

27. _____ is a school of macroeconomic thought that argues that economic growth can be most effectively created using incentives for people to produce (supply) goods and services, such as adjusting income tax and capital gains tax rates, and by allowing greater flexibility by reducing regulation. Consumers will then benefit from a greater supply of goods and services at lower prices.

The term _____ was coined by journalist Jude Wanniski in 1975, and popularized the ideas of economists Robert Mundell and Arthur Laffer.

   a. Commodity trading advisors
   b. Clap note
   c. Fiscal stimulus plans
   d. Supply-side economics

28. In economics, _____ is the total demand for final goods and services in the economy (Y) at a given time and price level. It is the amount of goods and services in the economy that will be purchased at all possible price levels. This is the demand for the gross domestic product of a country when inventory levels are static.
   a. Aggregate supply
   b. Aggregation problem
   c. Aggregate expenditure
   d. Aggregate demand

29. In economics, the _____ measures the payments that flow between any individual country and all other countries. It is used to summarize all international economic transactions for that country during a specific time period, usually a year. The _____ is determined by the country's exports and imports of goods, services, and financial capital, as well as financial transfers.
   a. Gross domestic product per barrel
   b. Gross world product
   c. Skyscraper Index
   d. Balance of payments

Chapter 1. Introduction

30. Economics:

    - _____, the desire to own something and the ability to pay for it
    - _____ curve, a graphic representation of a _____ schedule
    - _____ deposit, the money in checking accounts
    - _____ pull theory, the theory that inflation occurs when _____ for goods and services exceeds existing supplies
    - _____ schedule, a table that lists the quantity of a good a person will buy it each different price
    - _____ side economics, the school of economics at believes government spending and tax cuts open economy by raising _____

    a. Demand
    b. Production
    c. McKesson ' Robbins scandal
    d. Variability

31. A _____ is the transfer of wealth from one party (such as a person or company) to another. A _____ is usually made in exchange for the provision of goods, services or both, or to fulfill a legal obligation.

    The simplest and oldest form of _____ is barter, the exchange of one good or service for another.

    a. Going concern
    b. Social gravity
    c. Soft count
    d. Payment

32. _____ is a common concept in economics, and gives rise to derived concepts such as consumer debt. Generally _____ is defined by opposition to production. But the precise definition can vary because different schools of economists define production quite differently.

    a. Foreclosure data providers
    b. Consumption
    c. Federal Reserve Bank Notes
    d. Cash or share options

33. To _____ is to impose a financial charge or other levy upon a taxpayer by a state or the functional equivalent of a state.

    _____es are also imposed by many subnational entities. _____es consist of direct _____ or indirect _____, and may be paid in money or as its labour equivalent (often but not always unpaid.)

    a. 1921 recession
    b. 100-year flood
    c. Tax
    d. 130-30 fund

34. A _____ is an object whose consumption increases the utility of the consumer, for which the quantity demanded exceeds the quantity supplied at zero price. _____s are usually modeled as having diminishing marginal utility. The first individual purchase has high utility; the second has less.

    a. Composite good
    b. Merit good
    c. Pie method
    d. Good

35. In economics, economic output is divided into physical goods and intangible services. Consumption of _____ is assumed to produce utility. It is often used when referring to a _____ Tax.

a. Manufactured goods
b. Goods and services
c. Private good
d. Composite good

36. _____ is the increase in the amount of the goods and services produced by an economy over time. It is conventionally measured as the percent rate of increase in real gross domestic product, or real GDP. Growth is usually calculated in real terms, i.e. inflation-adjusted terms, in order to net out the effect of inflation on the price of the goods and services produced.
   a. ACEA agreement
   b. AD-IA Model
   c. ACCRA Cost of Living Index
   d. Economic growth

37. The _____ is the official currency of 16 of the 27 member states of the European Union (EU.) The states, known collectively as the Eurozone, are Austria, Belgium, Cyprus, Finland, France, Germany, Greece, Ireland, Italy, Luxembourg, Malta, the Netherlands, Portugal, Slovakia, Slovenia, and Spain. The currency is also used in a further five European countries, with and without formal agreements and is consequently used daily by some 327 million Europeans.
   a. Import and Export Price Indices
   b. Euro
   c. Equity capital market
   d. IRS Code 3401

38. In economics, _____ is the total amount of money available in an economy at a particular point in time. There are several ways to define 'money', but standard measures usually include currency in circulation and demand deposits.

_____ data are recorded and published, usually by the government or the central bank of the country.

   a. Veil of money
   b. Neutrality of money
   c. Money supply
   d. Velocity of money

39. _____ is that which is owed; usually referencing assets owed, but the term can also cover moral obligations and other interactions not requiring money. In the case of assets, _____ is a means of using future purchasing power in the present before a summation has been earned. Some companies and corporations use _____ as a part of their overall corporate finance strategy.
   a. Collateral Management
   b. Debenture
   c. Hard money loan
   d. Debt

Chapter 2. Measurement of Macroeconomic Variables

1. The _____ or gross domestic income (GDI), a basic measure of an economy's economic performance, is the market value of all final goods and services produced within the borders of a nation in a year. _____ can be defined in three ways, all of which are conceptually identical. First, it is equal to the total expenditures for all final goods and services produced within the country in a stipulated period of time (usually a 365-day year.)
   a. Monopolistic competition
   b. Countercyclical
   c. Gross domestic product
   d. Market structure

2. A variety of measures of national income and output are used in economics to estimate total economic activity in a country or region, including gross domestic product (GDP), _____ , and net national income (NNI.)

   There are three main ways of calculating these numbers; the output approach, the income approach and the expenditure approach. In theory, the three must yield the same, because total expenditures on goods and services must equal the total income paid to the producers (GNI), and that must also equal the total value of the output of goods and services (_____.)

   a. Purchasing power parity
   b. Gross national product
   c. Household final consumption expenditure
   d. Gross world product

3. _____ and Keynesian Theory) is a macroeconomic theory based on the ideas of 20th-century British economist John Maynard Keynes. _____ argues that private sector decisions sometimes lead to inefficient macroeconomic outcomes and therefore advocates active policy responses by the public sector, including monetary policy actions by the central bank and fiscal policy actions by the government to stabilize output over the business cycle.

   The theories forming the basis of _____ were first presented in The General Theory of Employment, Interest and Money, published in 1936.

   a. Rational choice theory
   b. Market failure
   c. Deflation
   d. Keynesian economics

4. A variety of measures of _____ and output are used in economics to estimate total economic activity in a country or region, including gross domestic product (GDP), gross national product (GNP), and net _____

   There are three main ways of calculating these numbers; the output approach, the income approach and the expenditure approach. In theory, the three must yield the same, because total expenditures on goods and services must equal the total income paid to the producers (Gnational income), and that must also equal the total value of the output of goods and services (GNP.)

   a. GNI per capita
   b. Gross world product
   c. Volume index
   d. National income

5. In microeconomics, _____ is quite simply the conversion of inputs into outputs. It is an economic process that uses resources to create a good or service that is suitable for exchange. This can include manufacturing, storing, shipping, and packaging.
   a. Production
   b. Solved
   c. MET
   d. Red Guards

Chapter 2. Measurement of Macroeconomic Variables

6. Economics:

    - _____, the desire to own something and the ability to pay for it
    - _____ curve, a graphic representation of a _____ schedule
    - _____ deposit, the money in checking accounts
    - _____ pull theory, the theory that inflation occurs when _____ for goods and services exceeds existing supplies
    - _____ schedule, a table that lists the quantity of a good a person will buy it each different price
    - _____ side economics, the school of economics at believes government spending and tax cuts open economy by raising _____

    a. Production
    b. Variability
    c. Demand
    d. McKesson ' Robbins scandal

7. In Marxian economics, _____ originally referred to the means of production. Individuals, organizations and governments use _____ in the production of other goods or commodities. _____ include factories, machinery, tools, equipment, and various buildings which are used to produce other products for consumption.

    a. Wealth inequality in the United States
    b. Capital goods
    c. Capital deepening
    d. Capital intensive

8. _____ is a term used in accounting, economics and finance to spread the cost of an asset over the span of several years.

    In simple words we can say that _____ is the reduction in the value of an asset due to usage, passage of time, wear and tear, technological outdating or obsolescence, depletion, inadequacy, rot, rust, decay or other such factors.

    In accounting, _____ is a term used to describe any method of attributing the historical or purchase cost of an asset across its useful life, roughly corresponding to normal wear and tear.

    a. Salvage value
    b. Net income per employee
    c. Historical cost
    d. Depreciation

9. In economics _____s are goods that are ultimately consumed rather than used in the production of another good. For example, a car sold to a consumer is a _____; the components such as tires sold to the car manufacturer are not; they are intermediate goods used to make the _____.

    When used in measures of national income and output the term _____s only includes new goods.

    a. Substitute good
    b. Goods and services
    c. Luxury good
    d. Final good

10. _____ or producer goods are goods used as inputs in the production of other goods, such as partly finished goods. They are goods used in production of final goods. A firm may make then use _____, or make then sell, or buy then use them.

a. Income distribution
b. Inflation adjustment
c. Economic forecasting
d. Intermediate goods

11. _____ relates to the composition of GDP. What is produced in a certain country is naturally also sold, but some of the goods produced in a given year may not be sold the same year, but in later years. Conversely, some of the goods sold in a given year might have been produced in an earlier year.
   a. Investment decisions
   b. Inventory investment
   c. Obelisk International
   d. Investment theory

12. _____, 1st Baron Keynes was a renowned economist from Britain whose many ideas on economic and political theories as well as on many governments' monetary policies influenced America. He advocated a government that played an active role in the lives of people regarding business, economy, etc. In this role, the government would use fiscal measures to reduce the consequences of recessions, economic depressions and booms.
   a. John Maynard Keynes
   b. Adolph Fischer
   c. Adolf Hitler
   d. Adam Smith

13. _____ is an economic concept with commonplace familiarity. It is the price that a good or service is offered at, or will fetch, in the marketplace. It is of interest mainly in the study of microeconomics.
   a. Market anomaly
   b. Noisy market hypothesis
   c. Paper trading
   d. Market price

14. A _____ is an object whose consumption increases the utility of the consumer, for which the quantity demanded exceeds the quantity supplied at zero price. _____s are usually modeled as having diminishing marginal utility. The first individual purchase has high utility; the second has less.
   a. Pie method
   b. Composite good
   c. Merit good
   d. Good

15. In economics, economic output is divided into physical goods and intangible services. Consumption of _____ is assumed to produce utility. It is often used when referring to a _____ Tax.
   a. Goods and services
   b. Private good
   c. Manufactured goods
   d. Composite good

16. _____ in economics and business is the result of an exchange and from that trade we assign a numerical monetary value to a good, service or asset. If Alice trades Bob 4 apples for an orange, the _____ of an orange is 4 apples. Inversely, the _____ of an apple is 1/4 oranges.
   a. Price book
   b. Price war
   c. Premium pricing
   d. Price

17. _____ is a common concept in economics, and gives rise to derived concepts such as consumer debt. Generally _____ is defined by opposition to production. But the precise definition can vary because different schools of economists define production quite differently.
   a. Consumption
   b. Federal Reserve Bank Notes
   c. Foreclosure data providers
   d. Cash or share options

Chapter 2. Measurement of Macroeconomic Variables

18. An _____, in economics, is the amount by which the real Gross domestic product exceeds potential GDP. The real GDP is also known as GDP 'adjusted for inflation', 'constant prices' GDP or 'constant dollar' GDP, because it measures the aggregate output in a country's income accounts in a given year, expressed in base-year prices. On the other hand, the potential GDP is the quantity of real GDP when a country's economy is at full-employment.
   a. AD-IA Model
   b. ACEA agreement
   c. ACCRA Cost of Living Index
   d. Inflationary gap

19. _____ is widely regarded as the first modern school of economic thought. It is the idea that free markets can regulate themselves. Its major developers include Adam Smith, David Ricardo, Thomas Malthus and John Stuart Mill. Sometimes the definition of _____ is expanded to include William Petty, Johann Heinrich von Thünen.
   a. Tendency of the rate of profit to fall
   b. Schools of economic thought
   c. Classical economics
   d. Marginalism

20. _____s is the social science that studies the production, distribution, and consumption of goods and services. The term _____s comes from the Ancient Greek oá¼°κονομῖα from oá¼¶κος (oikos, 'house') + νῖŒμος (nomos, 'custom' or 'law'), hence 'rules of the house(hold)'. Current _____ models developed out of the broader field of political economy in the late 19th century, owing to a desire to use an empirical approach more akin to the physical sciences.
   a. Economic
   b. Energy economics
   c. Inflation
   d. Opportunity cost

21. In economics, an _____ is any good or commodity, transported from one country to another country in a legitimate fashion, typically for use in trade. _____ goods or services are provided to foreign consumers by domestic producers. _____ is an important part of international trade.
   a. ACCRA Cost of Living Index
   b. AD-IA Model
   c. ACEA agreement
   d. Export

22. _____ refers to a business or organization attempting to acquire goods or services to accomplish the goals of the enterprise. Though there are several organizations that attempt to set standards in the _____ process, processes can vary greatly between organizations. Typically the word '_____' is not used interchangeably with the word 'procurement', since procurement typically includes Expediting, Supplier Quality, and Traffic and Logistics (T'L) in addition to _____.
   a. Free port
   b. 100-year flood
   c. 130-30 fund
   d. Purchasing

23. _____ refers to internal and external organizing and correcting factors that provide order to market and other types of societal institutions and organizations - economic, political, social and cultural - so that they may function efficiently and effectively as well as repair their failures.

The expression _____ is increasingly found in the title, abstract and text of articles, chapters and papers in the business, management, organization, strategy, social-issues, political-science and sociology literatures. The ABI/Inform Global source located 1748 such uses of both expressions in October 2008, compared with 31 in 1991 and 247 in 2002.

   a. Total revenue
   b. Private Benefits of Control
   c. Positive statement
   d. Nonmarket

Chapter 2. Measurement of Macroeconomic Variables

24. The _____ or black market is a market where all commerce is conducted without regard to taxation, law or regulations of trade. The term is also often known as the underdog, shadow economy, black economy, parallel economy or phantom trades.

In modern societies the _____ covers a vast array of activities.

 a. Autarky
 b. Information economy
 c. Information markets
 d. Underground economy

25. _____ is the total market value of all final goods and services produced by citizens of an economy during a given period of time (gross national product or GNP) minus depreciation. The _____ can be similarly applied at a country's domestic output level. The net domestic product (NDP) is the equivalent application of _____ within macroeconomics, and NDP is equal to gross domestic product (GDP) minus depreciation: NDP = GDP - depreciation.
 a. Gross private domestic investment
 b. Current account
 c. Compensation of employees
 d. Net national product

26. Total _____ is defined by the United States' Bureau of Economic Analysis as

income received by persons from all sources. It includes income received from participation in production as well as from government and business transfer payments. It is the sum of compensation of employees (received), supplements to wages and salaries, proprietors' income with inventory valuation adjustment (IVA) and capital consumption adjustment (CCAdj), rental income of persons with CCAdj, _____ receipts on assets, and personal current transfer receipts, less contributions for government social insurance.

 a. Personal income
 b. Bidding
 c. Greater fool theory
 d. Dividend Discount Model

27. A _____ product is a product designed for cheapness and short-term convenience rather than medium to long-term durability, with most products only intended for single use. The term is also sometimes used for products that may last several months (ex. _____ air filters) to distinguish from similar products that last indefinitely (ex.
 a. 1921 recession
 b. 130-30 fund
 c. 100-year flood
 d. Disposable

28. _____ is gross income minus income tax on that income.

Discretionary income is income after subtracting taxes and normal expenses (such as rent or mortgage, utilities, insurance, medical, transportation, property maintenance, child support, inflation, food and sundries, 'c.) to maintain a certain standard of living.

 a. Disposable personal income
 b. Taxation as theft
 c. Disposable income
 d. Stamp Act

29. _____ is a fee paid on borrowed assets. It is the price paid for the use of borrowed money , or, money earned by deposited funds . Assets that are sometimes lent with _____ include money, shares, consumer goods through hire purchase, major assets such as aircraft, and even entire factories in finance lease arrangements.

Chapter 2. Measurement of Macroeconomic Variables

a. Insolvency
c. Internal debt
b. Interest
d. Asset protection

30. The _____ is a theory of consumption that was developed by the American economist Milton Friedman. In its simplest form, the hypothesis states that the choices made by consumers regarding their consumption patterns are determined not by current income but by their longer-term income expectations. The key conclusion of this theory is that transitory, short-term changes in income have little effect on consumer spending behavior.
   a. Natural rate of unemployment
   c. Permanent income hypothesis
   b. Washington Consensus
   d. Balanced-growth equilibrium

31. In economics, a _____ is a redistribution of income in the market system. These payments are considered to be nonexhaustive because they do not directly absorb resources or create output. Examples of certain _____s include welfare (financial aid), social security, and government subsidies for certain businesses (firms.)
   a. 100-year flood
   c. Transfer payment
   b. 130-30 fund
   d. 1921 recession

32. In finance, a _____ is a debt security, in which the authorized issuer owes the holders a debt and, depending on the terms of the _____, is obliged to pay interest (the coupon) and/or to repay the principal at a later date, termed maturity. A _____ is a formal contract to repay borrowed money with interest at fixed intervals.

Thus a _____ is like a loan: the issuer is the borrower (debtor), the holder is the lender (creditor), and the coupon is the interest.

   a. Callable
   c. Zero-coupon
   b. Prize Bond
   d. Bond

33. In economics, the term _____ of income or _____ refers to a simple economic model which describes the reciprocal circulation of income between producers and consumers. In the _____ model, the inter-dependent entities of producer and consumer are referred to as 'firms' and 'households' respectively and provide each other with factors in order to facilitate the flow of income. Firms provide consumers with goods and services in exchange for consumer expenditure and 'factors of production' from households.
   a. 130-30 fund
   c. Circular flow
   b. 1921 recession
   d. 100-year flood

34. A _____ is the transfer of wealth from one party (such as a person or company) to another. A _____ is usually made in exchange for the provision of goods, services or both, or to fulfill a legal obligation.

The simplest and oldest form of _____ is barter, the exchange of one good or service for another.

   a. Social gravity
   c. Going concern
   b. Payment
   d. Soft count

35. To _____ is to impose a financial charge or other levy upon a taxpayer by a state or the functional equivalent of a state.

Chapter 2. Measurement of Macroeconomic Variables 15

_____es are also imposed by many subnational entities. _____es consist of direct _____ or indirect _____, and may be paid in money or as its labour equivalent (often but not always unpaid.)

a. 130-30 fund
b. 1921 recession
c. 100-year flood
d. Tax

36. To tax is to impose a financial charge or other levy upon a taxpayer by a state or the functional equivalent of a state.

_____ are also imposed by many subnational entities. _____ consist of direct tax or indirect tax, and may be paid in money or as its labour equivalent (often but not always unpaid.)

a. 100-year flood
b. 1921 recession
c. 130-30 fund
d. Taxes

37. The _____ was a worldwide economic downturn starting in most places in 1929 and ending at different times in the 1930s or early 1940s for different countries. It was the largest and most important economic depression in the 20th century, and is used in the 21st century as an example of how far the world's economy can fall. The _____ originated in the United States; historians most often use as a starting date the stock market crash on October 29, 1929, known as Black Tuesday.

a. British Empire Economic Conference
b. Wall Street Crash of 1929
c. Great Depression
d. Jarrow March

38. The term _____ has more than one meaning.

In the colloquial sense, an _____, or goods and services tax (GST)) is a tax collected by an intermediary (such as a retail store) from the person who bears the ultimate economic burden of the tax (such as the customer.) The intermediary later files a tax return and forwards the tax proceeds to government with the return.

a. Optimal tax
b. User charge
c. Indirect tax
d. Olivera-Tanzi effect

39. In statistics, _____ has two related meanings:

- the arithmetic _____
- the expected value of a random variable, which is also called the population _____.

It is sometimes stated that the '_____' _____s average. This is incorrect if '_____' is taken in the specific sense of 'arithmetic _____' as there are different types of averages: the _____, median, and mode. Other simple statistical analyses use measures of spread, such as range, interquartile range, or standard deviation. For a real-valued random variable X, the _____ is the expectation of X. Note that not every probability distribution has a defined _____ (or variance); see the Cauchy distribution for an example.

a. 130-30 fund
b. Mean
c. 1921 recession
d. 100-year flood

40. In statistics, a _____ is a value that allows data to be measured over time in terms of some base period usually through a price index in order to distinguish between changes in the money value of GNP which result from a change in prices and those which result from a change in physical output. It is the measure of the price level for some quantity. A _____ serves as a price index in which the effects of inflation are nulled.

a. Contingent employment
b. Blanket order
c. Market microstructure
d. Deflator

41. A _____ is a normalized average (typically a weighted average) of prices for a given class of goods or services in a given region, during a given interval of time. It is a statistic designed to help to compare how these prices, taken as a whole, differ between time periods or geographical locations.

Price indices have several potential uses.

a. Price index
b. Transactional Net Margin Method
c. Two-part tariff
d. Product sabotage

42. A _____ is a hypothetical measure of overall prices for some set of goods and services, in a given region during a given interval, normalized relative to some base set. Typically, a _____ is approximated with a price index.

The classical dichotomy is the assumption that there is a relatively clean distinction between overall increases or decreases in prices and underlying, e;reale; economic variables.

a. Price level
b. Discretionary spending
c. Discouraged worker
d. Price elasticity of supply

43. A consumer price index (_____) is a measure of the average price of consumer goods and services purchased by households. A consumer price index measures a price change for a constant market basket of goods and services from one period to the next within the same area (city, region, or nation.) It is a price index determined by measuring the price of a standard group of goods meant to represent the typical market basket of a typical urban consumer.

a. Cost-of-living index
b. Hedonic price index
c. CPI
d. Lipstick index

44. _____ is a broad label that refers to any individuals or households that use goods and services generated within the economy. The concept of a _____ is used in different contexts, so that the usage and significance of the term may vary.

Typically when business people and economists talk of _____s they are talking about person as _____, an aggregated commodity item with little individuality other than that expressed in the buy/not-buy decision.

a. 1921 recession
b. Consumer
c. 100-year flood
d. 130-30 fund

Chapter 2. Measurement of Macroeconomic Variables

45. A _____ is a measure of the average price of consumer goods and services purchased by households. A _____ measures a price change for a constant market basket of goods and services from one period to the next within the same area (city, region, or nation.) It is a price index determined by measuring the price of a standard group of goods meant to represent the typical market basket of a typical urban consumer.
   a. Consumer price index
   b. Cost-of-living index
   c. CPI
   d. Lipstick index

46. A _____ measures average changes in prices received by domestic producers for their output. It is one of several price indices

Its importance is being undermined by the steady decline in manufactured goods as a share of spending.

A number of countries that now report a _____ previously reported a Wholesale Price Index.

   a. Producer price index
   b. Visible balance
   c. Hemline index
   d. Gross national product

47. In economics, _____ is inflation that is very high or 'out of control', a condition in which prices increase rapidly as a currency loses its value. Definitions used by the media vary from a cumulative inflation rate over three years approaching 100% to 'inflation exceeding 50% a month.' In informal usage the term is often applied to much lower rates. As a rule of thumb, normal inflation is reported per year, but _____ is often reported for much shorter intervals, often per month.
   a. 100-year flood
   b. Hyperinflation
   c. 1921 recession
   d. 130-30 fund

48. The _____ is an expected return that the provider of capital plans to earn on their investment.

Capital (money) used for funding a business should earn returns for the capital providers who risk their capital. For an investment to be worthwhile, the expected return on capital must be greater than the _____.

   a. Modigliani-Miller theorem
   b. Capital intensive
   c. Capital expenditure
   d. Cost of capital

49. The _____ is a group of three respected economists who advise the President of the United States on economic policy. It is a part of the Executive Office of the President of the United States, and provides much of the economic policy of the White House. The council prepares the annual Economic Report of the President.
   a. Federal Reserve Bank Notes
   b. Hybrid renewable energy systems
   c. Constrained Pareto optimality
   d. Council of Economic Advisers

50. In economics, _____ refers to the highest level of real Gross Domestic Product output that can be sustained over the long term. The existence of a limit is due to natural and institutional constraints. If actual GDP rises and stays above _____, then (in the absence of wage and price controls) inflation tends to increase as demand exceeds supply.
   a. Monetary policy reaction function
   b. Monetary conditions index
   c. Potential output
   d. Fundamental psychological law

Chapter 2. Measurement of Macroeconomic Variables

51. In economics, the concept of the _____ refers to the decision-making time frame of a firm in which at least one factor of production is fixed. Costs which are fixed in the _____ have no impact on a firms decisions. For example a firm can raise output by increasing the amount of labour through overtime.
   a. Hicks-neutral technical change
   b. Product Pipeline
   c. Short-run
   d. Productivity model

52. _____ is a term used to described a tendency or preference towards a particular perspective, ideology or result, especially when the tendency interferes with the ability to be impartial, unprejudiced, or objective. The term _____ed is used to describe an action, judgment, or other outcome influenced by a prejudged perspective. It is also used to refer to a person or body of people whose actions or judgments exhibit _____.
   a. 1921 recession
   b. 100-year flood
   c. Bias
   d. 130-30 fund

53. The _____, a unit of the United States Department of Labor, is the principal fact-finding agency for the U.S. government in the broad field of labor economics and statistics. The BLS is an independent national statistical agency that collects, processes, analyzes, and disseminates essential statistical data to the American public, the U.S. Congress, other Federal agencies, State and local governments, business, and labor representatives. The BLS also serves as a statistical resource to the Department of Labor.
   a. Gross national product
   b. Bureau of Labor Statistics
   c. Gross Regional Product
   d. Gross world product

54. The term _____ or commodity bundle refers to a fixed list of items used specifically to track the progress of inflation in an economy or specific market.

The most common type of _____ is the basket of consumer goods, used to define the Consumer Price Index (CPI.) Other types of baskets are used to define

- Producer Price Index (PPI), previously known as Wholesale Price Index (WPI)
- various commodity price indices

The term _____ analysis in the retail business refers to research that provides the retailer with information to understand the purchase behaviour of a buyer. This information will enable the retailer to understand the buyer's needs and rewrite the store's layout accordingly, develop cross-promotional programs, or even capture new buyers (much like the cross-selling concept.)

   a. Market basket
   b. Cost-weighted activity index
   c. Robin Hood index
   d. Category Development Index

55. _____ describes a bias in gay economics index numbers arising from tendency to purchase inexpensive substitutes for expensive items when prices change.

_____ occurs when two or more items experience a change of price relative to each other. Consumers will consume more of the now comparatively inexpensive good and less of the now relatively more expensive good.

Chapter 2. Measurement of Macroeconomic Variables

a. Market basket
b. Constant dollars
c. State of World Liberty Index
d. Substitution bias

56. In economics, _____ is the total supply of goods and services produced by a national economy during a specific time period. It is the total amount of goods and services in the economy available at all possible price levels.
 a. Aggregation problem
 b. Aggregate demand
 c. Aggregate expenditure
 d. Aggregate supply

57. In economics, a _____ is a general slowdown in economic activity over a sustained period of time, or a business cycle contraction. During _____s, many macroeconomic indicators vary in a similar way. Production as measured by Gross Domestic Product (GDP), employment, investment spending, capacity utilization, household incomes and business profits all fall during _____s.
 a. Treasury View
 b. Monetary economics
 c. Leading indicators
 d. Recession

58. _____ is the process by which the government, central bank (ii) availability of money, and (iii) cost of money or rate of interest, in order to attain a set of objectives oriented towards the growth and stability of the economy. Monetary theory provides insight into how to craft optimal _____.

_____ is referred to as either being an expansionary policy where an expansionary policy increases the total supply of money in the economy, and a contractionary policy decreases the total money supply.

 a. 130-30 fund
 b. 1921 recession
 c. 100-year flood
 d. Monetary policy

59. In finance, the _____s between two currencies specifies how much one currency is worth in terms of the other. It is the value of a foreign natione;s currency in terms of the home natione;s currency. For example an _____ of 102 Japanese yen to the United States dollar means that JPY 102 is worth the same as USD 1.
 a. ACEA agreement
 b. ACCRA Cost of Living Index
 c. Interbank market
 d. Exchange rate

60. The term _____ refers to economy-wide fluctuations in production or economic activity over several months or years. These fluctuations occur around a long-term growth trend, and typically involve shifts over time between periods of relatively rapid economic growth (expansion or boom), and periods of relative stagnation or decline (contraction or recession.)

These fluctuations are often measured using the growth rate of real gross domestic product.

 a. Nominal value
 b. Consumer theory
 c. Business Cycle
 d. Tobit model

61. A _____ is something for which there is demand, but which is supplied without qualitative differentiation across a market. It is a product that is the same no matter who produces it, such as petroleum, notebook paper, or milk. In other words, copper is copper.

Chapter 2. Measurement of Macroeconomic Variables

a. 100-year flood
b. Hard commodity
c. Soft commodity
d. Commodity

62. The _____ is a US private, nonprofit research organization dedicated to studying the science and empirics of economics, especially the American economy. It is 'committed to undertaking and disseminating unbiased economic research among public policymakers, business professionals, and the academic community.' It publishes NBER Working Papers and books. The NBER is located in Cambridge, Massachusetts with branch offices in Palo Alto, California, and New York City.
   a. CEFTA
   b. Non-governmental organization
   c. Deutsche Bank
   d. National Bureau of Economic Research

63. _____ Theory (or _____ Theory) is a class of macroeconomic models in which business cycle fluctuations to a large extent can be accounted for by real (in contrast to nominal) shocks. (The four primary economic fluctuations are secular (trend), business cycle, seasonal, and random.) Unlike other leading theories of the business cycle, it sees recessions and periods of economic growth as the efficient response to exogenous changes in the real economic environment.
   a. SIMIC
   b. Balanced-growth equilibrium
   c. Monetary policy reaction function
   d. Real business cycle

64. A _____ occurs when an entity spends more money than it takes in. The opposite of a _____ is a budget surplus. Debt is essentially an accumulated flow of deficits.
   a. Funding body
   b. Budget deficit
   c. Lump-sum tax
   d. Public Financial Management

Chapter 3. Classical Macroeconomics (I): Equilibrium Output and Employment

1. _____ is widely regarded as the first modern school of economic thought. It is the idea that free markets can regulate themselves. Its major developers include Adam Smith, David Ricardo, Thomas Malthus and John Stuart Mill. Sometimes the definition of _____ is expanded to include William Petty, Johann Heinrich von Thünen.

   a. Schools of economic thought
   b. Tendency of the rate of profit to fall
   c. Marginalism
   d. Classical economics

2. _____s is the social science that studies the production, distribution, and consumption of goods and services. The term _____s comes from the Ancient Greek oá¼°κονομῖα from oá¼¶κος (oikos, 'house') + vÏŒμος (nomos, 'custom' or 'law'), hence 'rules of the house(hold)'. Current _____ models developed out of the broader field of political economy in the late 19th century, owing to a desire to use an empirical approach more akin to the physical sciences.

   a. Opportunity cost
   b. Inflation
   c. Energy economics
   d. Economic

3. _____ is the increase in the amount of the goods and services produced by an economy over time. It is conventionally measured as the percent rate of increase in real gross domestic product, or real GDP. Growth is usually calculated in real terms, i.e. inflation-adjusted terms, in order to net out the effect of inflation on the price of the goods and services produced.

   a. ACEA agreement
   b. ACCRA Cost of Living Index
   c. AD-IA Model
   d. Economic growth

4. _____, 1st Baron Keynes was a renowned economist from Britain whose many ideas on economic and political theories as well as on many governments' monetary policies influenced America. He advocated a government that played an active role in the lives of people regarding business, economy, etc. In this role, the government would use fiscal measures to reduce the consequences of recessions, economic depressions and booms.

   a. Adolph Fischer
   b. Adolf Hitler
   c. Adam Smith
   d. John Maynard Keynes

5. _____ is a branch of economics that deals with the performance, structure, and behavior of a national or regional economy as a whole. Along with microeconomics, _____ is one of the two most general fields in economics. It is the study of the behavior and decision-making of entire economies.

   a. Macroeconomics
   b. Nominal value
   c. Tobit model
   d. New Trade Theory

6. _____ is the view within monetary economics that variation in the money supply has major influences on national output in the short run and the price level over longer periods and that objectives of monetary policy are best met by targeting the growth rate of the money supply.

_____ today is mainly associated with the work of Milton Friedman, who was among the generation of economists to accept Keynesian economics and then criticize it on his own terms. Friedman and Anna Schwartz wrote an influential book, Monetary History of the United States 1867-1960, and argued that 'inflation is always and everywhere a monetary phenomenon.' Friedman advocated a central bank policy aimed at keeping the supply and demand for money at equilibrium, as measured by growth in productivity and demand.

   a. Historical school of economics
   b. Complexity economics
   c. Marginal revenue productivity theory of wages
   d. Monetarism

Chapter 3. Classical Macroeconomics (I): Equilibrium Output and Employment

7. _____ Theory (or _____ Theory) is a class of macroeconomic models in which business cycle fluctuations to a large extent can be accounted for by real (in contrast to nominal) shocks. (The four primary economic fluctuations are secular (trend), business cycle, seasonal, and random.) Unlike other leading theories of the business cycle, it sees recessions and periods of economic growth as the efficient response to exogenous changes in the real economic environment.
   a. Monetary policy reaction function   b. Real business cycle
   c. SIMIC   d. Balanced-growth equilibrium

8. In economics, _____ is the total supply of goods and services produced by a national economy during a specific time period. It is the total amount of goods and services in the economy available at all possible price levels.
   a. Aggregate demand   b. Aggregation problem
   c. Aggregate expenditure   d. Aggregate supply

9. The term _____ refers to economy-wide fluctuations in production or economic activity over several months or years. These fluctuations occur around a long-term growth trend, and typically involve shifts over time between periods of relatively rapid economic growth (expansion or boom), and periods of relative stagnation or decline (contraction or recession.)

These fluctuations are often measured using the growth rate of real gross domestic product.

   a. Nominal value   b. Consumer theory
   c. Tobit model   d. Business cycle

10. Economics:

- _____, the desire to own something and the ability to pay for it
- _____ curve, a graphic representation of a _____ schedule
- _____ deposit, the money in checking accounts
- _____ pull theory, the theory that inflation occurs when _____ for goods and services exceeds existing supplies
- _____ schedule, a table that lists the quantity of a good a person will buy it each different price
- _____ side economics, the school of economics at believes government spending and tax cuts open economy by raising _____

   a. Production   b. Demand
   c. McKesson ' Robbins scandal   d. Variability

11. _____ is an economic model based on price, utility and quantity in a market. It predicts that in a competitive market, price will function to equalize the quantity demanded by consumers, and the quantity supplied by producers, resulting in an economic equilibrium of price and quantity. The model incorporates other factors changing equilibrium as a shift of demand and/or supply.
   a. Deferred gratification   b. Joint demand
   c. Rational addiction   d. Supply and demand

Chapter 3. Classical Macroeconomics (I): Equilibrium Output and Employment

12. _____ was a survey conducted by the U.S. Department of Justice to gauge the prevalence of alcohol and illegal drug use among prior arrestees. It was a reformulation of the prior Drug Use Forecasting (DUF) program, focused on five drugs in particular: cocaine, marijuana, methamphetamine, opiates, and PCP.

Participants were randomly selected from arrest records in major metropolitan areas; because no personally identifying information is taken from each record chosen, the resulting data can be correlated to arrest rates, but not to the total population of persons charged.

   a. Arrestee Drug Abuse Monitoring
   b. ACCRA Cost of Living Index
   c. AD-IA Model
   d. ACEA agreement

13. _____ is an economic theory that defines wealth by the amount of precious metals owned. _____ is an early or primitive form of mercantilism. It was derived, in the 16th century, from the observation that the English state possessed large amounts of gold and silver, in spite of the fact that there was no mining of precious metals on English soil, because of its large trade surplus.

   a. Classical economics
   b. Cost-of-production theory of value
   c. Marginalism
   d. Bullionism

14. In macroeconomics, _____ is a condition of the national economy, where all or nearly all persons willing and able to work at the prevailing wages and working conditions are able to do so. It is defined either as 0% unemployment, literally, no unemployment (the rate of unemployment is the fraction of the work force unable to find work), as by James Tobin, or as the level of employment rates when there is no cyclical unemployment. It is defined by the majority of mainstream economists as being an acceptable level of natural unemployment above 0%, the discrepancy from 0% being due to non-cyclical types of unemployment.

   a. Marginal propensity to consume
   b. Harrod-Johnson diagram
   c. Full employment
   d. Demand shock

15. The _____ or gross domestic income (GDI), a basic measure of an economy's economic performance, is the market value of all final goods and services produced within the borders of a nation in a year. _____ can be defined in three ways, all of which are conceptually identical. First, it is equal to the total expenditures for all final goods and services produced within the country in a stipulated period of time (usually a 365-day year.)

   a. Gross domestic product
   b. Monopolistic competition
   c. Market structure
   d. Countercyclical

16. _____ and Keynesian Theory) is a macroeconomic theory based on the ideas of 20th-century British economist John Maynard Keynes. _____ argues that private sector decisions sometimes lead to inefficient macroeconomic outcomes and therefore advocates active policy responses by the public sector, including monetary policy actions by the central bank and fiscal policy actions by the government to stabilize output over the business cycle.

The theories forming the basis of _____ were first presented in The General Theory of Employment, Interest and Money, published in 1936.

   a. Deflation
   b. Keynesian economics
   c. Market failure
   d. Rational choice theory

Chapter 3. Classical Macroeconomics (I): Equilibrium Output and Employment

17. _____ is the price at which an asset would trade in a competitive Walrasian auction setting. _____ is often used interchangeably with open _____, fair value or fair _____, although these terms have distinct definitions in different standards, and may differ in some circumstances.

International Valuation Standards defines _____ as 'the estimated amount for which a property should exchange on the date of valuation between a willing buyer and a willing seller in an arm's-length transaction after proper marketing wherein the parties had each acted knowledgeably, prudently, and without compulsion.'

_____ is a concept distinct from market price, which is 'the price at which one can transact', while _____ is 'the true underlying value' according to theoretical standards.

- a. Market value
- b. Personal financial management
- c. Netting
- d. Secured loan

18. _____ is an economic theory that holds that the prosperity of a nation is dependent upon its supply of capital, and that the global volume of international trade is 'unchangeable.' Economic assets or capital, are represented by bullion (gold, silver, and trade value) held by the state, which is best increased through a positive balance of trade with other nations (exports minus imports.) _____ suggests that the ruling government should advance these goals by playing a protectionist role in the economy; by encouraging exports and discouraging imports, notably through the use of tariffs and subsidies.

_____ was the dominant school of thought throughout the early modern period (from the 16th to the 18th century.)

- a. Nominal value
- b. General equilibrium theory
- c. Consumer theory
- d. Mercantilism

19. _____ originally was the term for studying production, buying and selling, and their relations with law, custom, and government. _____ originated in moral philosophy. It developed in the 18th century as the study of the economies of states -- polities, hence _____.

- a. Political Economy
- b. Dirigisme
- c. Geoeconomics
- d. Productive and unproductive labour

20. _____ by John Stuart Mill was the most important economics or political economy textbook of the mid nineteenth century. It was revised until its seventh edition in 1871, shortly before Mill's death in 1873, and republished in numerous other editions.

Mill's Principles were written in a style of prose far flung from the introductory texts of today.

- a. Limits to Growth
- b. Principles of Political Economy and Taxation
- c. Principles of Political Economy
- d. The Rise and Fall of the Great Powers

21. In economics, the concept of the _____ refers to the decision-making time frame of a firm in which at least one factor of production is fixed. Costs which are fixed in the _____ have no impact on a firms decisions. For example a firm can raise output by increasing the amount of labour through overtime.

Chapter 3. Classical Macroeconomics (I): Equilibrium Output and Employment

a. Product Pipeline
b. Short-run
c. Productivity model
d. Hicks-neutral technical change

22. _____ was a Scottish moral philosopher and a pioneer of political economy. One of the key figures of the Scottish Enlightenment, Smith is the author of The Theory of Moral Sentiments and An Inquiry into the Nature and Causes of the Wealth of Nations. The latter, usually abbreviated as The Wealth of Nations, is considered his magnum opus and the first modern work of economics.

a. Adolph Fischer
b. Adolf Hitler
c. Alan Greenspan
d. Adam Smith

23. The _____ is the average frequency with which a unit of money is spent in a specific period of time. Velocity associates the amount of economic activity associated with a given money supply. When the period is understood, the velocity may be present as a pure number; otherwise it should be given as a pure number over time.

a. Neutrality of money
b. Money supply
c. Chartalism
d. Velocity of money

24. An Inquiry into the Nature and Causes of the _____ is the magnum opus of the Scottish economist Adam Smith. It is a clearly written account of economics at the dawn of the Industrial Revolution, as well as a rhetorical piece written for the generally educated individual of the 18th century - advocating a free market economy as more productive and more beneficial to society.

The work is credited as a watershed in history and economics due to its comprehensive, largely accurate characterization of economic mechanisms that survive in modern economics; and also for its effective use of rhetorical technique, including structuring the work to contrast real world examples of free and fettered markets.

a. Black Book of Communism
b. The Rise and Fall of the Great Powers
c. Wealth of Nations
d. The Bell Curve

25. In finance, a _____ is a debt security, in which the authorized issuer owes the holders a debt and, depending on the terms of the _____, is obliged to pay interest (the coupon) and/or to repay the principal at a later date, termed maturity. A _____ is a formal contract to repay borrowed money with interest at fixed intervals.

Thus a _____ is like a loan: the issuer is the borrower (debtor), the holder is the lender (creditor), and the coupon is the interest.

a. Prize Bond
b. Bond
c. Zero-coupon
d. Callable

26. _____ is the a method of technical and economic research of the systems for purpose to optimize a parity between system's consumer functions or properties and expenses to achieve those functions or properties.

26   *Chapter 3. Classical Macroeconomics (I): Equilibrium Output and Employment*

This methodology for continuous perfection of production, industrial technologies, organizational structures was developed by Juryj Sobolev in 1948 at the 'Perm telephone factory'

- 1948 Juryj Sobolev - the first success in application of a method analysis at the 'Perm telephone factory'.
- 1949 - the first application for the invention as result of use of the new method.

Today in economically developed countries practically each enterprise or the company use methodology of the kind of functional-cost analysis as a practice of the quality management, most full satisfying to principles of standards of series ISO 9000.

- Interest of consumer not in products itself, but the advantage which it will receive from its usage.
- The consumer aspires to reduce his expenses
- Functions needed by consumer can be executed in the various ways, and, hence, with various efficiency and expenses. Among possible alternatives of realization of functions exist such in which the parity of quality and the price is the optimal for the consumer.

The goal of _____ is achievement of the highest consumer satisfaction of production at simultaneous decrease in all kinds of industrial expenses Classical _____ has three English synonyms - Value Engineering, Value Management, Value Analysis.

 a. Monopoly wage
 c. Function cost analysis
 b. Willingness to pay
 d. Staple financing

27. In statistics, _____ has two related meanings:

- the arithmetic _____
- the expected value of a random variable, which is also called the population _____.

It is sometimes stated that the '_____' _____s average. This is incorrect if '_____' is taken in the specific sense of 'arithmetic _____' as there are different types of averages: the _____, median, and mode. Other simple statistical analyses use measures of spread, such as range, interquartile range, or standard deviation. For a real-valued random variable X, the _____ is the expectation of X. Note that not every probability distribution has a defined _____ (or variance); see the Cauchy distribution for an example.

 a. 1921 recession
 c. 130-30 fund
 b. 100-year flood
 d. Mean

28. In labor economics, the _____ hypothesis argues that wages, at least in some markets, are determined by more than simply supply and demand. Specifically, it points to the incentive for managers to pay their employees more than the market-clearing wage in order to increase their productivity or efficiency. This increased labor productivity pays for the relatively higher wages.

 a. Earnings calls
 c. Exogenous growth model
 b. Efficiency wage
 d. Inflatable rats

Chapter 3. Classical Macroeconomics (I): Equilibrium Output and Employment

29. The supply of labor is the number of total hours that workers wish to work at a given real wage rate.

    _____ curves are derived from the 'labor-leisure' trade-off. More hours worked earn higher incomes but necessitate a cut in the amount of leisure that workers enjoy.

    a. Human trafficking
    c. Late capitalism
    b. Creative capitalism
    d. Labor supply

30. In economics, the _____ or marginal physical product is the extra output produced by one more unit of an input (for instance, the difference in output when a firm's labour is increased from five to six units.) Assuming that no other inputs to production change, the _____ of a given input (X) can be expressed as:

    _____ = ΔY/ΔX = (the change of Y)/(the change of X.)

    -
      -
        - Pending approval by Thomas Sowell***

    In neoclassical economics, this is the mathematical derivative of the production function.... Note that the 'product' (Y) is typically defined ignoring external costs and benefits.

    a. Marginal product
    c. Productive capacity
    b. Labor problem
    d. Factor prices

31. In economics, the _____ also known as MPL or MPN is the change in output from hiring one additional unit of labor. It is the increase in output added by the last unit of labor. Assuming that no other inputs to production change, the marginal product of a given input (X) can be expressed as:

    MP = ΔY/ΔX = (the change of Y)/(the change of X.)

    a. Marginal product
    c. Product Pipeline
    b. Marginal product of labor
    d. Production function

32. In microeconomics, _____ is quite simply the conversion of inputs into outputs. It is an economic process that uses resources to create a good or service that is suitable for exchange. This can include manufacturing, storing, shipping, and packaging.
    a. MET
    c. Solved
    b. Production
    d. Red Guards

33. In economics, a _____ is a function that specifies the output of a firm, an industry, or an entire economy for all combinations of inputs. A meta-_____ compares the practice of the existing entities converting inputs X into output y to determine the most efficient practice _____ of the existing entities, whether the most efficient feasible practice production or the most efficient actual practice production. In either case, the maximum output of a technologically-determined production process is a mathematical function of input factors of production.

Chapter 3. Classical Macroeconomics (I): Equilibrium Output and Employment

   a. Production function
   c. Short-run
   b. Constant elasticity of substitution
   d. Post-Fordism

34. In economics, _____ and economies of scale are related terms that describe what happens as the scale of production increases. They are different terms and should not be used interchangeably.

_____ refers to a technical property of production that examines changes in output subsequent to a proportional change in all inputs (where all inputs increase by a constant factor.)

   a. Customer equity
   c. Returns to scale
   b. Constant returns to scale
   d. Necessity good

35. The term _____s refers to wages that have been adjusted for inflation. This term is used in contrast to nominal wages or unadjusted wages.

The use of adjusted figures is in undertaking some form of economic analysis.

   a. Federal Wage System
   c. Profit sharing
   b. Living wage
   d. Real wage

36. In economics, _____ is the total demand for final goods and services in the economy (Y) at a given time and price level. It is the amount of goods and services in the economy that will be purchased at all possible price levels. This is the demand for the gross domestic product of a country when inventory levels are static.
   a. Aggregate demand
   c. Aggregation problem
   b. Aggregate supply
   d. Aggregate expenditure

37. In economics and finance, _____ is the change in total cost that arises when the quantity produced changes by one unit. It is the cost of producing one more unit of a good. Mathematically, the _____ function is expressed as the first derivative of the total cost (TC) function with respect to quantity (Q.)
   a. Khozraschyot
   c. Quality costs
   b. Marginal cost
   d. Variable cost

38. In economics, _____ is the process by which a firm determines the price and output level that returns the greatest profit. There are several approaches to this problem. The total revenue--total cost method relies on the fact that profit equals revenue minus cost, and the marginal revenue--marginal cost method is based on the fact that total profit in a perfectly competitive market reaches its maximum point where marginal revenue equals marginal cost.
   a. 100-year flood
   c. Profit maximization
   b. Profit margin
   d. Normal profit

39. In economics, _____ is the total amount of money available in an economy at a particular point in time. There are several ways to define 'money', but standard measures usually include currency in circulation and demand deposits.

_____ data are recorded and published, usually by the government or the central bank of the country.

Chapter 3. Classical Macroeconomics (I): Equilibrium Output and Employment 29

a. Neutrality of money
b. Veil of money
c. Velocity of money
d. Money supply

40. _____ refers to an action or object coming from outside a system. It is the opposite of endogenous, something generated from within the system.

- In an economic model, an _____ change is one that comes from outside the model and is unexplained by the model. For example, in the simple supply and demand model, a change in consumer tastes or preferences is unexplained by the model and also leads to endogenous changes in demand that lead to changes in the equilibrium price. Put another way, an _____ change involves an alteration of a variable that is autonomous, i.e., unaffected by the workings of the model.

- In linear regression, it means that the variable is independent of all other response values.

- In biology, '_____' refers to an action or object coming from the outside of a system. For example, an _____ contrast agent in medical imaging refers to a liquid injected into the patient intravenously that enhances visibility of a pathology, such as a tumor.

a. Exogenous
b. ACCRA Cost of Living Index
c. AD-IA Model
d. ACEA agreement

41. _____ in economics and business is the result of an exchange and from that trade we assign a numerical monetary value to a good, service or asset. If Alice trades Bob 4 apples for an orange, the _____ of an orange is 4 apples. Inversely, the _____ of an apple is 1/4 oranges.

a. Price war
b. Price book
c. Premium pricing
d. Price

42. A _____ is a hypothetical measure of overall prices for some set of goods and services, in a given region during a given interval, normalized relative to some base set. Typically, a _____ is approximated with a price index.

The classical dichotomy is the assumption that there is a relatively clean distinction between overall increases or decreases in prices and underlying, e;reale; economic variables.

a. Discretionary spending
b. Price level
c. Price elasticity of supply
d. Discouraged worker

43. _____ is a macroeconomic theory that argues that private sector decisions sometimes lead to inefficient macroeconomic outcomes and therefore advocates active policy responses by the public sector, including monetary policy actions by the central bank and fiscal policy actions by the government to stabilize output over the business cycle.

The theories forming the basis of _____ were first presented in The General Theory of Employment, Interest and Money, published in 1936.

a. Keynesian theory
b. Tobit model
c. Mainstream economics
d. Human capital

Chapter 3. Classical Macroeconomics (I): Equilibrium Output and Employment

44. In economics, economic equilibrium is simply a state of the world where economic forces are balanced and in the absence of external influences the (equilibrium) values of economic variables will not change. It is the point at which quantity demanded and quantity supplied are equal. _____, for example, refers to a condition where a market price is established through competition such that the amount of goods or services sought by buyers is equal to the amount of goods or services produced by sellers.

   a. Market equilibrium   b. Regulated market
   c. Marketization   d. Product-Market Growth Matrix

45. In economics, the _____ can be defined as the graph depicting the relationship between the price of a certain commodity, and the amount of it that consumers are willing and able to purchase at that given price. It is a graphic representation of a demand schedule. The _____ for all consumers together follows from the _____ of every individual consumer: the individual demands at each price are added together.

   a. Kuznets curve   b. Demand Curve
   c. Wage curve   d. Cost curve

46. The Organization of the Petroleum Exporting Countries is a cartel of twelve countries made up of Algeria, Angola, Ecuador, Iran, Iraq, Kuwait, Libya, Nigeria, Qatar, Saudi Arabia, the United Arab Emirates, and Venezuela. The cartel has maintained its headquarters in Vienna since 1965, and hosts regular meetings among the oil ministers of its Member Countries. Indonesia withdrew its membership in _____ in 2008 after it became a net importer of oil, but stated it would likely return if it became a net exporter in the world.

   a. ACEA agreement   b. AD-IA Model
   c. ACCRA Cost of Living Index   d. OPEC

47. _____ is a term used in game theory. A game is said to have _____ if all players know all moves that have taken place.

Chess is an example of a game with _____ as each player can see all of the pieces on the board at all times.

   a. Parity game   b. Game theory
   c. Perfect rationality   d. Perfect information

48. A _____ measures average changes in prices received by domestic producers for their output. It is one of several price indices

Its importance is being undermined by the steady decline in manufactured goods as a share of spending.

A number of countries that now report a _____ previously reported a Wholesale Price Index.

   a. Visible balance   b. Gross national product
   c. Hemline index   d. Producer price index

49. _____ is an economic concept with commonplace familiarity. It is the price that a good or service is offered at, or will fetch, in the marketplace. It is of interest mainly in the study of microeconomics.

   a. Market anomaly   b. Noisy market hypothesis
   c. Paper trading   d. Market price

Chapter 3. Classical Macroeconomics (I): Equilibrium Output and Employment

50. A _____ is a normalized average (typically a weighted average) of prices for a given class of goods or services in a given region, during a given interval of time. It is a statistic designed to help to compare how these prices, taken as a whole, differ between time periods or geographical locations.

Price indices have several potential uses.

a. Price index
c. Transactional Net Margin Method
b. Product sabotage
d. Two-part tariff

Chapter 4. Classical Macroeconomics (II): Money, Prices, and Interest

1. _____ is widely regarded as the first modern school of economic thought. It is the idea that free markets can regulate themselves.Its major developers include Adam Smith, David Ricardo, Thomas Malthus and John Stuart Mill. Sometimes the definition of _____ is expanded to include William Petty, Johann Heinrich von Thünen.
   - a. Classical economics
   - b. Tendency of the rate of profit to fall
   - c. Marginalism
   - d. Schools of economic thought

2. _____s is the social science that studies the production, distribution, and consumption of goods and services. The term _____s comes from the Ancient Greek oá¼°κονομῖα from oá¼¶κος (oikos, 'house') + νÏŒμος (nomos, 'custom' or 'law'), hence 'rules of the house(hold)'. Current _____ models developed out of the broader field of political economy in the late 19th century, owing to a desire to use an empirical approach more akin to the physical sciences.
   - a. Inflation
   - b. Opportunity cost
   - c. Energy economics
   - d. Economic

3. _____ is the increase in the amount of the goods and services produced by an economy over time. It is conventionally measured as the percent rate of increase in real gross domestic product, or real GDP. Growth is usually calculated in real terms, i.e. inflation-adjusted terms, in order to net out the effect of inflation on the price of the goods and services produced.
   - a. Economic growth
   - b. AD-IA Model
   - c. ACEA agreement
   - d. ACCRA Cost of Living Index

4. _____ and Keynesian Theory) is a macroeconomic theory based on the ideas of 20th-century British economist John Maynard Keynes. _____ argues that private sector decisions sometimes lead to inefficient macroeconomic outcomes and therefore advocates active policy responses by the public sector, including monetary policy actions by the central bank and fiscal policy actions by the government to stabilize output over the business cycle.

   The theories forming the basis of _____ were first presented in The General Theory of Employment, Interest and Money, published in 1936.
   - a. Deflation
   - b. Rational choice theory
   - c. Market failure
   - d. Keynesian economics

5. _____ is a branch of economics that deals with the performance, structure, and behavior of a national or regional economy as a whole. Along with microeconomics, _____ is one of the two most general fields in economics. It is the study of the behavior and decision-making of entire economies.
   - a. Nominal value
   - b. New Trade Theory
   - c. Tobit model
   - d. Macroeconomics

6. In economics, the _____ of money is a theory emphasizing the positive relationship of overall prices or the nominal value of expenditures to the quantity of money.

   It is the mainstream economic theory of the price level. Alternative theories include the real bills doctrine and the more recent fiscal theory of the price level.
   - a. Romer Model
   - b. Real business cycle
   - c. Dishoarding
   - d. Quantity theory

Chapter 4. Classical Macroeconomics (II): Money, Prices, and Interest

7. In economics, the _____ is a theory emphasizing the positive relationship of overall prices or the nominal value of expenditures to the quantity of money.

It is the mainstream economic theory of the price level. Alternative theories include the real bills doctrine and the more recent fiscal theory of the price level.

   a. Fundamental psychological law
   b. Consumer spending
   c. Microsimulation
   d. Quantity theory of money

8. The _____ is the average frequency with which a unit of money is spent in a specific period of time. Velocity associates the amount of economic activity associated with a given money supply. When the period is understood, the velocity may be present as a pure number; otherwise it should be given as a pure number over time.

   a. Neutrality of money
   b. Chartalism
   c. Money supply
   d. Velocity of money

9. In economics, _____ is the total supply of goods and services produced by a national economy during a specific time period. It is the total amount of goods and services in the economy available at all possible price levels.

   a. Aggregate expenditure
   b. Aggregation problem
   c. Aggregate demand
   d. Aggregate supply

10. Economics:

    - _____, the desire to own something and the ability to pay for it
    - _____ curve, a graphic representation of a _____ schedule
    - _____ deposit, the money in checking accounts
    - _____ pull theory, the theory that inflation occurs when _____ for goods and services exceeds existing supplies
    - _____ schedule, a table that lists the quantity of a good a person will buy it each different price
    - _____ side economics, the school of economics at believes government spending and tax cuts open economy by raising _____

    a. Demand
    b. Production
    c. McKesson ' Robbins scandal
    d. Variability

11. _____ is a fee paid on borrowed assets. It is the price paid for the use of borrowed money, or, money earned by deposited funds . Assets that are sometimes lent with _____ include money, shares, consumer goods through hire purchase, major assets such as aircraft, and even entire factories in finance lease arrangements.

    a. Internal debt
    b. Insolvency
    c. Asset protection
    d. Interest

12. _____ in economics and business is the result of an exchange and from that trade we assign a numerical monetary value to a good, service or asset. If Alice trades Bob 4 apples for an orange, the _____ of an orange is 4 apples. Inversely, the _____ of an apple is 1/4 oranges.

Chapter 4. Classical Macroeconomics (II): Money, Prices, and Interest

a. Price book
b. Price war
c. Premium pricing
d. Price

13. _____ is an economic model based on price, utility and quantity in a market. It predicts that in a competitive market, price will function to equalize the quantity demanded by consumers, and the quantity supplied by producers, resulting in an economic equilibrium of price and quantity. The model incorporates other factors changing equilibrium as a shift of demand and/or supply.

a. Joint demand
b. Deferred gratification
c. Supply and demand
d. Rational addiction

14. The _____ or gross domestic income (GDI), a basic measure of an economy's economic performance, is the market value of all final goods and services produced within the borders of a nation in a year. _____ can be defined in three ways, all of which are conceptually identical. First, it is equal to the total expenditures for all final goods and services produced within the country in a stipulated period of time (usually a 365-day year.)

a. Countercyclical
b. Market structure
c. Monopolistic competition
d. Gross domestic product

15. In economics, the _____ is the relation:

$$M \cdot V = P \cdot Q$$

where, for a given period,

M is the total amount of money in circulation on average in an economy.
V is the velocity of money, that is the average frequency with which a unit of money is spent.
P is the price level.

a. Open market
b. Outside money
c. ACCRA Cost of Living Index
d. Equation of exchange

16. _____ is the a method of technical and economic research of the systems for purpose to optimize a parity between system's consumer functions or properties and expenses to achieve those functions or properties.

This methodology for continuous perfection of production, industrial technologies, organizational structures was developed by Juryj Sobolev in 1948 at the 'Perm telephone factory'

- 1948 Juryj Sobolev - the first success in application of a method analysis at the 'Perm telephone factory' .
- 1949 - the first application for the invention as result of use of the new method.

Today in economically developed countries practically each enterprise or the company use methodology of the kind of functional-cost analysis as a practice of the quality management, most full satisfying to principles of standards of series ISO 9000.

- Interest of consumer not in products itself, but the advantage which it will receive from its usage.
- The consumer aspires to reduce his expenses
- Functions needed by consumer can be executed in the various ways, and, hence, with various efficiency and expenses. Among possible alternatives of realization of functions exist such in which the parity of quality and the price is the optimal for the consumer.

The goal of _____ is achievement of the highest consumer satisfaction of production at simultaneous decrease in all kinds of industrial expenses Classical _____ has three English synonyms - Value Engineering, Value Management, Value Analysis.

   a. Function cost analysis   b. Willingness to pay
   c. Staple financing   d. Monopoly wage

17.   In economics, _____ is the total demand for final goods and services in the economy (Y) at a given time and price level. It is the amount of goods and services in the economy that will be purchased at all possible price levels. This is the demand for the gross domestic product of a country when inventory levels are static.

   a. Aggregation problem   b. Aggregate demand
   c. Aggregate supply   d. Aggregate expenditure

18.   _____ is the price at which an asset would trade in a competitive Walrasian auction setting. _____ is often used interchangeably with open _____, fair value or fair _____, although these terms have distinct definitions in different standards, and may differ in some circumstances.

International Valuation Standards defines _____ as 'the estimated amount for which a property should exchange on the date of valuation between a willing buyer and a willing seller in an arm's-length transaction after proper marketing wherein the parties had each acted knowledgeably, prudently, and without compulsion.'

_____ is a concept distinct from market price, which is 'the price at which one can transact', while _____ is 'the true underlying value' according to theoretical standards.

   a. Secured loan   b. Personal financial management
   c. Netting   d. Market value

19.   _____ is the view within monetary economics that variation in the money supply has major influences on national output in the short run and the price level over longer periods and that objectives of monetary policy are best met by targeting the growth rate of the money supply.

Chapter 4. Classical Macroeconomics (II): Money, Prices, and Interest

_____ today is mainly associated with the work of Milton Friedman, who was among the generation of economists to accept Keynesian economics and then criticize it on his own terms. Friedman and Anna Schwartz wrote an influential book, Monetary History of the United States 1867-1960, and argued that 'inflation is always and everywhere a monetary phenomenon.' Friedman advocated a central bank policy aimed at keeping the supply and demand for money at equilibrium, as measured by growth in productivity and demand.

a. Historical school of economics
b. Monetarism
c. Complexity economics
d. Marginal revenue productivity theory of wages

20. In economics, _____ is the total amount of money available in an economy at a particular point in time. There are several ways to define 'money', but standard measures usually include currency in circulation and demand deposits.

_____ data are recorded and published, usually by the government or the central bank of the country.

a. Money supply
b. Velocity of money
c. Neutrality of money
d. Veil of money

21. A _____ measures average changes in prices received by domestic producers for their output. It is one of several price indices

Its importance is being undermined by the steady decline in manufactured goods as a share of spending.

A number of countries that now report a _____ previously reported a Wholesale Price Index.

a. Producer price index
b. Visible balance
c. Hemline index
d. Gross national product

22. _____ is a common concept in economics, and gives rise to derived concepts such as consumer debt. Generally _____ is defined by opposition to production. But the precise definition can vary because different schools of economists define production quite differently.

a. Cash or share options
b. Foreclosure data providers
c. Federal Reserve Bank Notes
d. Consumption

23. A _____ is a normalized average (typically a weighted average) of prices for a given class of goods or services in a given region, during a given interval of time. It is a statistic designed to help to compare how these prices, taken as a whole, differ between time periods or geographical locations.

Price indices have several potential uses.

a. Product sabotage
b. Transactional Net Margin Method
c. Two-part tariff
d. Price index

Chapter 4. Classical Macroeconomics (II): Money, Prices, and Interest

24. In economics, the _____ can be defined as the graph depicting the relationship between the price of a certain commodity, and the amount of it that consumers are willing and able to purchase at that given price. It is a graphic representation of a demand schedule. The _____ for all consumers together follows from the _____ of every individual consumer: the individual demands at each price are added together.
    a. Kuznets curve
    b. Wage curve
    c. Demand curve
    d. Cost curve

25. In economics, _____ is inflation that is very high or 'out of control', a condition in which prices increase rapidly as a currency loses its value. Definitions used by the media vary from a cumulative inflation rate over three years approaching 100% to 'inflation exceeding 50% a month.' In informal usage the term is often applied to much lower rates. As a rule of thumb, normal inflation is reported per year, but _____ is often reported for much shorter intervals, often per month.
    a. 100-year flood
    b. 1921 recession
    c. 130-30 fund
    d. Hyperinflation

26. In finance, a _____ is a debt security, in which the authorized issuer owes the holders a debt and, depending on the terms of the _____, is obliged to pay interest (the coupon) and/or to repay the principal at a later date, termed maturity. A _____ is a formal contract to repay borrowed money with interest at fixed intervals.

    Thus a _____ is like a loan: the issuer is the borrower (debtor), the holder is the lender (creditor), and the coupon is the interest.

    a. Zero-coupon
    b. Prize Bond
    c. Bond
    d. Callable

27. An _____ is the price a borrower pays for the use of money they do not own, for instance a small company might borrow from a bank to kick start their business, and the return a lender receives for deferring the use of funds, by lending it to the borrower. _____s are normally expressed as a percentage rate over the period of one year.

    _____s targets are also a vital tool of monetary policy and are used to control variables like investment, inflation, and unemployment.

    a. Arrow-Debreu model
    b. Enterprise value
    c. ACCRA Cost of Living Index
    d. Interest rate

28. The _____ is a term used in economics to refer to a number of things:

    - The demand element of a supply and demand partial equilibrium diagram, in microeconomics
    - The aggregate demand in an economy, in macroeconomics
    - Economic policy actions which are designed to affect aggregate demand.
    - Demand-side learning referring to the incentive to learn how to use and modify free software as opposed to buying conventional software.

The term is also used broadly to distinguish supply-side economics from other schools, for instance Keynesian economics.

Chapter 4. Classical Macroeconomics (II): Money, Prices, and Interest

    a. CPFR
    b. Vendor Managed Inventory
    c. Demand-side
    d. Demand side

29. _____, 1st Baron Keynes was a renowned economist from Britain whose many ideas on economic and political theories as well as on many governments' monetary policies influenced America. He advocated a government that played an active role in the lives of people regarding business, economy, etc. In this role, the government would use fiscal measures to reduce the consequences of recessions, economic depressions and booms.
    a. Adolph Fischer
    b. Adam Smith
    c. Adolf Hitler
    d. John Maynard Keynes

30. In economics, the _____ market is a hypothetical market that brings savers and borrowers together, also bringing together the money available in commercial banks and lending institutions available for firms and households to finance expenditures, either investments or consumption. Savers supply the _____; for instance, buying bonds will transfer their money to the institution issuing the bond, which can be a firm or government. In return, borrowers demand _____; when an institution sells a bond, it is demanding _____.
    a. Reservation wage
    b. Buffer stock scheme
    c. Spatial inequality
    d. Loanable funds

31. The _____ is a financial market where participants buy and sell debt securities, usually in the form of bonds. As of 2006, the size of the international _____ is an estimated $44.9 trillion, of which the size of the outstanding U.S. _____ debt was $25.2 trillion.

Nearly all of the $923 billion average daily trading volume in the U.S. _____ takes place between broker-dealers and large institutions in a decentralized, over-the-counter market.

    a. 100-year flood
    b. Bond market
    c. 130-30 fund
    d. Pool factor

32. The _____ is the desired holding of money balances in the form of cash or bank deposits.

Money is dominated as store of value by interest bearing assets. However, money is necessary to carry out transactions, or in other words, it provides liquidity.

    a. Market neutral
    b. Demand for money
    c. Borrowing base
    d. Conglomerate merger

33. _____ is a concept found in moral, political, and bioethical philosophy. Within these contexts, it refers to the capacity of a rational individual to make an informed, un-coerced decision. In moral and political philosophy, _____ is often used as the basis for determining moral responsibility for one's actions.
    a. ACEA agreement
    b. ACCRA Cost of Living Index
    c. AD-IA Model
    d. Autonomy

34. A _____ represents the combinations of goods and services that a consumer can purchase given current prices and his income. Consumer theory uses the concepts of a _____ and a preference map to analyze consumer choices. Both concepts have a ready graphical representation in the two-good case.

Chapter 4. Classical Macroeconomics (II): Money, Prices, and Interest

a. Quality bias
c. Joint demand
b. Revealed preference
d. Budget constraint

35. The term _____ refers to government debt, expenditures and revenues, or to finance (particularly financial revenue) in general.

- _____ deficit is the budget deficit of federal or local government
- _____ policy is the discretionary spending of governments. Contrasts with monetary policy.
- _____ year and _____ quarter are reporting periods for firms and other agencies.

a. Drawdown
c. Procter ' Gamble
b. Bucket shop
d. Fiscal

36. In economics, _____ is the use of government spending and revenue collection to influence the economy.

_____ can be contrasted with the other main type of economic policy, monetary policy, which attempts to stabilize the economy by controlling interest rates and the supply of money. The two main instruments of _____ are government spending and taxation.

a. 100-year flood
c. Fiscalism
b. Sustainable investment rule
d. Fiscal policy

37. _____ or government expenditure is classified by economists into three main types. Government purchases of goods and services for current use are classed as government consumption. Government purchases of goods and services intended to create future benefits, such as infrastructure investment or research spending, are classed as government investment.
a. Government spending
c. 1921 recession
b. 100-year flood
d. 130-30 fund

38. Market _____ is a business, economics or investment term that refers to an asset's ability to be easily converted through an act of buying or selling without causing a significant movement in the price and with minimum loss of value. Money, or cash on hand, is the most liquid asset. An act of exchange of a less liquid asset with a more liquid asset is called liquidation.
a. 100-year flood
c. Liquidity
b. 130-30 fund
d. 1921 recession

39. The term _____ is used in macroeconomics to refer to a situation where a country's nominal interest rate has been lowered nearly to or equal to zero to avoid a recession, but the liquidity in the market created by these low interest rates does not stimulate the economy to full employment. In this situation, any further increase in the money supply will not stimulate the economy any further. This is because any further injection of liquidity will no longer lower the nominal interest rate, as the nominal interest rate cannot drop below zero.
a. Minimum wage
c. Liquidity trap
b. Macroeconomic models
d. Robertson lag

40. _____ is the process by which the government, central bank (ii) availability of money, and (iii) cost of money or rate of interest, in order to attain a set of objectives oriented towards the growth and stability of the economy. Monetary theory provides insight into how to craft optimal _____.

_____ is referred to as either being an expansionary policy where an expansionary policy increases the total supply of money in the economy, and a contractionary policy decreases the total money supply.

a. 130-30 fund
b. 1921 recession
c. Monetary policy
d. 100-year flood

41. A _____ is a package or set of measures introduced to stabilise a financial system or economy. The term can refer to policies in two distinct sets of circumstances: business cycle stabilization and crisis stabilization.

Stabilization can refer to correcting the normal behavior of the business cycle.

a. Stabilization policy
b. Volunteers for Economic Growth Alliance
c. New International Economic Order
d. Capacity Development

42. From a Keynesian point of view, a _____ in the public sector is achieved when the government equates the revenues with expenditure over the business cycles. In other words, a government's budget is balanced if its income is equal to its expenditure. It is a budget in which revenues are equal to spending.

a. Budget crisis
b. Budget support
c. Budget theory
d. Balanced budget

43. An _____ is a tax levied on the financial income of people, corporations, or other legal entities. Various _____ systems exist, with varying degrees of tax incidence. Income taxation can be progressive, proportional, or regressive.

a. ACEA agreement
b. ACCRA Cost of Living Index
c. Income tax
d. AD-IA Model

44. To _____ is to impose a financial charge or other levy upon a taxpayer by a state or the functional equivalent of a state.

_____es are also imposed by many subnational entities. _____es consist of direct _____ or indirect _____, and may be paid in money or as its labour equivalent (often but not always unpaid.)

a. 130-30 fund
b. Tax
c. 100-year flood
d. 1921 recession

45. _____ is the government's approach to taxation, both from the practical and normative side of the question.

Policymakers debate the nature of the tax structure they plan to implement (i.e., how progressive or regressive) and how they might affect individuals and businesses (i.e., tax incidence.)

The reason for such focus is economic efficiency as advisor to the Stuart King of England Richard Petty had noted that the government does not want to kill the goose that lays the golden egg.

Chapter 4. Classical Macroeconomics (II): Money, Prices, and Interest

a. Commuter tax
b. Tax policy
c. Tax-allocation district
d. Partnership taxation

46. The Demand side is a term used in economics to refer to a number of things:

- The demand element of a supply and demand partial equilibrium diagram, in microeconomics
- The aggregate demand in an economy, in macroeconomics
- Economic policy actions which are designed to affect aggregate demand.
- _____ learning referring to the incentive to learn how to use and modify free software as opposed to buying conventional software.

The term is also used broadly to distinguish supply-side economics from other schools, for instance Keynesian economics.

a. CPFR
b. Reverse auction
c. Delayed differentiation
d. Demand-side

47. A _____ is a reduction in taxes. Economic stimulus via _____s, along with interest rate intervention and deficit spending, are one of the central tenets of Keynesian economics.

The immediate effects of a _____ are, generally, a decrease in the real income of the government and an increase in the real income of those whose tax rate has been lowered.

a. Tax cut
b. Withholding tax
c. Popiwek
d. Direct taxes

48. _____ is a macroeconomic theory that argues that private sector decisions sometimes lead to inefficient macroeconomic outcomes and therefore advocates active policy responses by the public sector, including monetary policy actions by the central bank and fiscal policy actions by the government to stabilize output over the business cycle.

The theories forming the basis of _____ were first presented in The General Theory of Employment, Interest and Money, published in 1936.

a. Tobit model
b. Human capital
c. Mainstream economics
d. Keynesian theory

49. _____ is a school of macroeconomic thought that argues that economic growth can be most effectively created using incentives for people to produce (supply) goods and services, such as adjusting income tax and capital gains tax rates, and by allowing greater flexibility by reducing regulation. Consumers will then benefit from a greater supply of goods and services at lower prices.

The term _____ was coined by journalist Jude Wanniski in 1975, and popularized the ideas of economists Robert Mundell and Arthur Laffer.

Chapter 4. Classical Macroeconomics (II): Money, Prices, and Interest

a. Supply-side economics
b. Commodity trading advisors
c. Fiscal stimulus plans
d. Clap note

50. In economics, the _____ is a historical inverse relation between the rate of unemployment and the rate of inflation in an economy. Stated simply, the lower the unemployment in an economy, the higher the rate of increase in nominal wages in the economy. Rate of Change of Wages against Unemployment, United Kingdom 1913-1948 from Phillips (1958)

William Phillips, a New Zealand born economist, wrote a paper in 1958 titled The Relationship between Unemployment and the Rate of Change of Money Wages in the United Kingdom 1861-1957, which was published in the quarterly journal Economica.

a. Lorenz curve
b. Cost curve
c. Demand curve
d. Phillips curve

51. In microeconomics, _____ is quite simply the conversion of inputs into outputs. It is an economic process that uses resources to create a good or service that is suitable for exchange. This can include manufacturing, storing, shipping, and packaging.
a. MET
b. Solved
c. Production
d. Red Guards

52. In economics, a _____ is a function that specifies the output of a firm, an industry, or an entire economy for all combinations of inputs. A meta-_____ compares the practice of the existing entities converting inputs X into output y to determine the most efficient practice _____ of the existing entities, whether the most efficient feasible practice production or the most efficient actual practice production. In either case, the maximum output of a technologically-determined production process is a mathematical function of input factors of production.
a. Constant elasticity of substitution
b. Short-run
c. Post-Fordism
d. Production function

53. _____ is the process of changing the way taxes are collected or managed by the government.

_____ers have different goals. Some seek to reduce the level of taxation of all people by the government.

a. Special-purpose local-option sales tax
b. Nil-rate band
c. Tax break
d. Tax Reform

Chapter 5. Long-Run Economic Growth: Origins of the Wealth of Nations

1. _____ was a survey conducted by the U.S. Department of Justice to gauge the prevalence of alcohol and illegal drug use among prior arrestees. It was a reformulation of the prior Drug Use Forecasting (DUF) program, focused on five drugs in particular: cocaine, marijuana, methamphetamine, opiates, and PCP.

Participants were randomly selected from arrest records in major metropolitan areas; because no personally identifying information is taken from each record chosen, the resulting data can be correlated to arrest rates, but not to the total population of persons charged.

    a. ACCRA Cost of Living Index
    b. ACEA agreement
    c. AD-IA Model
    d. Arrestee Drug Abuse Monitoring

2. _____s is the social science that studies the production, distribution, and consumption of goods and services. The term _____s comes from the Ancient Greek oá¼°κονοµῖα from oá¼¶κος (oikos, 'house') + vίŒµος (nomos, 'custom' or 'law'), hence 'rules of the house(hold)'. Current _____ models developed out of the broader field of political economy in the late 19th century, owing to a desire to use an empirical approach more akin to the physical sciences.

    a. Opportunity cost
    b. Energy economics
    c. Economic
    d. Inflation

3. _____ is the increase in the amount of the goods and services produced by an economy over time. It is conventionally measured as the percent rate of increase in real gross domestic product, or real GDP. Growth is usually calculated in real terms, i.e. inflation-adjusted terms, in order to net out the effect of inflation on the price of the goods and services produced.

    a. ACCRA Cost of Living Index
    b. Economic growth
    c. AD-IA Model
    d. ACEA agreement

4. The _____ was a period in the late 18th and early 19th centuries when major changes in agriculture, manufacturing, mining, and transportation had a profound effect on the socioeconomic and cultural conditions in Britain. The changes subsequently spread throughout Europe, North America, and eventually the world. The onset of the _____ marked a major turning point in human society; almost every aspect of daily life was eventually influenced in some way.

    a. Adolf Hitler
    b. Adolph Fischer
    c. Adam Smith
    d. Industrial revolution

5. A fixed exchange rate, sometimes called a _____, is a type of exchange rate regime wherein a currency's value is matched to the value of another single currency or to a basket of other currencies such as gold.

A fixed exchange rate is usually used to stabilize the value of a currency, vis-a-vis the currency it is pegged to. This facilitates trade and investments between the two countries, and is especially useful for small economies where external trade forms a large part of their GDP.

    a. Leading indicators
    b. Mainstream economics
    c. Recession
    d. Pegged exchange rate

6. _____ was a Scottish moral philosopher and a pioneer of political economy. One of the key figures of the Scottish Enlightenment, Smith is the author of The Theory of Moral Sentiments and An Inquiry into the Nature and Causes of the Wealth of Nations. The latter, usually abbreviated as The Wealth of Nations, is considered his magnum opus and the first modern work of economics.

Chapter 5. Long-Run Economic Growth: Origins of the Wealth of Nations

a. Adam Smith
b. Adolph Fischer
c. Alan Greenspan
d. Adolf Hitler

7. An Inquiry into the Nature and Causes of the _____ is the magnum opus of the Scottish economist Adam Smith. It is a clearly written account of economics at the dawn of the Industrial Revolution, as well as a rhetorical piece written for the generally educated individual of the 18th century - advocating a free market economy as more productive and more beneficial to society.

The work is credited as a watershed in history and economics due to its comprehensive, largely accurate characterization of economic mechanisms that survive in modern economics; and also for its effective use of rhetorical technique, including structuring the work to contrast real world examples of free and fettered markets.

a. Black Book of Communism
b. The Rise and Fall of the Great Powers
c. The Bell Curve
d. Wealth of Nations

8. In finance, the _____s between two currencies specifies how much one currency is worth in terms of the other. It is the value of a foreign natione;s currency in terms of the home natione;s currency. For example an _____ of 102 Japanese yen to the United States dollar means that JPY 102 is worth the same as USD 1.

a. ACEA agreement
b. ACCRA Cost of Living Index
c. Interbank market
d. Exchange rate

9. _____ is a misspelled phrase from Latin 'pro capite' phrase meaning per head with pro meaning 'per' or 'for each' and capite meaning 'head.' Both words together equate to the phrase 'for each head.'

It is usually used in the field of statistics to indicate the average per person for any given concern, such as income, crime rate, etc.

It is also used in wills to indicate that each of the named beneficiaries should receive, by devise or bequest, equal shares of the estate. This is in contrast to a per stirpes division, in which each branch of the inheriting family inherits an equal share of the estate.

a. Population statistics
b. Per capita
c. False positive rate
d. Sargan test

10. _____ means how much each individual receives, in monetary terms, of the yearly income generated in the country. This is what each citizen is to receive if the yearly national income is divided equally among everyone. _____ is usually reported in units of currency per year.

a. Family income
b. Lerman ratio
c. Real income
d. Per capita income

11. In microeconomics, _____ is quite simply the conversion of inputs into outputs. It is an economic process that uses resources to create a good or service that is suitable for exchange. This can include manufacturing, storing, shipping, and packaging.

a. Solved
b. Production
c. MET
d. Red Guards

Chapter 5. Long-Run Economic Growth: Origins of the Wealth of Nations

12. In economics, a _____ is a function that specifies the output of a firm, an industry, or an entire economy for all combinations of inputs. A meta-_____ compares the practice of the existing entities converting inputs X into output y to determine the most efficient practice _____ of the existing entities, whether the most efficient feasible practice production or the most efficient actual practice production. In either case, the maximum output of a technologically-determined production process is a mathematical function of input factors of production.
    a. Post-Fordism
    b. Short-run
    c. Constant elasticity of substitution
    d. Production function

13. In production, returns to scale refers to changes in output subsequent to a proportional change in all inputs (where all inputs increase by a constant factor.) If output increases by that same proportional change then there are _____ If output increases by less than that proportional change, there are decreasing returns to scale (DRS.)
    a. Lexicographic preferences
    b. Consumer sovereignty
    c. Long term
    d. Constant returns to scale

14. In economics, _____ and economies of scale are related terms that describe what happens as the scale of production increases. They are different terms and should not be used interchangeably.

    _____ refers to a technical property of production that examines changes in output subsequent to a proportional change in all inputs (where all inputs increase by a constant factor.)

    a. Customer equity
    b. Constant returns to scale
    c. Necessity good
    d. Returns to scale

15. _____ is a term used in economics to describe an economy where capital per worker is increasing. A process of increasing the amount of capital per worker. It is an increase in the capital intensity.
    a. Capital expenditure
    b. Capital deepening
    c. Firm-specific infrastructure
    d. Capital formation

16. _____ is widely regarded as the first modern school of economic thought. It is the idea that free markets can regulate themselves.Its major developers include Adam Smith, David Ricardo, Thomas Malthus and John Stuart Mill. Sometimes the definition of _____ is expanded to include William Petty, Johann Heinrich von Thünen.
    a. Marginalism
    b. Tendency of the rate of profit to fall
    c. Classical economics
    d. Schools of economic thought

17. The _____ or gross domestic income (GDI), a basic measure of an economy's economic performance, is the market value of all final goods and services produced within the borders of a nation in a year. _____ can be defined in three ways, all of which are conceptually identical. First, it is equal to the total expenditures for all final goods and services produced within the country in a stipulated period of time (usually a 365-day year.)
    a. Market structure
    b. Monopolistic competition
    c. Countercyclical
    d. Gross domestic product

18. _____ and Keynesian Theory) is a macroeconomic theory based on the ideas of 20th-century British economist John Maynard Keynes. _____ argues that private sector decisions sometimes lead to inefficient macroeconomic outcomes and therefore advocates active policy responses by the public sector, including monetary policy actions by the central bank and fiscal policy actions by the government to stabilize output over the business cycle.

The theories forming the basis of _____ were first presented in The General Theory of Employment, Interest and Money, published in 1936.

a. Market failure
b. Deflation
c. Rational choice theory
d. Keynesian economics

19. In economics, the people in the _____ are the suppliers of labor. The _____ is all the nonmilitary people who are employed or unemployed. In 2005, the worldwide _____ was over 3 billion people.

a. Distributed workforce
b. Grenelle agreements
c. Departmentalization
d. Labor force

20. In economic models, the _____ time frame assumes no fixed factors of production. Firms can enter or leave the marketplace, and the cost (and availability) of land, labor, raw materials, and capital goods can be assumed to vary. In contrast, in the short-run time frame, certain factors are assumed to be fixed, because there is not sufficient time for them to change.

a. Productivity world
b. Price/performance ratio
c. Diseconomies of scale
d. Long-run

21. In economics, _____ is the total amount of money available in an economy at a particular point in time. There are several ways to define 'money', but standard measures usually include currency in circulation and demand deposits.

_____ data are recorded and published, usually by the government or the central bank of the country.

a. Money supply
b. Velocity of money
c. Neutrality of money
d. Veil of money

22. _____ is a term used in national accounts statistics and macroeconomics. It basically refers to the net additions to the (physical) capital stock in an accounting period, or, to the value of the increase of the capital stock; though it may occasionally also refer to the (growth of the) total stock of capital formed.

Thus, in UNSNA, _____ equals fixed capital investment, the increase in the value of inventories held, plus (net) lending to foreign countries, during an accounting period.

a. Capital intensity
b. Consumption of fixed capital
c. Capital flight
d. Capital formation

23. _____ is a term that is used to describe the overall process of invention, innovation and diffusion of technology or processes. The term is redundant with technological development, technological achievement, and technological progress. In essence _____ is the invention of a technology (or a process), the continuous process of improving a technology (in which it often becomes cheaper) and its diffusion throughout industry or society.

a. 1921 recession
b. 130-30 fund
c. 100-year flood
d. Technological change

Chapter 5. Long-Run Economic Growth: Origins of the Wealth of Nations

24. In labor economics, the _____ hypothesis argues that wages, at least in some markets, are determined by more than simply supply and demand. Specifically, it points to the incentive for managers to pay their employees more than the market-clearing wage in order to increase their productivity or efficiency. This increased labor productivity pays for the relatively higher wages.
   a. Earnings calls
   b. Exogenous growth model
   c. Efficiency wage
   d. Inflatable rats

25. The supply of labor is the number of total hours that workers wish to work at a given real wage rate.

   _____ curves are derived from the 'labor-leisure' trade-off. More hours worked earn higher incomes but necessitate a cut in the amount of leisure that workers enjoy.

   a. Late capitalism
   b. Creative capitalism
   c. Human trafficking
   d. Labor supply

26. The Organisation for Economic Co-operation and Development (_____) is an international organisation of 30 countries that accept the principles of representative democracy and free-market economy. Most _____ members are high-income economies with a high HDI and are regarded as developed countries.

   It originated in 1948 as the Organisation for European Economic Co-operation , led by Robert Marjolin of France, to help administer the Marshall Plan for the reconstruction of Europe after World War II.

   a. OECD
   b. AD-IA Model
   c. ACCRA Cost of Living Index
   d. ACEA agreement

27. The _____ is a theory of consumption that was developed by the American economist Milton Friedman. In its simplest form, the hypothesis states that the choices made by consumers regarding their consumption patterns are determined not by current income but by their longer-term income expectations. The key conclusion of this theory is that transitory, short-term changes in income have little effect on consumer spending behavior.
   a. Permanent income hypothesis
   b. Washington Consensus
   c. Natural rate of unemployment
   d. Balanced-growth equilibrium

28. An _____, in economics, is the amount by which the real Gross domestic product exceeds potential GDP. The real GDP is also known as GDP 'adjusted for inflation', 'constant prices' GDP or 'constant dollar' GDP, because it measures the aggregate output in a country's income accounts in a given year, expressed in base-year prices. On the other hand, the potential GDP is the quantity of real GDP when a country's economy is at full-employment.
   a. Inflationary gap
   b. AD-IA Model
   c. ACCRA Cost of Living Index
   d. ACEA agreement

29. In economics, the term _____ of income or _____ refers to a simple economic model which describes the reciprocal circulation of income between producers and consumers. In the _____ model, the inter-dependent entities of producer and consumer are referred to as 'firms' and 'households' respectively and provide each other with factors in order to facilitate the flow of income. Firms provide consumers with goods and services in exchange for consumer expenditure and 'factors of production' from households.

a. 1921 recession
b. 130-30 fund
c. 100-year flood
d. Circular flow

30. The _____ is where currency trading takes place. It is where banks and other official institutions facilitate the buying and selling of foreign currencies. FX transactions typically involve one party purchasing a quantity of one currency in exchange for paying a quantity of another.
    a. Floating currency
    b. Currency swap
    c. Covered interest arbitrage
    d. Foreign exchange market

Chapter 6. The Keynesian System (I): The Role of Aggregate Demand

1. A variety of measures of national income and output are used in economics to estimate total economic activity in a country or region, including gross domestic product (GDP), _____ , and net national income (NNI.)

There are three main ways of calculating these numbers; the output approach, the income approach and the expenditure approach. In theory, the three must yield the same, because total expenditures on goods and services must equal the total income paid to the producers (GNI), and that must also equal the total value of the output of goods and services (_____.)

   a. Household final consumption expenditure
   b. Gross world product
   c. Purchasing power parity
   d. Gross national product

2. _____, 1st Baron Keynes was a renowned economist from Britain whose many ideas on economic and political theories as well as on many governments' monetary policies influenced America. He advocated a government that played an active role in the lives of people regarding business, economy, etc. In this role, the government would use fiscal measures to reduce the consequences of recessions, economic depressions and booms.
   a. Adolph Fischer
   b. John Maynard Keynes
   c. Adolf Hitler
   d. Adam Smith

3. _____ and Keynesian Theory) is a macroeconomic theory based on the ideas of 20th-century British economist John Maynard Keynes. _____ argues that private sector decisions sometimes lead to inefficient macroeconomic outcomes and therefore advocates active policy responses by the public sector, including monetary policy actions by the central bank and fiscal policy actions by the government to stabilize output over the business cycle.

The theories forming the basis of _____ were first presented in The General Theory of Employment, Interest and Money, published in 1936.

   a. Rational choice theory
   b. Market failure
   c. Deflation
   d. Keynesian economics

4. _____s is the social science that studies the production, distribution, and consumption of goods and services. The term _____s comes from the Ancient Greek oἰκονομία from oἶκος (oikos, 'house') + νόμος (nomos, 'custom' or 'law'), hence 'rules of the house(hold)'. Current _____ models developed out of the broader field of political economy in the late 19th century, owing to a desire to use an empirical approach more akin to the physical sciences.
   a. Energy economics
   b. Opportunity cost
   c. Economic
   d. Inflation

5. _____ or government expenditure is classified by economists into three main types. Government purchases of goods and services for current use are classed as government consumption. Government purchases of goods and services intended to create future benefits, such as infrastructure investment or research spending, are classed as government investment.
   a. 130-30 fund
   b. 1921 recession
   c. Government spending
   d. 100-year flood

6. _____ is the price at which an asset would trade in a competitive Walrasian auction setting. _____ is often used interchangeably with open _____, fair value or fair _____, although these terms have distinct definitions in different standards, and may differ in some circumstances.

Chapter 6. The Keynesian System (I): The Role of Aggregate Demand

International Valuation Standards defines _____ as 'the estimated amount for which a property should exchange on the date of valuation between a willing buyer and a willing seller in an arm's-length transaction after proper marketing wherein the parties had each acted knowledgeably, prudently, and without compulsion.'

_____ is a concept distinct from market price, which is 'the price at which one can transact', while _____ is 'the true underlying value' according to theoretical standards.

    a. Secured loan
    c. Personal financial management
    b. Netting
    d. Market value

7. _____ is the view within monetary economics that variation in the money supply has major influences on national output in the short run and the price level over longer periods and that objectives of monetary policy are best met by targeting the growth rate of the money supply.

_____ today is mainly associated with the work of Milton Friedman, who was among the generation of economists to accept Keynesian economics and then criticize it on his own terms. Friedman and Anna Schwartz wrote an influential book, Monetary History of the United States 1867-1960, and argued that 'inflation is always and everywhere a monetary phenomenon.' Friedman advocated a central bank policy aimed at keeping the supply and demand for money at equilibrium, as measured by growth in productivity and demand.

    a. Marginal revenue productivity theory of wages
    c. Historical school of economics
    b. Complexity economics
    d. Monetarism

8. _____ is the process by which the government, central bank (ii) availability of money, and (iii) cost of money or rate of interest, in order to attain a set of objectives oriented towards the growth and stability of the economy. Monetary theory provides insight into how to craft optimal _____.

_____ is referred to as either being an expansionary policy where an expansionary policy increases the total supply of money in the economy, and a contractionary policy decreases the total money supply.

    a. 130-30 fund
    c. 1921 recession
    b. 100-year flood
    d. Monetary policy

9. _____ is a school of contemporary macroeconomics that strives to provide microeconomic foundations for Keynesian economics. It developed partly as a response to criticisms of Keynesian macroeconomics by adherents of New Classical macroeconomics.

    a. Keynesian theory
    c. Law of demand
    b. Mainstream economics
    d. New Keynesian economics

10. In economics, _____ is the total demand for final goods and services in the economy (Y) at a given time and price level. It is the amount of goods and services in the economy that will be purchased at all possible price levels. This is the demand for the gross domestic product of a country when inventory levels are static.

Chapter 6. The Keynesian System (I): The Role of Aggregate Demand

a. Aggregate demand
b. Aggregation problem
c. Aggregate supply
d. Aggregate expenditure

11. _____ is widely regarded as the first modern school of economic thought. It is the idea that free markets can regulate themselves. Its major developers include Adam Smith, David Ricardo, Thomas Malthus and John Stuart Mill. Sometimes the definition of _____ is expanded to include William Petty, Johann Heinrich von Thünen.
   a. Tendency of the rate of profit to fall
   b. Schools of economic thought
   c. Marginalism
   d. Classical economics

12. Economics:

   - _____, the desire to own something and the ability to pay for it
   - _____ curve, a graphic representation of a _____ schedule
   - _____ deposit, the money in checking accounts
   - _____ pull theory, the theory that inflation occurs when _____ for goods and services exceeds existing supplies
   - _____ schedule, a table that lists the quantity of a good a person will buy it each different price
   - _____ side economics, the school of economics at believes government spending and tax cuts open economy by raising _____

   a. Demand
   b. McKesson ' Robbins scandal
   c. Production
   d. Variability

13. _____ is a common concept in economics, and gives rise to derived concepts such as consumer debt. Generally _____ is defined by opposition to production. But the precise definition can vary because different schools of economists define production quite differently.
   a. Federal Reserve Bank Notes
   b. Foreclosure data providers
   c. Consumption
   d. Cash or share options

14. _____ is the a method of technical and economic research of the systems for purpose to optimize a parity between system's consumer functions or properties and expenses to achieve those functions or properties.

This methodology for continuous perfection of production, industrial technologies, organizational structures was developed by Juryj Sobolev in 1948 at the 'Perm telephone factory'

- 1948 Juryj Sobolev - the first success in application of a method analysis at the 'Perm telephone factory'.
- 1949 - the first application for the invention as result of use of the new method.

Chapter 6. The Keynesian System (I): The Role of Aggregate Demand

Today in economically developed countries practically each enterprise or the company use methodology of the kind of functional-cost analysis as a practice of the quality management, most full satisfying to principles of standards of series ISO 9000.

- Interest of consumer not in products itself, but the advantage which it will receive from its usage.
- The consumer aspires to reduce his expenses
- Functions needed by consumer can be executed in the various ways, and, hence, with various efficiency and expenses. Among possible alternatives of realization of functions exist such in which the parity of quality and the price is the optimal for the consumer.

The goal of _____ is achievement of the highest consumer satisfaction of production at simultaneous decrease in all kinds of industrial expenses Classical _____ has three English synonyms - Value Engineering, Value Management, Value Analysis.

a. Willingness to pay
c. Monopoly wage
b. Staple financing
d. Function cost analysis

15. The _____ or gross domestic income (GDI), a basic measure of an economy's economic performance, is the market value of all final goods and services produced within the borders of a nation in a year. _____ can be defined in three ways, all of which are conceptually identical. First, it is equal to the total expenditures for all final goods and services produced within the country in a stipulated period of time (usually a 365-day year.)

a. Monopolistic competition
c. Market structure
b. Countercyclical
d. Gross domestic product

16. _____ was the 31st President of the United States (1929-1933.) Besides his political career, Hoover was a professional mining engineer and author. As the United States Secretary of Commerce in the 1920s under Presidents Warren Harding and Calvin Coolidge, he promoted government intervention under the rubric 'economic modernization'.

a. Herbert Hoover
c. Adolph Fischer
b. Adolf Hitler
d. Adam Smith

17. _____, often referred to by his initials _____, was the 32nd President of the United States. He was a central figure of the 20th century during a time of worldwide economic crisis and world war. Elected to four terms in office, he served from 1933 to 1945 and is the only U.S. president to have served more than two terms.

a. Adolf Hitler
c. Adam Smith
b. Franklin Delano Roosevelt
d. Adolph Fischer

18. _____ is a branch of economics that deals with the performance, structure, and behavior of a national or regional economy as a whole. Along with microeconomics, _____ is one of the two most general fields in economics. It is the study of the behavior and decision-making of entire economies.

a. Macroeconomics
c. Nominal value
b. Tobit model
d. New Trade Theory

Chapter 6. The Keynesian System (I): The Role of Aggregate Demand

19. In economics, the term _____ of income or _____ refers to a simple economic model which describes the reciprocal circulation of income between producers and consumers. In the _____ model, the inter-dependent entities of producer and consumer are referred to as 'firms' and 'households' respectively and provide each other with factors in order to facilitate the flow of income. Firms provide consumers with goods and services in exchange for consumer expenditure and 'factors of production' from households.

    a. Circular flow
    b. 100-year flood
    c. 130-30 fund
    d. 1921 recession

20. The _____ is a theory of consumption that was developed by the American economist Milton Friedman. In its simplest form, the hypothesis states that the choices made by consumers regarding their consumption patterns are determined not by current income but by their longer-term income expectations. The key conclusion of this theory is that transitory, short-term changes in income have little effect on consumer spending behavior.

    a. Natural rate of unemployment
    b. Balanced-growth equilibrium
    c. Washington Consensus
    d. Permanent income hypothesis

21. To _____ is to impose a financial charge or other levy upon a taxpayer by a state or the functional equivalent of a state.

_____es are also imposed by many subnational entities. _____es consist of direct _____ or indirect _____, and may be paid in money or as its labour equivalent (often but not always unpaid.)

    a. 130-30 fund
    b. 100-year flood
    c. Tax
    d. 1921 recession

22. The term _____ describes two different concepts:

- The first is a recognition of partial payment already made towards taxes due.
- The second is a state benefit paid to workers through the tax system, which has the effect of increasing (rather than reducing) net income.

Within the Australian, Canadian, United Kingdom, and United States tax systems, a _____ is a recognition of partial payment already made towards taxes due. A similar concept exists (fr:Avoir fiscal) in the French tax system. This situation arises, for example, when standard rate tax has been deducted at source, but the tax-payer is subject to further taxation at a higher rate. It also applies in dividend imputation systems.

    a. 100-year flood
    b. 130-30 fund
    c. 1921 recession
    d. Tax credit

23. A _____ refers to any type debt instrument, such as a loan, bond, mortgage that does not have a fixed rate of interest over the life of the instrument. Such debt typically uses an index or other base rate for establishing the interest rate for each relevant period. One of the most common rates to use as the basis for applying interest rates is the London Inter-bank Offered Rate, or LIBOR

    a. Moneylender
    b. Disposal tax effect
    c. Money market
    d. Floating interest rate

Chapter 6. The Keynesian System (I): The Role of Aggregate Demand

24. _____ in economics and business is the result of an exchange and from that trade we assign a numerical monetary value to a good, service or asset. If Alice trades Bob 4 apples for an orange, the _____ of an orange is 4 apples. Inversely, the _____ of an apple is 1/4 oranges.
   a. Price war
   b. Premium pricing
   c. Price book
   d. Price

25. A _____ is a hypothetical measure of overall prices for some set of goods and services, in a given region during a given interval, normalized relative to some base set. Typically, a _____ is approximated with a price index.

The classical dichotomy is the assumption that there is a relatively clean distinction between overall increases or decreases in prices and underlying, e;reale; economic variables.

   a. Discretionary spending
   b. Price level
   c. Price elasticity of supply
   d. Discouraged worker

26. _____ relates to the composition of GDP. What is produced in a certain country is naturally also sold, but some of the goods produced in a given year may not be sold the same year, but in later years. Conversely, some of the goods sold in a given year might have been produced in an earlier year.
   a. Inventory investment
   b. Obelisk International
   c. Investment decisions
   d. Investment theory

27. In economics, the _____ is a single mathematical function used to express consumer spending. It was developed by John Maynard Keynes and detailed most famously in his book The General Theory of Employment, Interest, and Money. The function is used to calculate the amount of total consumption in an economy.
   a. Procyclical
   b. DAD-SAS model
   c. Liquidity preference
   d. Consumption function

28. In economics, the _____ is an empirical metric that quantifies induced consumption, the concept that the increase in personal consumer spending (consumption) that occurs with an increase in disposable income (income after taxes and transfers.) For example, if a household earns one extra dollar of disposable income, and the _____ is 0.65, then of that dollar, the household will spend 65 cents and save 35 cents.

Mathematically, the _____ (MPC) function is expressed as the derivative of the consumption (C) function with respect to disposable income (Y.)

   a. Technology shock
   b. Supply shock
   c. Marginal propensity to import
   d. Marginal propensity to consume

29. The _____ refers to the increase in saving (non-purchase of current goods and services) that results from an increase in income. For example, if a household earns one extra dollar, and the _____ is 0.35, then of that dollar, the household will spend 65 cents and save 35 cents. It can also go the other way, referring to the decrease in saving that results from a decrease in income.
   a. Marginal propensity to save
   b. Solow residual
   c. Robertson lag
   d. Real business cycle

Chapter 6. The Keynesian System (I): The Role of Aggregate Demand

30. _____ is a concept found in moral, political, and bioethical philosophy. Within these contexts, it refers to the capacity of a rational individual to make an informed, un-coerced decision. In moral and political philosophy, _____ is often used as the basis for determining moral responsibility for one's actions.
    a. AD-IA Model
    b. ACCRA Cost of Living Index
    c. ACEA agreement
    d. Autonomy

31. _____ is a fee paid on borrowed assets. It is the price paid for the use of borrowed money , or, money earned by deposited funds . Assets that are sometimes lent with _____ include money, shares, consumer goods through hire purchase, major assets such as aircraft, and even entire factories in finance lease arrangements.
    a. Asset protection
    b. Internal debt
    c. Insolvency
    d. Interest

32. An _____ is the price a borrower pays for the use of money they do not own, for instance a small company might borrow from a bank to kick start their business, and the return a lender receives for deferring the use of funds, by lending it to the borrower. _____s are normally expressed as a percentage rate over the period of one year.

    _____s targets are also a vital tool of monetary policy and are used to control variables like investment, inflation, and unemployment.

    a. Enterprise value
    b. ACCRA Cost of Living Index
    c. Interest rate
    d. Arrow-Debreu model

33. _____ is the process of estimation in unknown situations. Prediction is a similar, but more general term. Both can refer to estimation of time series, cross-sectional or longitudinal data.
    a. 130-30 fund
    b. 100-year flood
    c. Forecasting
    d. 1921 recession

34. To tax is to impose a financial charge or other levy upon a taxpayer by a state or the functional equivalent of a state.

    _____ are also imposed by many subnational entities. _____ consist of direct tax or indirect tax, and may be paid in money or as its labour equivalent (often but not always unpaid.)

    a. 130-30 fund
    b. 1921 recession
    c. Taxes
    d. 100-year flood

Chapter 6. The Keynesian System (I): The Role of Aggregate Demand

35. _____ refers to an action or object coming from outside a system. It is the opposite of endogenous, something generated from within the system.

- In an economic model, an _____ change is one that comes from outside the model and is unexplained by the model. For example, in the simple supply and demand model, a change in consumer tastes or preferences is unexplained by the model and also leads to endogenous changes in demand that lead to changes in the equilibrium price. Put another way, an _____ change involves an alteration of a variable that is autonomous, i.e., unaffected by the workings of the model.

- In linear regression, it means that the variable is independent of all other response values.

- In biology, '_____' refers to an action or object coming from the outside of a system. For example, an _____ contrast agent in medical imaging refers to a liquid injected into the patient intravenously that enhances visibility of a pathology, such as a tumor.

a. ACEA agreement
b. ACCRA Cost of Living Index
c. AD-IA Model
d. Exogenous

36. A variety of measures of _____ and output are used in economics to estimate total economic activity in a country or region, including gross domestic product (GDP), gross national product (GNP), and net _____

There are three main ways of calculating these numbers; the output approach, the income approach and the expenditure approach. In theory, the three must yield the same, because total expenditures on goods and services must equal the total income paid to the producers (Gnational income), and that must also equal the total value of the output of goods and services (GNP.)

a. Volume index
b. GNI per capita
c. Gross world product
d. National income

37. In economics, _____ is the total supply of goods and services produced by a national economy during a specific time period. It is the total amount of goods and services in the economy available at all possible price levels.

a. Aggregate supply
b. Aggregate demand
c. Aggregation problem
d. Aggregate expenditure

38. From a Keynesian point of view, a _____ in the public sector is achieved when the government equates the revenues with expenditure over the business cycles. In other words, a government's budget is balanced if its income is equal to its expenditure. It is a budget in which revenues are equal to spending.

a. Budget support
b. Balanced budget
c. Budget crisis
d. Budget theory

Chapter 6. The Keynesian System (I): The Role of Aggregate Demand

39. The term _____ refers to government debt, expenditures and revenues, or to finance (particularly financial revenue) in general.

- _____ deficit is the budget deficit of federal or local government
- _____ policy is the discretionary spending of governments. Contrasts with monetary policy.
- _____ year and _____ quarter are reporting periods for firms and other agencies.

  a. Bucket shop
  c. Procter ' Gamble
  b. Fiscal
  d. Drawdown

40. _____ is the increase in the amount of the goods and services produced by an economy over time. It is conventionally measured as the percent rate of increase in real gross domestic product, or real GDP. Growth is usually calculated in real terms, i.e. inflation-adjusted terms, in order to net out the effect of inflation on the price of the goods and services produced.

  a. AD-IA Model
  c. ACEA agreement
  b. ACCRA Cost of Living Index
  d. Economic growth

41. In economics, an _____ is any good or commodity, transported from one country to another country in a legitimate fashion, typically for use in trade. _____ goods or services are provided to foreign consumers by domestic producers. _____ is an important part of international trade.

  a. ACCRA Cost of Living Index
  c. AD-IA Model
  b. Export
  d. ACEA agreement

42. In economics, _____ is the use of government spending and revenue collection to influence the economy.

_____ can be contrasted with the other main type of economic policy, monetary policy, which attempts to stabilize the economy by controlling interest rates and the supply of money. The two main instruments of _____ are government spending and taxation.

  a. 100-year flood
  c. Fiscal policy
  b. Sustainable investment rule
  d. Fiscalism

43. In economics, an _____ is any good (e.g. a commodity) or service brought into one country from another country in a legitimate fashion, typically for use in trade. It is a good that is brought in from another country for sale. _____ goods or services are provided to domestic consumers by foreign producers. An _____ in the receiving country is an export to the sending country.

  a. Economic integration
  c. Import quota
  b. Incoterms
  d. Import

44. A _____ is a package or set of measures introduced to stabilise a financial system or economy. The term can refer to policies in two distinct sets of circumstances: business cycle stabilization and crisis stabilization.

Stabilization can refer to correcting the normal behavior of the business cycle.

a. Volunteers for Economic Growth Alliance
b. Stabilization policy
c. New International Economic Order
d. Capacity Development

45. An autarky is an economy that is self-sufficient and does not take part in international trade, or severely limits trade with the outside world. Likewise the term refers to an ecosystem not affected by influences from the outside, which relies entirely on its own resources. In the economic meaning, it is also referred to as a _____.
   a. Network Economy
   b. Transition economy
   c. Digital economy
   d. Closed economy

46. _____ is a broad label that refers to any individuals or households that use goods and services generated within the economy. The concept of a _____ is used in different contexts, so that the usage and significance of the term may vary.

Typically when business people and economists talk of _____s they are talking about person as _____, an aggregated commodity item with little individuality other than that expressed in the buy/not-buy decision.

   a. 100-year flood
   b. Consumer
   c. 130-30 fund
   d. 1921 recession

47. A _____ is a measure of the average price of consumer goods and services purchased by households. A _____ measures a price change for a constant market basket of goods and services from one period to the next within the same area (city, region, or nation.) It is a price index determined by measuring the price of a standard group of goods meant to represent the typical market basket of a typical urban consumer.
   a. CPI
   b. Cost-of-living index
   c. Lipstick index
   d. Consumer price index

48. An _____ is an economy in which people, including businesses, can trade in goods and services with other people and businesses in the international community at large. This contrasts with a closed economy in which international trade cannot take place.

The act of selling goods or services to a foreign country is called exporting.

   a. Attention work
   b. Information economy
   c. Indicative planning
   d. Open economy

49. A _____ is a normalized average (typically a weighted average) of prices for a given class of goods or services in a given region, during a given interval of time. It is a statistic designed to help to compare how these prices, taken as a whole, differ between time periods or geographical locations.

Price indices have several potential uses.

   a. Product sabotage
   b. Price index
   c. Two-part tariff
   d. Transactional Net Margin Method

Chapter 6. The Keynesian System (I): The Role of Aggregate Demand

50. A _____ is a reduction in taxes. Economic stimulus via _____s, along with interest rate intervention and deficit spending, are one of the central tenets of Keynesian economics.

The immediate effects of a _____ are, generally, a decrease in the real income of the government and an increase in the real income of those whose tax rate has been lowered.

a. Popiwek
c. Tax cut
b. Direct taxes
d. Withholding tax

51. A _____, reserve bank, or monetary authority is the entity responsible for the monetary policy of a country or of a group of member states. It is a bank that can lend money to other banks in times of need. Its primary responsibility is to maintain the stability of the national currency and money supply, but more active duties include controlling subsidized-loan interest rates, and acting as a lender of last resort to the banking sector during times of financial crisis (private banks often being integral to the national financial system.)

a. 1921 recession
c. 100-year flood
b. 130-30 fund
d. Central bank

Chapter 7. The Keynesian System (II): Money, Interest, and Income

1. _____ is a fee paid on borrowed assets. It is the price paid for the use of borrowed money, or, money earned by deposited funds. Assets that are sometimes lent with _____ include money, shares, consumer goods through hire purchase, major assets such as aircraft, and even entire factories in finance lease arrangements.
   a. Asset protection
   b. Internal debt
   c. Insolvency
   d. Interest

2. An _____ is the price a borrower pays for the use of money they do not own, for instance a small company might borrow from a bank to kick start their business, and the return a lender receives for deferring the use of funds, by lending it to the borrower. _____s are normally expressed as a percentage rate over the period of one year.

   _____s targets are also a vital tool of monetary policy and are used to control variables like investment, inflation, and unemployment.

   a. Arrow-Debreu model
   b. Enterprise value
   c. Interest rate
   d. ACCRA Cost of Living Index

3. _____ and Keynesian Theory) is a macroeconomic theory based on the ideas of 20th-century British economist John Maynard Keynes. _____ argues that private sector decisions sometimes lead to inefficient macroeconomic outcomes and therefore advocates active policy responses by the public sector, including monetary policy actions by the central bank and fiscal policy actions by the government to stabilize output over the business cycle.

   The theories forming the basis of _____ were first presented in The General Theory of Employment, Interest and Money, published in 1936.

   a. Keynesian economics
   b. Market failure
   c. Rational choice theory
   d. Deflation

4. In economics, _____ is the total demand for final goods and services in the economy (Y) at a given time and price level. It is the amount of goods and services in the economy that will be purchased at all possible price levels. This is the demand for the gross domestic product of a country when inventory levels are static.
   a. Aggregation problem
   b. Aggregate demand
   c. Aggregate supply
   d. Aggregate expenditure

5. Economics:

   - _____, the desire to own something and the ability to pay for it
   - _____ curve, a graphic representation of a _____ schedule
   - _____ deposit, the money in checking accounts
   - _____ pull theory, the theory that inflation occurs when _____ for goods and services exceeds existing supplies
   - _____ schedule, a table that lists the quantity of a good a person will buy it each different price
   - _____ side economics, the school of economics at believes government spending and tax cuts open economy by raising _____

Chapter 7. The Keynesian System (II): Money, Interest, and Income

    a. McKesson ' Robbins scandal
    b. Demand
    c. Production
    d. Variability

6. _____s is the social science that studies the production, distribution, and consumption of goods and services. The term _____s comes from the Ancient Greek oá¼°κονομῖα from oá¼¶κος (oikos, 'house') + vÏŒμος (nomos, 'custom' or 'law'), hence 'rules of the house(hold)'. Current _____ models developed out of the broader field of political economy in the late 19th century, owing to a desire to use an empirical approach more akin to the physical sciences.
    a. Energy economics
    b. Economic
    c. Inflation
    d. Opportunity cost

7. The _____ or gross domestic income (GDI), a basic measure of an economy's economic performance, is the market value of all final goods and services produced within the borders of a nation in a year. _____ can be defined in three ways, all of which are conceptually identical. First, it is equal to the total expenditures for all final goods and services produced within the country in a stipulated period of time (usually a 365-day year.)
    a. Market structure
    b. Monopolistic competition
    c. Countercyclical
    d. Gross domestic product

8. _____ or government expenditure is classified by economists into three main types. Government purchases of goods and services for current use are classed as government consumption. Government purchases of goods and services intended to create future benefits, such as infrastructure investment or research spending, are classed as government investment.
    a. 130-30 fund
    b. 100-year flood
    c. 1921 recession
    d. Government spending

9. An _____, in economics, is the amount by which the real Gross domestic product exceeds potential GDP. The real GDP is also known as GDP 'adjusted for inflation', 'constant prices' GDP or 'constant dollar' GDP, because it measures the aggregate output in a country's income accounts in a given year, expressed in base-year prices. On the other hand, the potential GDP is the quantity of real GDP when a country's economy is at full-employment.
    a. AD-IA Model
    b. ACCRA Cost of Living Index
    c. Inflationary gap
    d. ACEA agreement

10. _____ is a common concept in economics, and gives rise to derived concepts such as consumer debt. Generally _____ is defined by opposition to production. But the precise definition can vary because different schools of economists define production quite differently.
    a. Federal Reserve Bank Notes
    b. Foreclosure data providers
    c. Cash or share options
    d. Consumption

11. In finance, a _____ is a debt security, in which the authorized issuer owes the holders a debt and, depending on the terms of the _____, is obliged to pay interest (the coupon) and/or to repay the principal at a later date, termed maturity. A _____ is a formal contract to repay borrowed money with interest at fixed intervals.

Thus a _____ is like a loan: the issuer is the borrower (debtor), the holder is the lender (creditor), and the coupon is the interest.

a. Bond
b. Zero-coupon
c. Prize Bond
d. Callable

12. _____, 1st Baron Keynes was a renowned economist from Britain whose many ideas on economic and political theories as well as on many governments' monetary policies influenced America. He advocated a government that played an active role in the lives of people regarding business, economy, etc. In this role, the government would use fiscal measures to reduce the consequences of recessions, economic depressions and booms.
   a. Adolf Hitler
   b. John Maynard Keynes
   c. Adam Smith
   d. Adolph Fischer

13. _____ is the view within monetary economics that variation in the money supply has major influences on national output in the short run and the price level over longer periods and that objectives of monetary policy are best met by targeting the growth rate of the money supply.

_____ today is mainly associated with the work of Milton Friedman, who was among the generation of economists to accept Keynesian economics and then criticize it on his own terms. Friedman and Anna Schwartz wrote an influential book, Monetary History of the United States 1867-1960, and argued that 'inflation is always and everywhere a monetary phenomenon.' Friedman advocated a central bank policy aimed at keeping the supply and demand for money at equilibrium, as measured by growth in productivity and demand.

   a. Complexity economics
   b. Marginal revenue productivity theory of wages
   c. Monetarism
   d. Historical school of economics

14. _____ is the process by which the government, central bank (ii) availability of money, and (iii) cost of money or rate of interest, in order to attain a set of objectives oriented towards the growth and stability of the economy. Monetary theory provides insight into how to craft optimal _____.

_____ is referred to as either being an expansionary policy where an expansionary policy increases the total supply of money in the economy, and a contractionary policy decreases the total money supply.

   a. 130-30 fund
   b. 1921 recession
   c. 100-year flood
   d. Monetary policy

15. _____ is a school of contemporary macroeconomics that strives to provide microeconomic foundations for Keynesian economics. It developed partly as a response to criticisms of Keynesian macroeconomics by adherents of New Classical macroeconomics.
   a. Mainstream economics
   b. New Keynesian economics
   c. Keynesian theory
   d. Law of demand

16. The _____ is the average frequency with which a unit of money is spent in a specific period of time. Velocity associates the amount of economic activity associated with a given money supply. When the period is understood, the velocity may be present as a pure number; otherwise it should be given as a pure number over time.
   a. Neutrality of money
   b. Money supply
   c. Chartalism
   d. Velocity of money

Chapter 7. The Keynesian System (II): Money, Interest, and Income

17. _____ is widely regarded as the first modern school of economic thought. It is the idea that free markets can regulate themselves. Its major developers include Adam Smith, David Ricardo, Thomas Malthus and John Stuart Mill. Sometimes the definition of _____ is expanded to include William Petty, Johann Heinrich von Thünen.
   a. Marginalism
   b. Classical economics
   c. Schools of economic thought
   d. Tendency of the rate of profit to fall

18. In economics, _____ is the total amount of money available in an economy at a particular point in time. There are several ways to define 'money', but standard measures usually include currency in circulation and demand deposits.

   _____ data are recorded and published, usually by the government or the central bank of the country.

   a. Neutrality of money
   b. Veil of money
   c. Velocity of money
   d. Money supply

19. In economics, _____ is the total supply of goods and services produced by a national economy during a specific time period. It is the total amount of goods and services in the economy available at all possible price levels.
   a. Aggregate demand
   b. Aggregate expenditure
   c. Aggregation problem
   d. Aggregate supply

20. _____ is the demand for financial assets, e.g., securities, money or foreign currency. It is used for purposes of business transactions and personal consumption.

   The need to accommodate a firm's expected cash transactions.

   a. Spending multiplier
   b. Keynesian cross
   c. Transactions demand
   d. Multiplier effect

21. _____ is the increase in the amount of the goods and services produced by an economy over time. It is conventionally measured as the percent rate of increase in real gross domestic product, or real GDP. Growth is usually calculated in real terms, i.e. inflation-adjusted terms, in order to net out the effect of inflation on the price of the goods and services produced.
   a. AD-IA Model
   b. ACCRA Cost of Living Index
   c. Economic growth
   d. ACEA agreement

22. _____ is the demand for financial assets, such as securities, money or foreign currency; it is money people want in case of emergency.

   In economic theory, specifically Keynesian economics, _____ is one of the determinants of demand for money (and credit), the others being transactions demand and Speculative demand.

   a. Kinked demand
   b. Marshallian demand function
   c. Kinked demand curve
   d. Precautionary demand

23. A _____ measures average changes in prices received by domestic producers for their output. It is one of several price indices

Its importance is being undermined by the steady decline in manufactured goods as a share of spending.

A number of countries that now report a _____ previously reported a Wholesale Price Index.

- a. Visible balance
- b. Hemline index
- c. Producer price index
- d. Gross national product

24. _____ in economics and business is the result of an exchange and from that trade we assign a numerical monetary value to a good, service or asset. If Alice trades Bob 4 apples for an orange, the _____ of an orange is 4 apples. Inversely, the _____ of an apple is 1/4 oranges.
- a. Price
- b. Price book
- c. Premium pricing
- d. Price war

25. A _____ is a normalized average (typically a weighted average) of prices for a given class of goods or services in a given region, during a given interval of time. It is a statistic designed to help to compare how these prices, taken as a whole, differ between time periods or geographical locations.

Price indices have several potential uses.

- a. Price index
- b. Two-part tariff
- c. Transactional Net Margin Method
- d. Product sabotage

26. _____ is the demand for financial assets, such as securities, money or foreign currency that is not dictated by real transactions such as trade, or financing.

The need for cash to take advantage of investment opportunities that may arise.

In economic theory, specifically Keynesian economics, _____ is one of the determinants of demand for money (and credit), the others being transactions demand and precautionary demand.

- a. Spending multiplier
- b. Keynesian Revolution
- c. Speculative demand
- d. Multiplier effect

27. In finance, _____ is a financial action that does not promise safety of the initial investment along with the return on the principal sum. _____ typically involves the lending of money or the purchase of assets, equity or debt but in a manner that has not been given thorough analysis or is deemed to have low margin of safety or a significant risk of the loss of the principal investment. The term, '_____,' which is formally defined as above in Graham and Dodd's 1934 text, Security Analysis, contrasts with the term 'investment,' which is a financial operation that, upon thorough analysis, promises safety of principal and a satisfactory return.
- a. Municipal Bond Arbitrage
- b. Global Financial Centres Index
- c. Hybrid market
- d. Speculation

Chapter 7. The Keynesian System (II): Money, Interest, and Income

28. In economics, the _____ can be defined as the graph depicting the relationship between the price of a certain commodity, and the amount of it that consumers are willing and able to purchase at that given price. It is a graphic representation of a demand schedule. The _____ for all consumers together follows from the _____ of every individual consumer: the individual demands at each price are added together.
   a. Kuznets curve
   b. Wage curve
   c. Cost curve
   d. Demand curve

29. _____ is the difference between a lower selling price and a higher purchase price, resulting in a financial loss for the seller. Pursuant to IRS TAX TIP 2009-35 'If your _____es exceed your capital gains, the excess can be deducted on your tax return, up to an annual limit of $3,000 ($1,500 if you are married filing separately.)'.
   a. Capital loss
   b. 100-year flood
   c. 1921 recession
   d. 130-30 fund

30. Market _____ is a business, economics or investment term that refers to an asset's ability to be easily converted through an act of buying or selling without causing a significant movement in the price and with minimum loss of value. Money, or cash on hand, is the most liquid asset. An act of exchange of a less liquid asset with a more liquid asset is called liquidation.
   a. 130-30 fund
   b. 1921 recession
   c. Liquidity
   d. 100-year flood

31. The term _____ is used in macroeconomics to refer to a situation where a country's nominal interest rate has been lowered nearly to or equal to zero to avoid a recession, but the liquidity in the market created by these low interest rates does not stimulate the economy to full employment. In this situation, any further increase in the money supply will not stimulate the economy any further. This is because any further injection of liquidity will no longer lower the nominal interest rate, as the nominal interest rate cannot drop below zero.
   a. Robertson lag
   b. Minimum wage
   c. Macroeconomic models
   d. Liquidity trap

32. The _____ is the desired holding of money balances in the form of cash or bank deposits.

Money is dominated as store of value by interest bearing assets. However, money is necessary to carry out transactions, or in other words, it provides liquidity.

   a. Borrowing base
   b. Conglomerate merger
   c. Market neutral
   d. Demand for money

33. In finance, the _____ is the global financial market for short-term borrowing and lending. It provides short-term liquidity funding for the global financial system. The _____ is where short-term obligations such as Treasury bills, commercial paper and bankers' acceptances are bought and sold.
   a. Consignment stock
   b. Money market
   c. Deferred compensation
   d. T-Model

Chapter 7. The Keynesian System (II): Money, Interest, and Income

34. In economics, economic equilibrium is simply a state of the world where economic forces are balanced and in the absence of external influences the (equilibrium) values of economic variables will not change. It is the point at which quantity demanded and quantity supplied are equal. _____, for example, refers to a condition where a market price is established through competition such that the amount of goods or services sought by buyers is equal to the amount of goods or services produced by sellers.
   a. Regulated market
   b. Marketization
   c. Market equilibrium
   d. Product-Market Growth Matrix

35. The _____ is the central banking system of the United States. Created in 1913 by the enactment of the Federal Reserve Act (signed by Woodrow Wilson), it is a quasi-public and quasi-private (government entity with private components) banking system that comprises (1) the presidentially appointed Board of Governors of the _____ in Washington, D.C.; (2) the Federal Open Market Committee; (3) twelve regional Federal Reserve Banks located in major cities throughout the nation acting as fiscal agents for the U.S. Treasury, each with its own nine-member board of directors; (4) numerous other private U.S. member banks, which subscribe to required amounts of non-transferable stock in their regional Federal Reserve Banks; and (5) various advisory councils. Since February 2006, Ben Bernanke has served as the Chairman of the Board of Governors of the _____.
   a. Monetary Policy Report to the Congress
   b. Term auction facility
   c. Federal Reserve System
   d. Federal Reserve System Open Market Account

36. _____ are banks' holdings of deposits in accounts with their central bank (for instance the European Central Bank or the Federal Reserve, in the latter case including federal funds), plus currency that is physically held in bank vaults (vault cash.) The central banks of some nations set minimum reserve requirements. Even when no requirements are set, banks commonly wish to hold some reserves, called desired reserves, against unexpected events.
   a. Sweep account
   b. Bilateral netting
   c. Structuring
   d. Bank reserves

37. The _____ is a financial market where participants buy and sell debt securities, usually in the form of bonds. As of 2006, the size of the international _____ is an estimated $44.9 trillion, of which the size of the outstanding U.S. _____ debt was $25.2 trillion.

Nearly all of the $923 billion average daily trading volume in the U.S. _____ takes place between broker-dealers and large institutions in a decentralized, over-the-counter market.

   a. 130-30 fund
   b. Bond market
   c. Pool factor
   d. 100-year flood

38. In finance, the _____s between two currencies specifies how much one currency is worth in terms of the other. It is the value of a foreign natione;s currency in terms of the home natione;s currency. For example an _____ of 102 Japanese yen to the United States dollar means that JPY 102 is worth the same as USD 1.
   a. Exchange rate
   b. Interbank market
   c. ACEA agreement
   d. ACCRA Cost of Living Index

39. In economics, _____ is the ratio of the percent change in one variable to the percent change in another variable. It is a tool for measuring the responsiveness of a function to changes in parameters in a relative way. Commonly analyzed are _____ of substitution, price and wealth.

Chapter 7. The Keynesian System (II): Money, Interest, and Income

a. ACCRA Cost of Living Index
b. Elasticity of demand
c. ACEA agreement
d. Elasticity

40. _____ in macroeconomic theory refers to the demand for money, considered as liquidity. The concept was first developed by John Maynard Keynes in his book The General Theory of Employment, Interest and Money (1936) to explain determination of the interest rate by the supply and demand for money. The demand for money as an asset was theorized to depend on the interest foregone by not holding bonds.
   a. DAD-SAS model
   b. Liquidity preference
   c. Forward premium anomaly
   d. Consumption function

41. _____ is a mechanism that allows people easily to buy and sell products. Services are often included in the scope of the term. _____ regulation is an economic term that describes restrictions in the market.
   a. Product market
   b. Financialization
   c. Fixed exchange rate system
   d. Market dominance

42. A _____ product is a product designed for cheapness and short-term convenience rather than medium to long-term durability, with most products only intended for single use. The term is also sometimes used for products that may last several months (ex. _____ air filters) to distinguish from similar products that last indefinitely (ex.
   a. 130-30 fund
   b. Disposable
   c. 100-year flood
   d. 1921 recession

43. _____ is gross income minus income tax on that income.

Discretionary income is income after subtracting taxes and normal expenses (such as rent or mortgage, utilities, insurance, medical, transportation, property maintenance, child support, inflation, food and sundries, 'c.) to maintain a certain standard of living.

   a. Taxation as theft
   b. Disposable personal income
   c. Disposable income
   d. Stamp Act

Chapter 8. The Keynesian System (III): Policy Effects in the IS-LM Model

1. In finance, the _____s between two currencies specifies how much one currency is worth in terms of the other. It is the value of a foreign natione;s currency in terms of the home natione;s currency. For example an _____ of 102 Japanese yen to the United States dollar means that JPY 102 is worth the same as USD 1.
   a. ACEA agreement
   b. Interbank market
   c. Exchange rate
   d. ACCRA Cost of Living Index

2. The term _____ refers to government debt, expenditures and revenues, or to finance (particularly financial revenue) in general.

   - _____ deficit is the budget deficit of federal or local government
   - _____ policy is the discretionary spending of governments. Contrasts with monetary policy.
   - _____ year and _____ quarter are reporting periods for firms and other agencies.

   a. Bucket shop
   b. Fiscal
   c. Procter ' Gamble
   d. Drawdown

3. In economics, _____ is the use of government spending and revenue collection to influence the economy.

   _____ can be contrasted with the other main type of economic policy, monetary policy, which attempts to stabilize the economy by controlling interest rates and the supply of money. The two main instruments of _____ are government spending and taxation.

   a. 100-year flood
   b. Fiscalism
   c. Fiscal policy
   d. Sustainable investment rule

4. _____ is a fee paid on borrowed assets. It is the price paid for the use of borrowed money , or, money earned by deposited funds . Assets that are sometimes lent with _____ include money, shares, consumer goods through hire purchase, major assets such as aircraft, and even entire factories in finance lease arrangements.
   a. Internal debt
   b. Asset protection
   c. Insolvency
   d. Interest

5. An _____ is the price a borrower pays for the use of money they do not own, for instance a small company might borrow from a bank to kick start their business, and the return a lender receives for deferring the use of funds, by lending it to the borrower. _____s are normally expressed as a percentage rate over the period of one year.

   _____s targets are also a vital tool of monetary policy and are used to control variables like investment, inflation, and unemployment.

   a. Arrow-Debreu model
   b. Enterprise value
   c. ACCRA Cost of Living Index
   d. Interest rate

6. _____ and Keynesian Theory) is a macroeconomic theory based on the ideas of 20th-century British economist John Maynard Keynes. _____ argues that private sector decisions sometimes lead to inefficient macroeconomic outcomes and therefore advocates active policy responses by the public sector, including monetary policy actions by the central bank and fiscal policy actions by the government to stabilize output over the business cycle.

Chapter 8. The Keynesian System (III): Policy Effects in the IS-LM Model

The theories forming the basis of _____ were first presented in The General Theory of Employment, Interest and Money, published in 1936.

a. Deflation
b. Rational choice theory
c. Market failure
d. Keynesian economics

7. _____ is the process by which the government, central bank (ii) availability of money, and (iii) cost of money or rate of interest, in order to attain a set of objectives oriented towards the growth and stability of the economy. Monetary theory provides insight into how to craft optimal _____.

_____ is referred to as either being an expansionary policy where an expansionary policy increases the total supply of money in the economy, and a contractionary policy decreases the total money supply.

a. 1921 recession
b. Monetary policy
c. 130-30 fund
d. 100-year flood

8. In economics, _____ is the total demand for final goods and services in the economy (Y) at a given time and price level. It is the amount of goods and services in the economy that will be purchased at all possible price levels. This is the demand for the gross domestic product of a country when inventory levels are static.

a. Aggregation problem
b. Aggregate supply
c. Aggregate expenditure
d. Aggregate demand

9. An autarky is an economy that is self-sufficient and does not take part in international trade, or severely limits trade with the outside world. Likewise the term refers to an ecosystem not affected by influences from the outside, which relies entirely on its own resources. In the economic meaning, it is also referred to as a _____.

a. Transition economy
b. Closed economy
c. Digital economy
d. Network Economy

10. Economics:

- _____, the desire to own something and the ability to pay for it
- _____ curve, a graphic representation of a _____ schedule
- _____ deposit, the money in checking accounts
- _____ pull theory, the theory that inflation occurs when _____ for goods and services exceeds existing supplies
- _____ schedule, a table that lists the quantity of a good a person will buy it each different price
- _____ side economics, the school of economics at believes government spending and tax cuts open economy by raising _____

a. Variability
b. Production
c. Demand
d. McKesson ' Robbins scandal

11. In economics, _____ is the total amount of money available in an economy at a particular point in time. There are several ways to define 'money', but standard measures usually include currency in circulation and demand deposits.

_____ data are recorded and published, usually by the government or the central bank of the country.

a. Velocity of money
c. Neutrality of money
b. Veil of money
d. Money supply

12. A _____ product is a product designed for cheapness and short-term convenience rather than medium to long-term durability, with most products only intended for single use. The term is also sometimes used for products that may last several months (ex. _____ air filters) to distinguish from similar products that last indefinitely (ex.
a. 130-30 fund
c. 100-year flood
b. 1921 recession
d. Disposable

13. _____ is gross income minus income tax on that income.

Discretionary income is income after subtracting taxes and normal expenses (such as rent or mortgage, utilities, insurance, medical, transportation, property maintenance, child support, inflation, food and sundries, 'c.) to maintain a certain standard of living.

a. Taxation as theft
c. Stamp Act
b. Disposable income
d. Disposable personal income

14. _____ or government expenditure is classified by economists into three main types. Government purchases of goods and services for current use are classed as government consumption. Government purchases of goods and services intended to create future benefits, such as infrastructure investment or research spending, are classed as government investment.
a. 130-30 fund
c. Government spending
b. 1921 recession
d. 100-year flood

15. _____ is a common concept in economics, and gives rise to derived concepts such as consumer debt. Generally _____ is defined by opposition to production. But the precise definition can vary because different schools of economists define production quite differently.
a. Cash or share options
c. Foreclosure data providers
b. Federal Reserve Bank Notes
d. Consumption

16. _____ is a concept found in moral, political, and bioethical philosophy. Within these contexts, it refers to the capacity of a rational individual to make an informed, un-coerced decision. In moral and political philosophy, _____ is often used as the basis for determining moral responsibility for one's actions.
a. Autonomy
c. AD-IA Model
b. ACCRA Cost of Living Index
d. ACEA agreement

17. A variety of measures of national income and output are used in economics to estimate total economic activity in a country or region, including gross domestic product (GDP), _____ , and net national income (NNI.)

There are three main ways of calculating these numbers; the output approach, the income approach and the expenditure approach. In theory, the three must yield the same, because total expenditures on goods and services must equal the total income paid to the producers (GNI), and that must also equal the total value of the output of goods and services (_____.)

a. Gross world product
b. Household final consumption expenditure
c. Purchasing power parity
d. Gross national product

18. Market _____ is a business, economics or investment term that refers to an asset's ability to be easily converted through an act of buying or selling without causing a significant movement in the price and with minimum loss of value. Money, or cash on hand, is the most liquid asset. An act of exchange of a less liquid asset with a more liquid asset is called liquidation.

a. Liquidity
b. 1921 recession
c. 100-year flood
d. 130-30 fund

19. The term _____ is used in macroeconomics to refer to a situation where a country's nominal interest rate has been lowered nearly to or equal to zero to avoid a recession, but the liquidity in the market created by these low interest rates does not stimulate the economy to full employment. In this situation, any further increase in the money supply will not stimulate the economy any further. This is because any further injection of liquidity will no longer lower the nominal interest rate, as the nominal interest rate cannot drop below zero.

a. Minimum wage
b. Robertson lag
c. Macroeconomic models
d. Liquidity trap

20. _____, 1st Baron Keynes was a renowned economist from Britain whose many ideas on economic and political theories as well as on many governments' monetary policies influenced America. He advocated a government that played an active role in the lives of people regarding business, economy, etc. In this role, the government would use fiscal measures to reduce the consequences of recessions, economic depressions and booms.

a. John Maynard Keynes
b. Adolph Fischer
c. Adam Smith
d. Adolf Hitler

21. _____ is the view within monetary economics that variation in the money supply has major influences on national output in the short run and the price level over longer periods and that objectives of monetary policy are best met by targeting the growth rate of the money supply.

_____ today is mainly associated with the work of Milton Friedman, who was among the generation of economists to accept Keynesian economics and then criticize it on his own terms. Friedman and Anna Schwartz wrote an influential book, Monetary History of the United States 1867-1960, and argued that 'inflation is always and everywhere a monetary phenomenon.' Friedman advocated a central bank policy aimed at keeping the supply and demand for money at equilibrium, as measured by growth in productivity and demand.

a. Marginal revenue productivity theory of wages
b. Historical school of economics
c. Complexity economics
d. Monetarism

Chapter 8. The Keynesian System (III): Policy Effects in the IS-LM Model

22. _____ is a school of contemporary macroeconomics that strives to provide microeconomic foundations for Keynesian economics. It developed partly as a response to criticisms of Keynesian macroeconomics by adherents of New Classical macroeconomics.
   a. Mainstream economics
   b. New Keynesian economics
   c. Keynesian theory
   d. Law of demand

23. _____ is widely regarded as the first modern school of economic thought. It is the idea that free markets can regulate themselves. Its major developers include Adam Smith, David Ricardo, Thomas Malthus and John Stuart Mill. Sometimes the definition of _____ is expanded to include William Petty, Johann Heinrich von Thünen.
   a. Schools of economic thought
   b. Tendency of the rate of profit to fall
   c. Marginalism
   d. Classical economics

24. _____s is the social science that studies the production, distribution, and consumption of goods and services. The term _____s comes from the Ancient Greek oá¼°κονομῖα from oá¼¶κος (oikos, 'house') + vÏŒμος (nomos, 'custom' or 'law'), hence 'rules of the house(hold)'. Current _____ models developed out of the broader field of political economy in the late 19th century, owing to a desire to use an empirical approach more akin to the physical sciences.
   a. Inflation
   b. Energy economics
   c. Opportunity cost
   d. Economic

25. In economics, _____ is the ratio of the percent change in one variable to the percent change in another variable. It is a tool for measuring the responsiveness of a function to changes in parameters in a relative way. Commonly analyzed are _____ of substitution, price and wealth.
   a. ACCRA Cost of Living Index
   b. ACEA agreement
   c. Elasticity of demand
   d. Elasticity

26. In economics, a _____ is a general slowdown in economic activity over a sustained period of time, or a business cycle contraction. During _____s, many macroeconomic indicators vary in a similar way. Production as measured by Gross Domestic Product (GDP), employment, investment spending, capacity utilization, household incomes and business profits all fall during _____s.
   a. Treasury View
   b. Monetary economics
   c. Leading indicators
   d. Recession

27. A _____ occurs when an entity spends more money than it takes in. The opposite of a _____ is a budget surplus. Debt is essentially an accumulated flow of deficits.
   a. Public Financial Management
   b. Funding body
   c. Lump-sum tax
   d. Budget deficit

28. _____ is the increase in the amount of the goods and services produced by an economy over time. It is conventionally measured as the percent rate of increase in real gross domestic product, or real GDP. Growth is usually calculated in real terms, i.e. inflation-adjusted terms, in order to net out the effect of inflation on the price of the goods and services produced.
   a. ACEA agreement
   b. AD-IA Model
   c. ACCRA Cost of Living Index
   d. Economic growth

Chapter 9. The Keynesian System (IV): Aggregate Supply and Demand

1. _____ or government expenditure is classified by economists into three main types. Government purchases of goods and services for current use are classed as government consumption. Government purchases of goods and services intended to create future benefits, such as infrastructure investment or research spending, are classed as government investment.
   - a. 1921 recession
   - b. 100-year flood
   - c. 130-30 fund
   - d. Government spending

2. _____, 1st Baron Keynes was a renowned economist from Britain whose many ideas on economic and political theories as well as on many governments' monetary policies influenced America. He advocated a government that played an active role in the lives of people regarding business, economy, etc. In this role, the government would use fiscal measures to reduce the consequences of recessions, economic depressions and booms.
   - a. Adolph Fischer
   - b. John Maynard Keynes
   - c. Adolf Hitler
   - d. Adam Smith

3. _____ and Keynesian Theory) is a macroeconomic theory based on the ideas of 20th-century British economist John Maynard Keynes. _____ argues that private sector decisions sometimes lead to inefficient macroeconomic outcomes and therefore advocates active policy responses by the public sector, including monetary policy actions by the central bank and fiscal policy actions by the government to stabilize output over the business cycle.

   The theories forming the basis of _____ were first presented in The General Theory of Employment, Interest and Money, published in 1936.

   - a. Deflation
   - b. Rational choice theory
   - c. Market failure
   - d. Keynesian economics

4. _____ is the view within monetary economics that variation in the money supply has major influences on national output in the short run and the price level over longer periods and that objectives of monetary policy are best met by targeting the growth rate of the money supply.

   _____ today is mainly associated with the work of Milton Friedman, who was among the generation of economists to accept Keynesian economics and then criticize it on his own terms. Friedman and Anna Schwartz wrote an influential book, Monetary History of the United States 1867-1960, and argued that 'inflation is always and everywhere a monetary phenomenon.' Friedman advocated a central bank policy aimed at keeping the supply and demand for money at equilibrium, as measured by growth in productivity and demand.

   - a. Complexity economics
   - b. Historical school of economics
   - c. Marginal revenue productivity theory of wages
   - d. Monetarism

5. _____ is the process by which the government, central bank (ii) availability of money, and (iii) cost of money or rate of interest, in order to attain a set of objectives oriented towards the growth and stability of the economy. Monetary theory provides insight into how to craft optimal _____.

   _____ is referred to as either being an expansionary policy where an expansionary policy increases the total supply of money in the economy, and a contractionary policy decreases the total money supply.

a. Monetary policy
b. 100-year flood
c. 1921 recession
d. 130-30 fund

6. _____ is a school of contemporary macroeconomics that strives to provide microeconomic foundations for Keynesian economics. It developed partly as a response to criticisms of Keynesian macroeconomics by adherents of New Classical macroeconomics.
   a. Keynesian theory
   b. New Keynesian economics
   c. Mainstream economics
   d. Law of demand

7. In economics, _____ is the total demand for final goods and services in the economy (Y) at a given time and price level. It is the amount of goods and services in the economy that will be purchased at all possible price levels. This is the demand for the gross domestic product of a country when inventory levels are static.
   a. Aggregate expenditure
   b. Aggregation problem
   c. Aggregate supply
   d. Aggregate demand

8. In economics, _____ is the total supply of goods and services produced by a national economy during a specific time period. It is the total amount of goods and services in the economy available at all possible price levels.
   a. Aggregate expenditure
   b. Aggregation problem
   c. Aggregate demand
   d. Aggregate supply

9. _____ is widely regarded as the first modern school of economic thought. It is the idea that free markets can regulate themselves. Its major developers include Adam Smith, David Ricardo, Thomas Malthus and John Stuart Mill. Sometimes the definition of _____ is expanded to include William Petty, Johann Heinrich von Thünen.
   a. Tendency of the rate of profit to fall
   b. Classical economics
   c. Marginalism
   d. Schools of economic thought

10. Economics:

    - _____, the desire to own something and the ability to pay for it
    - _____ curve, a graphic representation of a _____ schedule
    - _____ deposit, the money in checking accounts
    - _____ pull theory, the theory that inflation occurs when _____ for goods and services exceeds existing supplies
    - _____ schedule, a table that lists the quantity of a good a person will buy it each different price
    - _____ side economics, the school of economics at believes government spending and tax cuts open economy by raising _____

    a. Variability
    b. McKesson ' Robbins scandal
    c. Production
    d. Demand

11. _____s is the social science that studies the production, distribution, and consumption of goods and services. The term _____s comes from the Ancient Greek οἰκονομία from οἶκος (oikos, 'house') + νόμος (nomos, 'custom' or 'law'), hence 'rules of the house(hold)'. Current _____ models developed out of the broader field of political economy in the late 19th century, owing to a desire to use an empirical approach more akin to the physical sciences.

Chapter 9. The Keynesian System (IV): Aggregate Supply and Demand

a. Inflation
b. Opportunity cost
c. Economic
d. Energy economics

12. _____ is a common concept in economics, and gives rise to derived concepts such as consumer debt. Generally _____ is defined by opposition to production. But the precise definition can vary because different schools of economists define production quite differently.

a. Foreclosure data providers
b. Cash or share options
c. Federal Reserve Bank Notes
d. Consumption

13. _____ is an economic model based on price, utility and quantity in a market. It predicts that in a competitive market, price will function to equalize the quantity demanded by consumers, and the quantity supplied by producers, resulting in an economic equilibrium of price and quantity. The model incorporates other factors changing equilibrium as a shift of demand and/or supply.

a. Rational addiction
b. Joint demand
c. Deferred gratification
d. Supply and demand

14. In labor economics, the _____ hypothesis argues that wages, at least in some markets, are determined by more than simply supply and demand. Specifically, it points to the incentive for managers to pay their employees more than the market-clearing wage in order to increase their productivity or efficiency. This increased labor productivity pays for the relatively higher wages.

a. Earnings calls
b. Efficiency wage
c. Exogenous growth model
d. Inflatable rats

15. The _____ or gross domestic income (GDI), a basic measure of an economy's economic performance, is the market value of all final goods and services produced within the borders of a nation in a year. _____ can be defined in three ways, all of which are conceptually identical. First, it is equal to the total expenditures for all final goods and services produced within the country in a stipulated period of time (usually a 365-day year.)

a. Monopolistic competition
b. Countercyclical
c. Market structure
d. Gross domestic product

16. The supply of labor is the number of total hours that workers wish to work at a given real wage rate.

_____ curves are derived from the 'labor-leisure' trade-off. More hours worked earn higher incomes but necessitate a cut in the amount of leisure that workers enjoy.

a. Late capitalism
b. Human trafficking
c. Creative capitalism
d. Labor supply

17. In economics, the _____ or marginal physical product is the extra output produced by one more unit of an input (for instance, the difference in output when a firm's labour is increased from five to six units.) Assuming that no other inputs to production change, the _____ of a given input (X) can be expressed as:

Chapter 9. The Keynesian System (IV): Aggregate Supply and Demand

_____ = ΔY/ΔX = (the change of Y)/(the change of X.)

-
  -
    - Pending approval by Thomas Sowell***

In neoclassical economics, this is the mathematical derivative of the production function.... Note that the 'product' (Y) is typically defined ignoring external costs and benefits.

a. Marginal product
c. Factor prices
b. Productive capacity
d. Labor problem

18. In economics, the _____ also known as MPL or MPN is the change in output from hiring one additional unit of labor. It is the increase in output added by the last unit of labor. Assuming that no other inputs to production change, the marginal product of a given input (X) can be expressed as:

MP = ΔY/ΔX = (the change of Y)/(the change of X.)

a. Marginal product of labor
c. Product Pipeline
b. Marginal product
d. Production function

19. In economics, the _____ can be defined as the graph depicting the relationship between the price of a certain commodity, and the amount of it that consumers are willing and able to purchase at that given price. It is a graphic representation of a demand schedule. The _____ for all consumers together follows from the _____ of every individual consumer: the individual demands at each price are added together.

a. Wage curve
c. Kuznets curve
b. Demand curve
d. Cost curve

20. In finance, the _____s between two currencies specifies how much one currency is worth in terms of the other. It is the value of a foreign natione;s currency in terms of the home natione;s currency. For example an _____ of 102 Japanese yen to the United States dollar means that JPY 102 is worth the same as USD 1.

a. ACEA agreement
c. ACCRA Cost of Living Index
b. Interbank market
d. Exchange rate

21. In economics, _____ is the total amount of money available in an economy at a particular point in time. There are several ways to define 'money', but standard measures usually include currency in circulation and demand deposits.

_____ data are recorded and published, usually by the government or the central bank of the country.

a. Velocity of money
c. Neutrality of money
b. Veil of money
d. Money supply

22. _____, in economics, is the quantity of money measured in a particular currency and is directly proportional to the price level.

This means, among other things, that if the price level rises by 10%, 10% more money than before is necessary in order to maintain stability. For example, if it costs $20 to buy an item, and the price level increases by 10%, the dollar amount necessary to buy the item increases by 10% (in this case by $2), which brings the total cost of the item to $22.

   a. Limping bimetallism   b. Silver Thursday
   c. Money of account   d. Nominal money

23. The _____ is the average frequency with which a unit of money is spent in a specific period of time. Velocity associates the amount of economic activity associated with a given money supply. When the period is understood, the velocity may be present as a pure number; otherwise it should be given as a pure number over time.

   a. Velocity of money   b. Chartalism
   c. Money supply   d. Neutrality of money

24. _____ is the increase in the amount of the goods and services produced by an economy over time. It is conventionally measured as the percent rate of increase in real gross domestic product, or real GDP. Growth is usually calculated in real terms, i.e. inflation-adjusted terms, in order to net out the effect of inflation on the price of the goods and services produced.

   a. ACCRA Cost of Living Index   b. AD-IA Model
   c. Economic growth   d. ACEA agreement

25. In economics, a _____ is a table that lists the quantity of a good a person will buy it each different price See Demand curve.

   a. Federal Reserve districts   b. Rational irrationality
   c. Free contract   d. Demand schedule

26. _____ is a branch of economics that deals with the performance, structure, and behavior of a national or regional economy as a whole. Along with microeconomics, _____ is one of the two most general fields in economics. It is the study of the behavior and decision-making of entire economies.

   a. Nominal value   b. New Trade Theory
   c. Tobit model   d. Macroeconomics

27. _____ is a macroeconomic theory that argues that private sector decisions sometimes lead to inefficient macroeconomic outcomes and therefore advocates active policy responses by the public sector, including monetary policy actions by the central bank and fiscal policy actions by the government to stabilize output over the business cycle.

The theories forming the basis of _____ were first presented in The General Theory of Employment, Interest and Money, published in 1936.

   a. Tobit model   b. Human capital
   c. Mainstream economics   d. Keynesian theory

Chapter 9. The Keynesian System (IV): Aggregate Supply and Demand

28. A trade union or _____ is an organization of workers who have banded together to achieve common goals in key areas and working conditions. The trade union, through its leadership, bargains with the employer on behalf of union members (rank and file members) and negotiates labor contracts (Collective bargaining) with employers. This may include the negotiation of wages, work rules, complaint procedures, rules governing hiring, firing and promotion of workers, benefits, workplace safety and policies.
   a. Demand-side technologies
   b. Business valuation standards
   c. Basis of futures
   d. Labor union

29. A _____ or labor union is an organization of workers who have banded together to achieve common goals in key areas and working conditions. The _____, through its leadership, bargains with the employer on behalf of union members (rank and file members) and negotiates labor contracts (Collective bargaining) with employers. This may include the negotiation of wages, work rules, complaint procedures, rules governing hiring, firing and promotion of workers, benefits, workplace safety and policies.
   a. Case-Shiller Home Price Indices
   b. Trade union
   c. Guaranteed investment contracts
   d. Consumer goods

30. A _____ measures average changes in prices received by domestic producers for their output. It is one of several price indices

Its importance is being undermined by the steady decline in manufactured goods as a share of spending.

A number of countries that now report a _____ previously reported a Wholesale Price Index.

   a. Gross national product
   b. Producer price index
   c. Hemline index
   d. Visible balance

31. In economics, the concept of _____ refers to one possible result of supply and demand disequilibrium in a market, either due to or in the absence of external constraints on the market. In the textbook story, if the quantity demanded does not equal the quantity supplied in a market, price adjustment is the rule: if there is a market surplus or glut (excess supply), prices fall, ending the glut, while a shortage (excess demand) causes price rises. However, instead of price adjustment -- or, more likely, simultaneously with price adjustment -- quantities may adjust: a market surplus leads to a cut-back in the quantity supplied, while a shortage causes a cut-back in the quantity demanded.
   a. Sonnenschein-Mantel-Debreu Theorem
   b. Differential tax analysis
   c. Regular economy
   d. Quantity adjustment

32. _____ in economics and business is the result of an exchange and from that trade we assign a numerical monetary value to a good, service or asset. If Alice trades Bob 4 apples for an orange, the _____ of an orange is 4 apples. Inversely, the _____ of an apple is 1/4 oranges.
   a. Price
   b. Price book
   c. Premium pricing
   d. Price war

33. A _____ is a normalized average (typically a weighted average) of prices for a given class of goods or services in a given region, during a given interval of time. It is a statistic designed to help to compare how these prices, taken as a whole, differ between time periods or geographical locations.

Price indices have several potential uses.

a. Price index
b. Transactional Net Margin Method
c. Product sabotage
d. Two-part tariff

34. The term _____s refers to wages that have been adjusted for inflation. This term is used in contrast to nominal wages or unadjusted wages.

The use of adjusted figures is in undertaking some form of economic analysis.

a. Federal Wage System
b. Living wage
c. Profit sharing
d. Real wage

35. A _____ is a hypothetical measure of overall prices for some set of goods and services, in a given region during a given interval, normalized relative to some base set. Typically, a _____ is approximated with a price index.

The classical dichotomy is the assumption that there is a relatively clean distinction between overall increases or decreases in prices and underlying, e;reale; economic variables.

a. Price elasticity of supply
b. Discouraged worker
c. Discretionary spending
d. Price level

36. The term _____, 'the state or characteristic of being variable', _____ describes how spread out or closely clustered a set of data is. may be applied to many different subjects:

- Climate _____
- Genetic _____
- Heart rate _____
- Human _____
- Solar van
- Spatial _____
- Statistical _____
- _____

a. Demand
b. Variability
c. Characteristic
d. Total product

37. A variety of measures of national income and output are used in economics to estimate total economic activity in a country or region, including gross domestic product (GDP), _____ , and net national income (NNI.)

There are three main ways of calculating these numbers; the output approach, the income approach and the expenditure approach. In theory, the three must yield the same, because total expenditures on goods and services must equal the total income paid to the producers (GNI), and that must also equal the total value of the output of goods and services (_____.)

Chapter 9. The Keynesian System (IV): Aggregate Supply and Demand

a. Household final consumption expenditure
b. Purchasing power parity
c. Gross world product
d. Gross national product

38. In economics and finance, _____ is the change in total cost that arises when the quantity produced changes by one unit. It is the cost of producing one more unit of a good. Mathematically, the _____ function is expressed as the first derivative of the total cost (TC) function with respect to quantity (Q.)
   a. Quality costs
   b. Marginal cost
   c. Khozraschyot
   d. Variable cost

39. _____ is a concept found in moral, political, and bioethical philosophy. Within these contexts, it refers to the capacity of a rational individual to make an informed, un-coerced decision. In moral and political philosophy, _____ is often used as the basis for determining moral responsibility for one's actions.
   a. AD-IA Model
   b. ACCRA Cost of Living Index
   c. Autonomy
   d. ACEA agreement

40. A _____ is an expression that compares quantities relative to each other. The most common examples involve two quantities, but any number of quantities can be compared. _____s are represented mathematically by separating each quantity with a colon, for example the _____ 2:3, which is read as the _____ 'two to three'.
   a. Ratio
   b. 130-30 fund
   c. Y-intercept
   d. 100-year flood

41. A _____ is an event that suddenly changes the price of a commodity or service. It may be caused by a sudden increase or decrease in the supply of a particular good. This sudden change affects the equilibrium price.
   a. Supply shock
   b. Demand shock
   c. Friedman rule
   d. SIMIC

42. _____ is the term denoting either an entrance or changes which are inserted into a system and which activate/modify a process. It is an abstract concept, used in the modeling, system(s) design and system(s) exploitation. It is usually connected with other terms, e.g., _____ field, _____ variable, _____ parameter, _____ value, _____ signal, _____ device and _____ file.
   a. Input
   b. ACCRA Cost of Living Index
   c. ACEA agreement
   d. AD-IA Model

43. A _____ is something that is acted upon or used by or by human labor or industry, for use as a building material to create some product or structure. Often the term is used to denote material that came from nature and is in an unprocessed or minimally processed state. Iron ore, logs, and crude oil, would be examples.
   a. 1921 recession
   b. 130-30 fund
   c. 100-year flood
   d. Raw material

44. _____ is a broad label that refers to any individuals or households that use goods and services generated within the economy. The concept of a _____ is used in different contexts, so that the usage and significance of the term may vary.

Typically when business people and economists talk of _____s they are talking about person as _____, an aggregated commodity item with little individuality other than that expressed in the buy/not-buy decision.

Chapter 9. The Keynesian System (IV): Aggregate Supply and Demand

a. 1921 recession
b. 130-30 fund
c. Consumer
d. 100-year flood

45. In economics, the _____ is a historical inverse relation between the rate of unemployment and the rate of inflation in an economy. Stated simply, the lower the unemployment in an economy, the higher the rate of increase in nominal wages in the economy. Rate of Change of Wages against Unemployment, United Kingdom 1913-1948 from Phillips (1958)

William Phillips, a New Zealand born economist, wrote a paper in 1958 titled The Relationship between Unemployment and the Rate of Change of Money Wages in the United Kingdom 1861-1957, which was published in the quarterly journal Economica.

a. Phillips curve
b. Demand curve
c. Cost curve
d. Lorenz curve

46. An _____, in economics, is the amount by which the real Gross domestic product exceeds potential GDP. The real GDP is also known as GDP 'adjusted for inflation', 'constant prices' GDP or 'constant dollar' GDP, because it measures the aggregate output in a country's income accounts in a given year, expressed in base-year prices. On the other hand, the potential GDP is the quantity of real GDP when a country's economy is at full-employment.

a. Inflationary gap
b. ACCRA Cost of Living Index
c. AD-IA Model
d. ACEA agreement

47. In economics, a _____ is a general slowdown in economic activity over a sustained period of time, or a business cycle contraction. During _____s, many macroeconomic indicators vary in a similar way. Production as measured by Gross Domestic Product (GDP), employment, investment spending, capacity utilization, household incomes and business profits all fall during _____s.

a. Monetary economics
b. Leading indicators
c. Treasury View
d. Recession

48. _____ is an economic situation in which inflation and economic stagnation occur simultaneously and remain unchecked for a period of time. The portmanteau _____ is generally attributed to British politician Iain Macleod, who coined the term in a speech to Parliament in 1965. The concept is notable partly because, in postwar macroeconomic theory, inflation and recession were regarded as mutually exclusive, and also because _____ has generally proven to be difficult and costly to eradicate once it gets started.

a. Stagflation
b. Chronic inflation
c. Real interest rate
d. Price/wage spiral

49. A _____ occurs when an entity spends more money than it takes in. The opposite of a _____ is a budget surplus. Debt is essentially an accumulated flow of deficits.

a. Public Financial Management
b. Lump-sum tax
c. Funding body
d. Budget deficit

50. The post-Soviet states, also commonly known as the _____ or former Soviet republics, are the 15 independent nations that split off from the Union of Soviet Socialist Republics in its breakup in December 1991. Excluding the Baltic states (which were independent before World War II and already in 1989 signalled their political intention to dissociate themselves from the rest of the Soviet Union), they were also referred to as the Newly Independent States (NIS) Post-Soviet states in English alphabetical order:1.

Chapter 9. The Keynesian System (IV): Aggregate Supply and Demand

a. 130-30 fund
b. 100-year flood
c. 1921 recession
d. Former Soviet Union

51. In economics, _____ is a rise in the general level of prices of goods and services in an economy over a period of time. When the general price level rises, each unit of currency buys fewer goods and services; consequently, _____ is also a decline in the real value of money--a loss of purchasing power in the medium of exchange which is also the monetary unit of account in the economy. A chief measure of general price-level _____ is the general _____ rate, which is the percentage change in a general price index (normally the Consumer Price Index) over time.

a. Opportunity cost
b. Economic
c. Energy economics
d. Inflation

52. In economics, the _____ of money is a theory emphasizing the positive relationship of overall prices or the nominal value of expenditures to the quantity of money.

It is the mainstream economic theory of the price level. Alternative theories include the real bills doctrine and the more recent fiscal theory of the price level.

a. Quantity theory
b. Romer Model
c. Real business cycle
d. Dishoarding

53. In economics, the _____ is a theory emphasizing the positive relationship of overall prices or the nominal value of expenditures to the quantity of money.

It is the mainstream economic theory of the price level. Alternative theories include the real bills doctrine and the more recent fiscal theory of the price level.

a. Microsimulation
b. Consumer spending
c. Fundamental psychological law
d. Quantity theory of money

54. In macroeconomics, _____ is a condition of the national economy, where all or nearly all persons willing and able to work at the prevailing wages and working conditions are able to do so. It is defined either as 0% unemployment, literally, no unemployment (the rate of unemployment is the fraction of the work force unable to find work), as by James Tobin, or as the level of employment rates when there is no cyclical unemployment. It is defined by the majority of mainstream economists as being an acceptable level of natural unemployment above 0%, the discrepancy from 0% being due to non-cyclical types of unemployment.

a. Full employment
b. Marginal propensity to consume
c. Demand shock
d. Harrod-Johnson diagram

Chapter 10. The Monetarist Counterrevolution

1. The _____ was a worldwide economic downturn starting in most places in 1929 and ending at different times in the 1930s or early 1940s for different countries. It was the largest and most important economic depression in the 20th century, and is used in the 21st century as an example of how far the world's economy can fall. The _____ originated in the United States; historians most often use as a starting date the stock market crash on October 29, 1929, known as Black Tuesday.

   a. British Empire Economic Conference
   b. Wall Street Crash of 1929
   c. Jarrow March
   d. Great Depression

2. _____ and Keynesian Theory) is a macroeconomic theory based on the ideas of 20th-century British economist John Maynard Keynes. _____ argues that private sector decisions sometimes lead to inefficient macroeconomic outcomes and therefore advocates active policy responses by the public sector, including monetary policy actions by the central bank and fiscal policy actions by the government to stabilize output over the business cycle.

   The theories forming the basis of _____ were first presented in The General Theory of Employment, Interest and Money, published in 1936.

   a. Deflation
   b. Keynesian economics
   c. Rational choice theory
   d. Market failure

3. _____ is the view within monetary economics that variation in the money supply has major influences on national output in the short run and the price level over longer periods and that objectives of monetary policy are best met by targeting the growth rate of the money supply.

   _____ today is mainly associated with the work of Milton Friedman, who was among the generation of economists to accept Keynesian economics and then criticize it on his own terms. Friedman and Anna Schwartz wrote an influential book, Monetary History of the United States 1867-1960, and argued that 'inflation is always and everywhere a monetary phenomenon.' Friedman advocated a central bank policy aimed at keeping the supply and demand for money at equilibrium, as measured by growth in productivity and demand.

   a. Historical school of economics
   b. Complexity economics
   c. Marginal revenue productivity theory of wages
   d. Monetarism

4. _____ is the process by which the government, central bank (ii) availability of money, and (iii) cost of money or rate of interest, in order to attain a set of objectives oriented towards the growth and stability of the economy. Monetary theory provides insight into how to craft optimal _____.

   _____ is referred to as either being an expansionary policy where an expansionary policy increases the total supply of money in the economy, and a contractionary policy decreases the total money supply.

   a. 100-year flood
   b. 130-30 fund
   c. 1921 recession
   d. Monetary policy

5. In economics, _____ is the total supply of goods and services produced by a national economy during a specific time period. It is the total amount of goods and services in the economy available at all possible price levels.

   a. Aggregation problem
   b. Aggregate supply
   c. Aggregate expenditure
   d. Aggregate demand

Chapter 10. The Monetarist Counterrevolution

6. _____ has several particular meanings:

   - in mathematics
     - _____ function
     - Euler _____
     - _____
     - _____ subgroup
     - method of _____s (partial differential equations)
   - in physics and engineering
     - any _____ curve that shows the relationship between certain input- and output parameters, e.g.
     - an I-V or current-voltage _____ is the current in a circuit as a function of the applied voltage
     - Receiver-Operator _____
   - in fiction
     - in Dungeons ' Dragons, _____ is another name for ability score

   a. Technocracy
   b. Russian financial crisis
   c. Demand
   d. Characteristic

7. _____ is widely regarded as the first modern school of economic thought. It is the idea that free markets can regulate themselves. Its major developers include Adam Smith, David Ricardo, Thomas Malthus and John Stuart Mill. Sometimes the definition of _____ is expanded to include William Petty, Johann Heinrich von Thünen.

   a. Classical economics
   b. Schools of economic thought
   c. Marginalism
   d. Tendency of the rate of profit to fall

8. Economics:

   - _____, the desire to own something and the ability to pay for it
   - _____ curve, a graphic representation of a _____ schedule
   - _____ deposit, the money in checking accounts
   - _____ pull theory, the theory that inflation occurs when _____ for goods and services exceeds existing supplies
   - _____ schedule, a table that lists the quantity of a good a person will buy it each different price
   - _____ side economics, the school of economics at believes government spending and tax cuts open economy by raising _____

   a. Production
   b. Variability
   c. McKesson ' Robbins scandal
   d. Demand

9. _____s is the social science that studies the production, distribution, and consumption of goods and services. The term _____s comes from the Ancient Greek οἰκονομῐ́α from οἶκος (oikos, 'house') + νόμος (nomos, 'custom' or 'law'), hence 'rules of the house(hold)'. Current _____ models developed out of the broader field of political economy in the late 19th century, owing to a desire to use an empirical approach more akin to the physical sciences.

Chapter 10. The Monetarist Counterrevolution

a. Inflation
b. Energy economics
c. Economic
d. Opportunity cost

10. _____ is an economic model based on price, utility and quantity in a market. It predicts that in a competitive market, price will function to equalize the quantity demanded by consumers, and the quantity supplied by producers, resulting in an economic equilibrium of price and quantity. The model incorporates other factors changing equilibrium as a shift of demand and/or supply.

a. Joint demand
b. Deferred gratification
c. Rational addiction
d. Supply and demand

11. In economics, _____ is the total demand for final goods and services in the economy (Y) at a given time and price level. It is the amount of goods and services in the economy that will be purchased at all possible price levels. This is the demand for the gross domestic product of a country when inventory levels are static.

a. Aggregate expenditure
b. Aggregation problem
c. Aggregate supply
d. Aggregate demand

12. In economics, _____ is the total amount of money available in an economy at a particular point in time. There are several ways to define 'money', but standard measures usually include currency in circulation and demand deposits.

_____ data are recorded and published, usually by the government or the central bank of the country.

a. Money supply
b. Veil of money
c. Neutrality of money
d. Velocity of money

13. In economics, the _____ is that part of the economy which is both run for private profit and is not controlled by the state. By contrast, enterprises that are part of the state are part of the public sector; private, non-profit organizations are regarded as part of the voluntary sector.

A variety of legal structures exist for _____ business organizations, depending on the jurisdiction in which they have their legal domicile.

a. Standard Industrial Classification
b. Primary products
c. Secondary sector of the economy
d. Private sector

14. A _____ measures average changes in prices received by domestic producers for their output. It is one of several price indices

Its importance is being undermined by the steady decline in manufactured goods as a share of spending.

A number of countries that now report a _____ previously reported a Wholesale Price Index.

a. Visible balance
b. Producer price index
c. Hemline index
d. Gross national product

15. In finance, a _____ is a debt security, in which the authorized issuer owes the holders a debt and, depending on the terms of the _____, is obliged to pay interest (the coupon) and/or to repay the principal at a later date, termed maturity. A _____ is a formal contract to repay borrowed money with interest at fixed intervals.

Thus a _____ is like a loan: the issuer is the borrower (debtor), the holder is the lender (creditor), and the coupon is the interest.

a. Callable
b. Zero-coupon
c. Prize Bond
d. Bond

16. _____ in economics and business is the result of an exchange and from that trade we assign a numerical monetary value to a good, service or asset. If Alice trades Bob 4 apples for an orange, the _____ of an orange is 4 apples. Inversely, the _____ of an apple is 1/4 oranges.

a. Price war
b. Price book
c. Price
d. Premium pricing

17. A _____ is a normalized average (typically a weighted average) of prices for a given class of goods or services in a given region, during a given interval of time. It is a statistic designed to help to compare how these prices, taken as a whole, differ between time periods or geographical locations.

Price indices have several potential uses.

a. Transactional Net Margin Method
b. Two-part tariff
c. Price index
d. Product sabotage

18. In economics, the _____ of money is a theory emphasizing the positive relationship of overall prices or the nominal value of expenditures to the quantity of money.

It is the mainstream economic theory of the price level. Alternative theories include the real bills doctrine and the more recent fiscal theory of the price level.

a. Quantity theory
b. Real business cycle
c. Romer Model
d. Dishoarding

19. In economics, the _____ is a theory emphasizing the positive relationship of overall prices or the nominal value of expenditures to the quantity of money.

It is the mainstream economic theory of the price level. Alternative theories include the real bills doctrine and the more recent fiscal theory of the price level.

a. Fundamental psychological law
b. Consumer spending
c. Microsimulation
d. Quantity theory of money

20. In business and accounting, _____ are everything of value that is owned by a person or company. It is a claim on the property your income of a borrower. The balance sheet of a firm records the monetary value of the _____ owned by the firm.

a. Assets
b. Amortization schedule
c. ACEA agreement
d. ACCRA Cost of Living Index

21. _____ is the increase in the amount of the goods and services produced by an economy over time. It is conventionally measured as the percent rate of increase in real gross domestic product, or real GDP. Growth is usually calculated in real terms, i.e. inflation-adjusted terms, in order to net out the effect of inflation on the price of the goods and services produced.
   a. ACEA agreement
   b. AD-IA Model
   c. ACCRA Cost of Living Index
   d. Economic growth

22. In finance, the _____s between two currencies specifies how much one currency is worth in terms of the other. It is the value of a foreign natione;s currency in terms of the home natione;s currency. For example an _____ of 102 Japanese yen to the United States dollar means that JPY 102 is worth the same as USD 1.
   a. ACCRA Cost of Living Index
   b. ACEA agreement
   c. Interbank market
   d. Exchange rate

23. _____ is a fee paid on borrowed assets. It is the price paid for the use of borrowed money , or, money earned by deposited funds . Assets that are sometimes lent with _____ include money, shares, consumer goods through hire purchase, major assets such as aircraft, and even entire factories in finance lease arrangements.
   a. Internal debt
   b. Insolvency
   c. Asset protection
   d. Interest

24. A _____ product is a product designed for cheapness and short-term convenience rather than medium to long-term durability, with most products only intended for single use. The term is also sometimes used for products that may last several months (ex. _____ air filters) to distinguish from similar products that last indefinitely (ex.
   a. 1921 recession
   b. 130-30 fund
   c. 100-year flood
   d. Disposable

25. _____ is gross income minus income tax on that income.

Discretionary income is income after subtracting taxes and normal expenses (such as rent or mortgage, utilities, insurance, medical, transportation, property maintenance, child support, inflation, food and sundries, 'c.) to maintain a certain standard of living.

   a. Taxation as theft
   b. Stamp Act
   c. Disposable personal income
   d. Disposable income

26. In economics, _____ is the ratio of the percent change in one variable to the percent change in another variable. It is a tool for measuring the responsiveness of a function to changes in parameters in a relative way. Commonly analyzed are _____ of substitution, price and wealth.
   a. ACCRA Cost of Living Index
   b. ACEA agreement
   c. Elasticity of demand
   d. Elasticity

27. _____ was an American economist, statistician and public intellectual, and a recipient of the Nobel Memorial Prize in Economic Sciences. He is best known among scholars for his theoretical and empirical research, especially consumption analysis, monetary history and theory, and for his demonstration of the complexity of stabilization policy. A global public followed his restatement of a political philosophy that insisted on minimizing the role of government in favor of the private sector.
   a. Milton Friedman
   b. Adam Smith
   c. Adolph Fischer
   d. Adolf Hitler

28. _____ or government expenditure is classified by economists into three main types. Government purchases of goods and services for current use are classed as government consumption. Government purchases of goods and services intended to create future benefits, such as infrastructure investment or research spending, are classed as government investment.
   a. 100-year flood
   b. 130-30 fund
   c. 1921 recession
   d. Government spending

29. _____, 1st Baron Keynes was a renowned economist from Britain whose many ideas on economic and political theories as well as on many governments' monetary policies influenced America. He advocated a government that played an active role in the lives of people regarding business, economy, etc. In this role, the government would use fiscal measures to reduce the consequences of recessions, economic depressions and booms.
   a. Adolph Fischer
   b. Adam Smith
   c. Adolf Hitler
   d. John Maynard Keynes

30. _____ is a school of contemporary macroeconomics that strives to provide microeconomic foundations for Keynesian economics. It developed partly as a response to criticisms of Keynesian macroeconomics by adherents of New Classical macroeconomics.
   a. Keynesian theory
   b. Mainstream economics
   c. Law of demand
   d. New Keynesian economics

31. The term _____ refers to government debt, expenditures and revenues, or to finance (particularly financial revenue) in general.

   - _____ deficit is the budget deficit of federal or local government
   - _____ policy is the discretionary spending of governments. Contrasts with monetary policy.
   - _____ year and _____ quarter are reporting periods for firms and other agencies.

   a. Drawdown
   b. Fiscal
   c. Bucket shop
   d. Procter ' Gamble

32. In economics, _____ is the use of government spending and revenue collection to influence the economy.

_____ can be contrasted with the other main type of economic policy, monetary policy, which attempts to stabilize the economy by controlling interest rates and the supply of money. The two main instruments of _____ are government spending and taxation.

Chapter 10. The Monetarist Counterrevolution 89

a. Fiscal policy
c. Sustainable investment rule

b. Fiscalism
d. 100-year flood

33. A _____ is:

- Rewrite _____, in generative grammar and computer science
- Standardization, a formal and widely-accepted statement, fact, definition, or qualification
- Operation, a determinate _____ for performing a mathematical operation and obtaining a certain result (Mathematics, Logic)
    - Unary operation
    - Binary operation
- _____ of inference, a function from sets of formulae to formulae (Mathematics, Logic)
- _____ of thumb, principle with broad application that is not intended to be strictly accurate or reliable for every situation. Also often simply referred to as a _____
- Moral, an atomic element of a moral code for guiding choices in human behavior
- Heuristic, a quantized '_____' which shows a tendency or probability for successful function
- A regulation, as in sports
- A Production _____, as in computer science
- Procedural law, a _____ set governing the application of laws to cases
    - A law, which may informally be called a '_____'
    - A court ruling, a decision by a court
- In the U.S. Government, a regulation mandated by Congress, but written or expanded upon by the Executive Branch.
- Norm (sociology), an informal but widely accepted _____, concept, truth, definition, or qualification (social norms, legal norms, coding norms)
- Norm (philosophy), a kind of sentence or a reason to act, feel or believe
- 'Rulership' is the concept of governance by a government:
    - Military _____, governance by a military body
    - Monastic _____, a collection of precepts that guides the life of monks or nuns in a religious order where the superior holds the place of Christ
- Slide _____

- '_____,' a song by Ayumi Hamasaki
- '_____,' a song by rapper Nas
- '_____s,' an album by the band The Whitest Boy Alive
- _____s: Pyaar Ka Superhit Formula, a 2003 Bollywood film
- ruler, an instrument for measuring lengths
- _____, a component of an astrolabe, circumferator or similar instrument
- The _____s, a bestselling self-help book
- _____ Project (Run Up-to-date Linux Everywhere), a project that aims to use up-to-date Linux software on old PCs
- _____ engine, a software system that helps managing business _____s
- Ja _____, a hip hop artist
    - R.U.L.E., a 2005 greatest hits album by rapper Ja _____
- '_____s,' a KMFDM song

a. Rule
b. Demand
c. Technocracy
d. Procter ' Gamble

34. _____ is a common concept in economics, and gives rise to derived concepts such as consumer debt. Generally _____ is defined by opposition to production. But the precise definition can vary because different schools of economists define production quite differently.

a. Federal Reserve Bank Notes
b. Cash or share options
c. Consumption
d. Foreclosure data providers

Chapter 11. Output, Inflation, and Unemployment: Alternative Views

1. _____ is widely regarded as the first modern school of economic thought. It is the idea that free markets can regulate themselves. Its major developers include Adam Smith, David Ricardo, Thomas Malthus and John Stuart Mill. Sometimes the definition of _____ is expanded to include William Petty, Johann Heinrich von Thünen.
    a. Tendency of the rate of profit to fall
    b. Schools of economic thought
    c. Marginalism
    d. Classical economics

2. The _____ was a worldwide economic downturn starting in most places in 1929 and ending at different times in the 1930s or early 1940s for different countries. It was the largest and most important economic depression in the 20th century, and is used in the 21st century as an example of how far the world's economy can fall. The _____ originated in the United States; historians most often use as a starting date the stock market crash on October 29, 1929, known as Black Tuesday.
    a. Jarrow March
    b. Wall Street Crash of 1929
    c. British Empire Economic Conference
    d. Great Depression

3. The _____ or gross domestic income (GDI), a basic measure of an economy's economic performance, is the market value of all final goods and services produced within the borders of a nation in a year. _____ can be defined in three ways, all of which are conceptually identical. First, it is equal to the total expenditures for all final goods and services produced within the country in a stipulated period of time (usually a 365-day year.)
    a. Market structure
    b. Gross domestic product
    c. Countercyclical
    d. Monopolistic competition

4. _____ and Keynesian Theory) is a macroeconomic theory based on the ideas of 20th-century British economist John Maynard Keynes. _____ argues that private sector decisions sometimes lead to inefficient macroeconomic outcomes and therefore advocates active policy responses by the public sector, including monetary policy actions by the central bank and fiscal policy actions by the government to stabilize output over the business cycle.

The theories forming the basis of _____ were first presented in The General Theory of Employment, Interest and Money, published in 1936.

    a. Keynesian economics
    b. Rational choice theory
    c. Market failure
    d. Deflation

5. In economics, the _____ is a historical inverse relation between the rate of unemployment and the rate of inflation in an economy. Stated simply, the lower the unemployment in an economy, the higher the rate of increase in nominal wages in the economy. Rate of Change of Wages against Unemployment, United Kingdom 1913-1948 from Phillips (1958)

William Phillips, a New Zealand born economist, wrote a paper in 1958 titled The Relationship between Unemployment and the Rate of Change of Money Wages in the United Kingdom 1861-1957, which was published in the quarterly journal Economica.

    a. Cost curve
    b. Demand curve
    c. Lorenz curve
    d. Phillips curve

6. _____s is the social science that studies the production, distribution, and consumption of goods and services. The term _____s comes from the Ancient Greek οἰκονομῖα from οἶκος (oikos, 'house') + νόμος (nomos, 'custom' or 'law'), hence 'rules of the house(hold)'. Current _____ models developed out of the broader field of political economy in the late 19th century, owing to a desire to use an empirical approach more akin to the physical sciences.

Chapter 11. Output, Inflation, and Unemployment: Alternative Views

a. Opportunity cost
b. Energy economics
c. Inflation
d. Economic

7. In economics, _____ is a rise in the general level of prices of goods and services in an economy over a period of time. When the general price level rises, each unit of currency buys fewer goods and services; consequently, _____ is also a decline in the real value of money--a loss of purchasing power in the medium of exchange which is also the monetary unit of account in the economy. A chief measure of general price-level _____ is the general _____ rate, which is the percentage change in a general price index (normally the Consumer Price Index) over time.
   a. Energy economics
   b. Economic
   c. Opportunity cost
   d. Inflation

8. _____, 1st Baron Keynes was a renowned economist from Britain whose many ideas on economic and political theories as well as on many governments' monetary policies influenced America. He advocated a government that played an active role in the lives of people regarding business, economy, etc. In this role, the government would use fiscal measures to reduce the consequences of recessions, economic depressions and booms.
   a. Adolph Fischer
   b. Adolf Hitler
   c. Adam Smith
   d. John Maynard Keynes

9. Economics:

   - _____, the desire to own something and the ability to pay for it
   - _____ curve, a graphic representation of a _____ schedule
   - _____ deposit, the money in checking accounts
   - _____ pull theory, the theory that inflation occurs when _____ for goods and services exceeds existing supplies
   - _____ schedule, a table that lists the quantity of a good a person will buy it each different price
   - _____ side economics, the school of economics at believes government spending and tax cuts open economy by raising _____

   a. McKesson ' Robbins scandal
   b. Production
   c. Variability
   d. Demand

10. In economics, a _____ is a table that lists the quantity of a good a person will buy it each different price See Demand curve.
    a. Free contract
    b. Federal Reserve districts
    c. Rational irrationality
    d. Demand schedule

11. The supply of labor is the number of total hours that workers wish to work at a given real wage rate.

    _____ curves are derived from the 'labor-leisure' trade-off. More hours worked earn higher incomes but necessitate a cut in the amount of leisure that workers enjoy.

    a. Late capitalism
    b. Labor supply
    c. Creative capitalism
    d. Human trafficking

Chapter 11. Output, Inflation, and Unemployment: Alternative Views

12. _____ is the process by which the government, central bank (ii) availability of money, and (iii) cost of money or rate of interest, in order to attain a set of objectives oriented towards the growth and stability of the economy. Monetary theory provides insight into how to craft optimal _____.

_____ is referred to as either being an expansionary policy where an expansionary policy increases the total supply of money in the economy, and a contractionary policy decreases the total money supply.

a. Monetary policy
b. 1921 recession
c. 100-year flood
d. 130-30 fund

13. Market _____ is a business, economics or investment term that refers to an asset's ability to be easily converted through an act of buying or selling without causing a significant movement in the price and with minimum loss of value. Money, or cash on hand, is the most liquid asset. An act of exchange of a less liquid asset with a more liquid asset is called liquidation.

a. 100-year flood
b. 130-30 fund
c. 1921 recession
d. Liquidity

14. The term _____ is used in macroeconomics to refer to a situation where a country's nominal interest rate has been lowered nearly to or equal to zero to avoid a recession, but the liquidity in the market created by these low interest rates does not stimulate the economy to full employment. In this situation, any further increase in the money supply will not stimulate the economy any further. This is because any further injection of liquidity will no longer lower the nominal interest rate, as the nominal interest rate cannot drop below zero.

a. Macroeconomic models
b. Minimum wage
c. Robertson lag
d. Liquidity trap

15. A _____ is a situation that involves losing one quality or aspect of something in return for gaining another quality or aspect. It implies a decision to be made with full comprehension of both the upside and downside of a particular choice.

In economics the term is expressed as opportunity cost, referring the most preferred alternative given up.

a. Nonmarket
b. Friedman-Savage utility function
c. Whitemail
d. Trade-off

16. In economics, the concept of the _____ refers to the decision-making time frame of a firm in which at least one factor of production is fixed. Costs which are fixed in the _____ have no impact on a firms decisions. For example a firm can raise output by increasing the amount of labour through overtime.

a. Productivity model
b. Hicks-neutral technical change
c. Short-run
d. Product Pipeline

17. In economics, _____ is inflation that is very high or 'out of control', a condition in which prices increase rapidly as a currency loses its value. Definitions used by the media vary from a cumulative inflation rate over three years approaching 100% to 'inflation exceeding 50% a month.' In informal usage the term is often applied to much lower rates. As a rule of thumb, normal inflation is reported per year, but _____ is often reported for much shorter intervals, often per month.

a. 1921 recession
b. 130-30 fund
c. 100-year flood
d. Hyperinflation

18. The _____ is an expected return that the provider of capital plans to earn on their investment.

Capital (money) used for funding a business should earn returns for the capital providers who risk their capital. For an investment to be worthwhile, the expected return on capital must be greater than the _____.

a. Capital intensive
b. Capital expenditure
c. Modigliani-Miller theorem
d. Cost of capital

19. _____ or government expenditure is classified by economists into three main types. Government purchases of goods and services for current use are classed as government consumption. Government purchases of goods and services intended to create future benefits, such as infrastructure investment or research spending, are classed as government investment.

a. Government spending
b. 100-year flood
c. 1921 recession
d. 130-30 fund

20. In economic models, the _____ time frame assumes no fixed factors of production. Firms can enter or leave the marketplace, and the cost (and availability) of land, labor, raw materials, and capital goods can be assumed to vary. In contrast, in the short-run time frame, certain factors are assumed to be fixed, because there is not sufficient time for them to change.

a. Productivity world
b. Diseconomies of scale
c. Price/performance ratio
d. Long-run

21. _____ is the view within monetary economics that variation in the money supply has major influences on national output in the short run and the price level over longer periods and that objectives of monetary policy are best met by targeting the growth rate of the money supply.

_____ today is mainly associated with the work of Milton Friedman, who was among the generation of economists to accept Keynesian economics and then criticize it on his own terms. Friedman and Anna Schwartz wrote an influential book, Monetary History of the United States 1867-1960, and argued that 'inflation is always and everywhere a monetary phenomenon.' Friedman advocated a central bank policy aimed at keeping the supply and demand for money at equilibrium, as measured by growth in productivity and demand.

a. Marginal revenue productivity theory of wages
b. Historical school of economics
c. Complexity economics
d. Monetarism

22. _____ is a school of contemporary macroeconomics that strives to provide microeconomic foundations for Keynesian economics. It developed partly as a response to criticisms of Keynesian macroeconomics by adherents of New Classical macroeconomics.

a. Law of demand
b. Keynesian theory
c. Mainstream economics
d. New Keynesian economics

23. In economics, _____ is the total demand for final goods and services in the economy (Y) at a given time and price level. It is the amount of goods and services in the economy that will be purchased at all possible price levels. This is the demand for the gross domestic product of a country when inventory levels are static.

a. Aggregation problem
b. Aggregate supply
c. Aggregate expenditure
d. Aggregate demand

24. _____ is a common concept in economics, and gives rise to derived concepts such as consumer debt. Generally _____ is defined by opposition to production. But the precise definition can vary because different schools of economists define production quite differently.
   a. Federal Reserve Bank Notes
   b. Cash or share options
   c. Foreclosure data providers
   d. Consumption

25. In economics, _____ is the total supply of goods and services produced by a national economy during a specific time period. It is the total amount of goods and services in the economy available at all possible price levels.
   a. Aggregate demand
   b. Aggregation problem
   c. Aggregate expenditure
   d. Aggregate supply

26. In algebra, a _____ is a function depending on n that associates a scalar, det(A), to an n×n square matrix A. The fundamental geometric meaning of a _____ is a scale factor for measure when A is regarded as a linear transformation. _____s are important both in calculus, where they enter the substitution rule for several variables, and in multilinear algebra.

For a fixed nonnegative integer n, there is a unique _____ function for the n×n matrices over any commutative ring R. In particular, this function exists when R is the field of real or complex numbers.

   a. 130-30 fund
   b. 1921 recession
   c. Determinant
   d. 100-year flood

27. The _____ is a concept of economic activity developed in particular by Milton Friedman and Edmund Phelps in the 1960s, both recipients of the Nobel prize in economics. In both cases, the development of the concept is cited as a main motivation behind the prize. It represents the hypothetical unemployment rate consistent with aggregate production being at the 'long-run' level.
   a. Robertson lag
   b. Romer Model
   c. Real Business Cycle Theory
   d. Natural rate of unemployment

28. The _____ is the official currency of 16 of the 27 member states of the European Union (EU.) The states, known collectively as the Eurozone, are Austria, Belgium, Cyprus, Finland, France, Germany, Greece, Ireland, Italy, Luxembourg, Malta, the Netherlands, Portugal, Slovakia, Slovenia, and Spain. The currency is also used in a further five European countries, with and without formal agreements and is consequently used daily by some 327 million Europeans.
   a. Euro
   b. Equity capital market
   c. Import and Export Price Indices
   d. IRS Code 3401

29. The _____ is an economic and political union of 27 member states, located primarily in Europe. It was established by the Treaty of Maastricht on 1 November 1993, upon the foundations of the pre-existing European Economic Community. With a population of almost 500 million, the _____ generates an estimated 30% share (US$18.4 trillion in 2008) of the nominal gross world product.
   a. European Court of Justice
   b. ACEA agreement
   c. European Union
   d. ACCRA Cost of Living Index

Chapter 11. Output, Inflation, and Unemployment: Alternative Views

30. A _____, reserve bank, or monetary authority is the entity responsible for the monetary policy of a country or of a group of member states. It is a bank that can lend money to other banks in times of need. Its primary responsibility is to maintain the stability of the national currency and money supply, but more active duties include controlling subsidized-loan interest rates, and acting as a lender of last resort to the banking sector during times of financial crisis (private banks often being integral to the national financial system.)
   a. 100-year flood
   b. 130-30 fund
   c. Central bank
   d. 1921 recession

31. In economics, a _____ is a general slowdown in economic activity over a sustained period of time, or a business cycle contraction. During _____s, many macroeconomic indicators vary in a similar way. Production as measured by Gross Domestic Product (GDP), employment, investment spending, capacity utilization, household incomes and business profits all fall during _____s.
   a. Monetary economics
   b. Recession
   c. Treasury View
   d. Leading indicators

32. A _____ occurs when an entity spends more money than it takes in. The opposite of a _____ is a budget surplus. Debt is essentially an accumulated flow of deficits.
   a. Public Financial Management
   b. Funding body
   c. Lump-sum tax
   d. Budget deficit

Chapter 12. New Classical Economics

1. _____ is widely regarded as the first modern school of economic thought. It is the idea that free markets can regulate themselves. Its major developers include Adam Smith, David Ricardo, Thomas Malthus and John Stuart Mill. Sometimes the definition of _____ is expanded to include William Petty, Johann Heinrich von Thünen.
   - a. Schools of economic thought
   - b. Tendency of the rate of profit to fall
   - c. Marginalism
   - d. Classical economics

2. _____s is the social science that studies the production, distribution, and consumption of goods and services. The term _____s comes from the Ancient Greek οἰκονομῖα from οἶκος (oikos, 'house') + νόμος (nomos, 'custom' or 'law'), hence 'rules of the house(hold)'. Current _____ models developed out of the broader field of political economy in the late 19th century, owing to a desire to use an empirical approach more akin to the physical sciences.
   - a. Energy economics
   - b. Opportunity cost
   - c. Inflation
   - d. Economic

3. In economics, _____ is the total supply of goods and services produced by a national economy during a specific time period. It is the total amount of goods and services in the economy available at all possible price levels.
   - a. Aggregate demand
   - b. Aggregate expenditure
   - c. Aggregate supply
   - d. Aggregation problem

4. _____ and Keynesian Theory) is a macroeconomic theory based on the ideas of 20th-century British economist John Maynard Keynes. _____ argues that private sector decisions sometimes lead to inefficient macroeconomic outcomes and therefore advocates active policy responses by the public sector, including monetary policy actions by the central bank and fiscal policy actions by the government to stabilize output over the business cycle.

   The theories forming the basis of _____ were first presented in The General Theory of Employment, Interest and Money, published in 1936.
   - a. Keynesian economics
   - b. Deflation
   - c. Market failure
   - d. Rational choice theory

5. The supply of labor is the number of total hours that workers wish to work at a given real wage rate.

   _____ curves are derived from the 'labor-leisure' trade-off. More hours worked earn higher incomes but necessitate a cut in the amount of leisure that workers enjoy.
   - a. Late capitalism
   - b. Labor supply
   - c. Creative capitalism
   - d. Human trafficking

6. The _____ is a new classical theory proposed in 1976 by Thomas J. Sargent and Neil Wallace based upon the theory of rational expectations. It posits that governments are powerless in the management of output and employment in an economy.

   Prior to the work of Sargent and Wallace, macroeconomic models were largely based on the adaptive expectations assumption.
   - a. Developmentalism
   - b. Non-Accelerating Inflation Rate of Unemployment
   - c. Policy ineffectiveness proposition
   - d. Dominant Design

Chapter 12. New Classical Economics

7. _____ in economics and business is the result of an exchange and from that trade we assign a numerical monetary value to a good, service or asset. If Alice trades Bob 4 apples for an orange, the _____ of an orange is 4 apples. Inversely, the _____ of an apple is 1/4 oranges.
   a. Price book
   b. Price
   c. Premium pricing
   d. Price war

8. A _____ is a hypothetical measure of overall prices for some set of goods and services, in a given region during a given interval, normalized relative to some base set. Typically, a _____ is approximated with a price index.

The classical dichotomy is the assumption that there is a relatively clean distinction between overall increases or decreases in prices and underlying, e;reale; economic variables.

   a. Price level
   b. Discretionary spending
   c. Price elasticity of supply
   d. Discouraged worker

9. _____ is an assumption used in many contemporary macroeconomic models, and also in other areas of contemporary economics and game theory and in other applications of rational choice theory.

Since most macroeconomic models today study decisions over many periods, the expectations of workers, consumers, and firms about future economic conditions are an essential part of the model. How to model these expectations has long been controversial, and it is well known that the macroeconomic predictions of the model may differ depending on the assumptions made about expectations

   a. Potential output
   b. Balanced-growth equilibrium
   c. Rational expectations
   d. Minimum wage

10. In labor economics, the _____ hypothesis argues that wages, at least in some markets, are determined by more than simply supply and demand. Specifically, it points to the incentive for managers to pay their employees more than the market-clearing wage in order to increase their productivity or efficiency. This increased labor productivity pays for the relatively higher wages.
    a. Exogenous growth model
    b. Earnings calls
    c. Inflatable rats
    d. Efficiency wage

11. A _____ measures average changes in prices received by domestic producers for their output. It is one of several price indices

Its importance is being undermined by the steady decline in manufactured goods as a share of spending.

A number of countries that now report a _____ previously reported a Wholesale Price Index.

   a. Visible balance
   b. Gross national product
   c. Hemline index
   d. Producer price index

12. A _____ is a normalized average (typically a weighted average) of prices for a given class of goods or services in a given region, during a given interval of time. It is a statistic designed to help to compare how these prices, taken as a whole, differ between time periods or geographical locations.

Chapter 12. New Classical Economics

Price indices have several potential uses.

a. Transactional Net Margin Method
c. Product sabotage

b. Two-part tariff
d. Price index

13. A _____ is a public market for the trading of company stock and derivatives at an agreed price; these are securities listed on a stock exchange as well as those only traded privately.

The size of the world _____ was estimated at about $36.6 trillion US at the beginning of October 2008 . The total world derivatives market has been estimated at about $791 trillion face or nominal value, 11 times the size of the entire world economy.

a. Adam Smith
c. Adolf Hitler

b. Adolph Fischer
d. Stock market

14. _____ is the process by which the government, central bank (ii) availability of money, and (iii) cost of money or rate of interest, in order to attain a set of objectives oriented towards the growth and stability of the economy. Monetary theory provides insight into how to craft optimal _____.

_____ is referred to as either being an expansionary policy where an expansionary policy increases the total supply of money in the economy, and a contractionary policy decreases the total money supply.

a. 100-year flood
c. 130-30 fund

b. Monetary policy
d. 1921 recession

15. _____ is an American economist and was the Chairman of the Federal Reserve of the United States from 1987 to 2006. He currently works as a private advisor and providing consulting for firms through his company, Greenspan Associates LLC.

First appointed Federal Reserve chairman by President Ronald Reagan in August 1987, he was reappointed at successive four-year intervals until retiring on January 31, 2006 after the second-longest tenure in the position.

a. Adolf Hitler
c. Alan Greenspan

b. Adam Smith
d. Adolph Fischer

16. The _____ is an American stock exchange. It is the largest electronic screen-based equity securities trading market in the United States. With approximately 3,800 companies, it has more trading volume per hour than any other stock exchange in the world.

a. NASDAQ
c. 1921 recession

b. 100-year flood
d. 130-30 fund

17. _____ or government expenditure is classified by economists into three main types. Government purchases of goods and services for current use are classed as government consumption. Government purchases of goods and services intended to create future benefits, such as infrastructure investment or research spending, are classed as government investment.

Chapter 12. New Classical Economics

a. 100-year flood
b. 1921 recession
c. Government spending
d. 130-30 fund

18. _____, 1st Baron Keynes was a renowned economist from Britain whose many ideas on economic and political theories as well as on many governments' monetary policies influenced America. He advocated a government that played an active role in the lives of people regarding business, economy, etc. In this role, the government would use fiscal measures to reduce the consequences of recessions, economic depressions and booms.
   a. John Maynard Keynes
   b. Adolf Hitler
   c. Adam Smith
   d. Adolph Fischer

19. _____ is the view within monetary economics that variation in the money supply has major influences on national output in the short run and the price level over longer periods and that objectives of monetary policy are best met by targeting the growth rate of the money supply.

   _____ today is mainly associated with the work of Milton Friedman, who was among the generation of economists to accept Keynesian economics and then criticize it on his own terms. Friedman and Anna Schwartz wrote an influential book, Monetary History of the United States 1867-1960, and argued that 'inflation is always and everywhere a monetary phenomenon.' Friedman advocated a central bank policy aimed at keeping the supply and demand for money at equilibrium, as measured by growth in productivity and demand.
   a. Historical school of economics
   b. Complexity economics
   c. Marginal revenue productivity theory of wages
   d. Monetarism

20. _____ is a school of contemporary macroeconomics that strives to provide microeconomic foundations for Keynesian economics. It developed partly as a response to criticisms of Keynesian macroeconomics by adherents of New Classical macroeconomics.
   a. Keynesian theory
   b. Mainstream economics
   c. New Keynesian economics
   d. Law of demand

21. In economics, _____ is the total demand for final goods and services in the economy (Y) at a given time and price level. It is the amount of goods and services in the economy that will be purchased at all possible price levels. This is the demand for the gross domestic product of a country when inventory levels are static.
   a. Aggregate demand
   b. Aggregate supply
   c. Aggregation problem
   d. Aggregate expenditure

Chapter 12. New Classical Economics

22. Economics:

- _____, the desire to own something and the ability to pay for it
- _____ curve, a graphic representation of a _____ schedule
- _____ deposit, the money in checking accounts
- _____ pull theory, the theory that inflation occurs when _____ for goods and services exceeds existing supplies
- _____ schedule, a table that lists the quantity of a good a person will buy it each different price
- _____ side economics, the school of economics at believes government spending and tax cuts open economy by raising _____

   a. Variability
   b. McKesson ' Robbins scandal
   c. Production
   d. Demand

23. _____ is a common concept in economics, and gives rise to derived concepts such as consumer debt. Generally _____ is defined by opposition to production. But the precise definition can vary because different schools of economists define production quite differently.

   a. Foreclosure data providers
   b. Consumption
   c. Federal Reserve Bank Notes
   d. Cash or share options

24. The _____ was a worldwide economic downturn starting in most places in 1929 and ending at different times in the 1930s or early 1940s for different countries. It was the largest and most important economic depression in the 20th century, and is used in the 21st century as an example of how far the world's economy can fall. The _____ originated in the United States; historians most often use as a starting date the stock market crash on October 29, 1929, known as Black Tuesday.

   a. British Empire Economic Conference
   b. Wall Street Crash of 1929
   c. Jarrow March
   d. Great Depression

25. The _____ or gross domestic income (GDI), a basic measure of an economy's economic performance, is the market value of all final goods and services produced within the borders of a nation in a year. _____ can be defined in three ways, all of which are conceptually identical. First, it is equal to the total expenditures for all final goods and services produced within the country in a stipulated period of time (usually a 365-day year.)

   a. Monopolistic competition
   b. Market structure
   c. Countercyclical
   d. Gross domestic product

26. A _____, reserve bank, or monetary authority is the entity responsible for the monetary policy of a country or of a group of member states. It is a bank that can lend money to other banks in times of need. Its primary responsibility is to maintain the stability of the national currency and money supply, but more active duties include controlling subsidized-loan interest rates, and acting as a lender of last resort to the banking sector during times of financial crisis (private banks often being integral to the national financial system.)

   a. 1921 recession
   b. 130-30 fund
   c. 100-year flood
   d. Central bank

27. _____ is the increase in the amount of the goods and services produced by an economy over time. It is conventionally measured as the percent rate of increase in real gross domestic product, or real GDP. Growth is usually calculated in real terms, i.e. inflation-adjusted terms, in order to net out the effect of inflation on the price of the goods and services produced.

    a. ACEA agreement
    b. ACCRA Cost of Living Index
    c. AD-IA Model
    d. Economic growth

28. In economics, the _____ is the term economists use to describe the self-regulating nature of the marketplace. The _____ is a metaphor coined by the economist Adam Smith in The Wealth of Nations.

Adam Smith mentions the metaphor in Book IV of The Wealth of Nations, arguing that people in any society will certainly employ their capital in foreign trading only if the profits available by that method far exceed those available locally, and that in such a case it is better for society as a whole if they so did.

    a. Invisible hand
    b. ACCRA Cost of Living Index
    c. AD-IA Model
    d. ACEA agreement

Chapter 13. Real Business Cycles and New Keynesian Economics

1. _____ Theory (or _____ Theory) is a class of macroeconomic models in which business cycle fluctuations to a large extent can be accounted for by real (in contrast to nominal) shocks. (The four primary economic fluctuations are secular (trend), business cycle, seasonal, and random.) Unlike other leading theories of the business cycle, it sees recessions and periods of economic growth as the efficient response to exogenous changes in the real economic environment.
   a. Monetary policy reaction function
   b. SIMIC
   c. Balanced-growth equilibrium
   d. Real business cycle

2. The term _____ refers to economy-wide fluctuations in production or economic activity over several months or years. These fluctuations occur around a long-term growth trend, and typically involve shifts over time between periods of relatively rapid economic growth (expansion or boom), and periods of relative stagnation or decline (contraction or recession.)

   These fluctuations are often measured using the growth rate of real gross domestic product.

   a. Tobit model
   b. Nominal value
   c. Consumer theory
   d. Business cycle

3. _____ is widely regarded as the first modern school of economic thought. It is the idea that free markets can regulate themselves. Its major developers include Adam Smith, David Ricardo, Thomas Malthus and John Stuart Mill. Sometimes the definition of _____ is expanded to include William Petty, Johann Heinrich von Thünen.
   a. Schools of economic thought
   b. Marginalism
   c. Tendency of the rate of profit to fall
   d. Classical economics

4. The _____ or gross domestic income (GDI), a basic measure of an economy's economic performance, is the market value of all final goods and services produced within the borders of a nation in a year. _____ can be defined in three ways, all of which are conceptually identical. First, it is equal to the total expenditures for all final goods and services produced within the country in a stipulated period of time (usually a 365-day year.)
   a. Countercyclical
   b. Market structure
   c. Monopolistic competition
   d. Gross domestic product

5. _____, 1st Baron Keynes was a renowned economist from Britain whose many ideas on economic and political theories as well as on many governments' monetary policies influenced America. He advocated a government that played an active role in the lives of people regarding business, economy, etc. In this role, the government would use fiscal measures to reduce the consequences of recessions, economic depressions and booms.
   a. Adolph Fischer
   b. Adolf Hitler
   c. Adam Smith
   d. John Maynard Keynes

6. _____ and Keynesian Theory) is a macroeconomic theory based on the ideas of 20th-century British economist John Maynard Keynes. _____ argues that private sector decisions sometimes lead to inefficient macroeconomic outcomes and therefore advocates active policy responses by the public sector, including monetary policy actions by the central bank and fiscal policy actions by the government to stabilize output over the business cycle.

The theories forming the basis of _____ were first presented in The General Theory of Employment, Interest and Money, published in 1936.

Chapter 13. Real Business Cycles and New Keynesian Economics

a. Rational choice theory
b. Market failure
c. Keynesian economics
d. Deflation

7. _____s is the social science that studies the production, distribution, and consumption of goods and services. The term _____s comes from the Ancient Greek oá¼°κονομῖα from oá¼¶κος (oikos, 'house') + vĭŒμος (nomos, 'custom' or 'law'), hence 'rules of the house(hold)'. Current _____ models developed out of the broader field of political economy in the late 19th century, owing to a desire to use an empirical approach more akin to the physical sciences.

a. Inflation
b. Energy economics
c. Economic
d. Opportunity cost

8. _____ is a class of macroeconomic models in which business cycle fluctuations to a large extent can be accounted for by real (in contrast to nominal) shocks. (The four primary economic fluctuations are secular (trend), business cycle, seasonal, and random.) Unlike other leading theories of the business cycle, it sees recessions and periods of economic growth as the efficient response to exogenous changes in the real economic environment.

a. Real business cycle theory
b. Consumer spending
c. War economy
d. Solow residual

9. Economists use the term _____ to refer to the typical decision-maker of a certain type (for example, the typical consumer, or the typical firm.)

More technically, an economic model is said to have a _____ if all agents of the same type are identical. Also, economists sometimes say a model has a _____ when agents differ, but act in such a way that the sum of their choices is mathematically equivalent to the decision of one individual or many identical individuals.

a. Representative agent
b. Classical general equilibrium model
c. Harrod-Domar model
d. Rostovian take-off model

10. _____s are events in a macroeconomic model, that change the production function. Usually this is modelled with an aggregate production function that has a scaling factor.

A _____ affects an industry or firm's productivity, this may be a positive shock - increasing the output for a given set of inputs, or a negative shock - decreasing the output for a given set of inputs.

a. Potential output
b. Supply shock
c. Technology shock
d. Macroeconomic models

11. _____ is the net revenue derived from the issuing of currency.

_____ derived from specie - metal coins - arises from the difference between the face value of a coin and the cost of producing, distributing and retiring it from circulation.

_____ derived from notes is more indirect, being the difference between interest earned on securities acquired in exchange for bank notes and the costs of producing and distributing those notes.

Chapter 13. Real Business Cycles and New Keynesian Economics

a. Money Tracker
c. 130-30 fund
b. Seigniorage
d. 100-year flood

12. _____ is a school of macroeconomic thought that argues that economic growth can be most effectively created using incentives for people to produce (supply) goods and services, such as adjusting income tax and capital gains tax rates, and by allowing greater flexibility by reducing regulation. Consumers will then benefit from a greater supply of goods and services at lower prices.

The term _____ was coined by journalist Jude Wanniski in 1975, and popularized the ideas of economists Robert Mundell and Arthur Laffer.

a. Fiscal stimulus plans
c. Clap note
b. Commodity trading advisors
d. Supply-side economics

13. A _____, reserve bank, or monetary authority is the entity responsible for the monetary policy of a country or of a group of member states. It is a bank that can lend money to other banks in times of need. Its primary responsibility is to maintain the stability of the national currency and money supply, but more active duties include controlling subsidized-loan interest rates, and acting as a lender of last resort to the banking sector during times of financial crisis (private banks often being integral to the national financial system.)

a. 1921 recession
c. 100-year flood
b. 130-30 fund
d. Central Bank

14. Market _____ is a business, economics or investment term that refers to an asset's ability to be easily converted through an act of buying or selling without causing a significant movement in the price and with minimum loss of value. Money, or cash on hand, is the most liquid asset. An act of exchange of a less liquid asset with a more liquid asset is called liquidation.

a. 1921 recession
c. 130-30 fund
b. 100-year flood
d. Liquidity

15. The term _____ is used in macroeconomics to refer to a situation where a country's nominal interest rate has been lowered nearly to or equal to zero to avoid a recession, but the liquidity in the market created by these low interest rates does not stimulate the economy to full employment. In this situation, any further increase in the money supply will not stimulate the economy any further. This is because any further injection of liquidity will no longer lower the nominal interest rate, as the nominal interest rate cannot drop below zero.

a. Robertson lag
c. Macroeconomic models
b. Minimum wage
d. Liquidity trap

16. _____ is the process by which the government, central bank (ii) availability of money, and (iii) cost of money or rate of interest, in order to attain a set of objectives oriented towards the growth and stability of the economy. Monetary theory provides insight into how to craft optimal _____.

_____ is referred to as either being an expansionary policy where an expansionary policy increases the total supply of money in the economy, and a contractionary policy decreases the total money supply.

a. 130-30 fund
b. Monetary policy
c. 1921 recession
d. 100-year flood

17. In economics, a _____ is a general slowdown in economic activity over a sustained period of time, or a business cycle contraction. During _____s, many macroeconomic indicators vary in a similar way. Production as measured by Gross Domestic Product (GDP), employment, investment spending, capacity utilization, household incomes and business profits all fall during _____s.
   a. Leading indicators
   b. Monetary economics
   c. Recession
   d. Treasury View

18. In financial accounting, a _____ or statement of financial position is a summary of a person's or organization's balances. Assets, liabilities and ownership equity are listed as of a specific date, such as the end of its financial year. A _____ is often described as a snapshot of a company's financial condition.
   a. 1921 recession
   b. 100-year flood
   c. 130-30 fund
   d. Balance sheet

19. A _____ occurs when an entity spends more money than it takes in. The opposite of a _____ is a budget surplus. Debt is essentially an accumulated flow of deficits.
   a. Funding body
   b. Lump-sum tax
   c. Public Financial Management
   d. Budget deficit

20. _____ is a macroeconomic theory that argues that private sector decisions sometimes lead to inefficient macroeconomic outcomes and therefore advocates active policy responses by the public sector, including monetary policy actions by the central bank and fiscal policy actions by the government to stabilize output over the business cycle.

The theories forming the basis of _____ were first presented in The General Theory of Employment, Interest and Money, published in 1936.

   a. Tobit model
   b. Keynesian theory
   c. Mainstream economics
   d. Human capital

21. _____ is a school of contemporary macroeconomics that strives to provide microeconomic foundations for Keynesian economics. It developed partly as a response to criticisms of Keynesian macroeconomics by adherents of New Classical macroeconomics.
   a. Mainstream economics
   b. Law of demand
   c. New Keynesian economics
   d. Keynesian theory

22. In economics, _____ is the total demand for final goods and services in the economy (Y) at a given time and price level. It is the amount of goods and services in the economy that will be purchased at all possible price levels. This is the demand for the gross domestic product of a country when inventory levels are static.
   a. Aggregate expenditure
   b. Aggregate supply
   c. Aggregate demand
   d. Aggregation problem

23. In economics, _____ is the total supply of goods and services produced by a national economy during a specific time period. It is the total amount of goods and services in the economy available at all possible price levels.

Chapter 13. Real Business Cycles and New Keynesian Economics

a. Aggregate supply
b. Aggregate expenditure
c. Aggregation problem
d. Aggregate demand

24. Economics:

- _____, the desire to own something and the ability to pay for it
- _____ curve, a graphic representation of a _____ schedule
- _____ deposit, the money in checking accounts
- _____ pull theory, the theory that inflation occurs when _____ for goods and services exceeds existing supplies
- _____ schedule, a table that lists the quantity of a good a person will buy it each different price
- _____ side economics, the school of economics at believes government spending and tax cuts open economy by raising _____

a. Variability
b. McKesson ' Robbins scandal
c. Production
d. Demand

25. _____ is the increase in the amount of the goods and services produced by an economy over time. It is conventionally measured as the percent rate of increase in real gross domestic product, or real GDP. Growth is usually calculated in real terms, i.e. inflation-adjusted terms, in order to net out the effect of inflation on the price of the goods and services produced.
   a. ACCRA Cost of Living Index
   b. Economic growth
   c. AD-IA Model
   d. ACEA agreement

26. _____ in economics and business is the result of an exchange and from that trade we assign a numerical monetary value to a good, service or asset. If Alice trades Bob 4 apples for an orange, the _____ of an orange is 4 apples. Inversely, the _____ of an apple is 1/4 oranges.
   a. Price book
   b. Price war
   c. Premium pricing
   d. Price

27. _____ is an economic model based on price, utility and quantity in a market. It predicts that in a competitive market, price will function to equalize the quantity demanded by consumers, and the quantity supplied by producers, resulting in an economic equilibrium of price and quantity. The model incorporates other factors changing equilibrium as a shift of demand and/or supply.
   a. Deferred gratification
   b. Joint demand
   c. Rational addiction
   d. Supply and demand

28. In labor economics, the _____ hypothesis argues that wages, at least in some markets, are determined by more than simply supply and demand. Specifically, it points to the incentive for managers to pay their employees more than the market-clearing wage in order to increase their productivity or efficiency. This increased labor productivity pays for the relatively higher wages.
   a. Inflatable rats
   b. Earnings calls
   c. Exogenous growth model
   d. Efficiency wage

29. A _____ or a flexible exchange rate is a type of exchange rate regime wherein a currency's value is allowed to fluctuate according to the foreign exchange market. A currency that uses a _____ is known as a floating currency. The opposite of a _____ is a fixed exchange rate.
   a. Trade Weighted US dollar Index
   b. Floating exchange rate
   c. Floating currency
   d. Foreign exchange market

30. In finance, the _____s between two currencies specifies how much one currency is worth in terms of the other. It is the value of a foreign natione;s currency in terms of the home natione;s currency. For example an _____ of 102 Japanese yen to the United States dollar means that JPY 102 is worth the same as USD 1.
   a. ACCRA Cost of Living Index
   b. Interbank market
   c. ACEA agreement
   d. Exchange rate

Chapter 14. Macroeconomic Models: A Summary

1. In economics, _____ is the total supply of goods and services produced by a national economy during a specific time period. It is the total amount of goods and services in the economy available at all possible price levels.
   a. Aggregation problem
   b. Aggregate demand
   c. Aggregate expenditure
   d. Aggregate supply

2. _____ and Keynesian Theory) is a macroeconomic theory based on the ideas of 20th-century British economist John Maynard Keynes. _____ argues that private sector decisions sometimes lead to inefficient macroeconomic outcomes and therefore advocates active policy responses by the public sector, including monetary policy actions by the central bank and fiscal policy actions by the government to stabilize output over the business cycle.

   The theories forming the basis of _____ were first presented in The General Theory of Employment, Interest and Money, published in 1936.

   a. Keynesian economics
   b. Market failure
   c. Rational choice theory
   d. Deflation

3. A model in macroeconomics is a logical, mathematical, and/or computational framework designed to describe the operation of a national or regional economy, and especially the dynamics of aggregate quantities such as the total amount of goods and services produced, total income earned, the level of employment of productive resources, and the level of prices.

   There are different types of _____ that serve different purposes and have different advantages and disadvantages. Models are used to clarify and illustrate basic theoretical principles in macroeconomics; they are used to test, compare, and quantify different theories of the macroeconomy; they are used to produce 'what if' scenarios, and especially to evaluate the possible effects of changes in monetary, fiscal, or other macroeconomic policies; and they are used for generating economic forecasts.

   a. High-powered money
   b. Natural rate of unemployment
   c. Factor shares
   d. Macroeconomic models

4. In economics, _____ is the total demand for final goods and services in the economy (Y) at a given time and price level. It is the amount of goods and services in the economy that will be purchased at all possible price levels. This is the demand for the gross domestic product of a country when inventory levels are static.
   a. Aggregate expenditure
   b. Aggregation problem
   c. Aggregate supply
   d. Aggregate demand

5. _____ is widely regarded as the first modern school of economic thought. It is the idea that free markets can regulate themselves. Its major developers include Adam Smith, David Ricardo, Thomas Malthus and John Stuart Mill. Sometimes the definition of _____ is expanded to include William Petty, Johann Heinrich von Thünen.
   a. Tendency of the rate of profit to fall
   b. Classical economics
   c. Schools of economic thought
   d. Marginalism

Chapter 14. Macroeconomic Models: A Summary

6. Economics:

   - _____, the desire to own something and the ability to pay for it
   - _____ curve, a graphic representation of a _____ schedule
   - _____ deposit, the money in checking accounts
   - _____ pull theory, the theory that inflation occurs when _____ for goods and services exceeds existing supplies
   - _____ schedule, a table that lists the quantity of a good a person will buy it each different price
   - _____ side economics, the school of economics at believes government spending and tax cuts open economy by raising _____

   a. McKesson ' Robbins scandal
   b. Production
   c. Variability
   d. Demand

7. _____s is the social science that studies the production, distribution, and consumption of goods and services. The term _____s comes from the Ancient Greek oá¼°κονομΓ α from oá¼¶κος (oikos, 'house') + vΪŒμος (nomos, 'custom' or 'law'), hence 'rules of the house(hold)'. Current _____ models developed out of the broader field of political economy in the late 19th century, owing to a desire to use an empirical approach more akin to the physical sciences.

   a. Opportunity cost
   b. Economic
   c. Inflation
   d. Energy economics

8. In economics, a model is a theoretical construct that represents economic processes by a set of variables and a set of logical and/or quantitative relationships between them. The _____ is a simplified framework designed to illustrate complex processes, often but not always using mathematical techniques. Frequently, _____s use structural parameters.

   a. AD-IA Model
   b. ACEA agreement
   c. Economic model
   d. ACCRA Cost of Living Index

9. _____ is a branch of economics that deals with the performance, structure, and behavior of a national or regional economy as a whole. Along with microeconomics, _____ is one of the two most general fields in economics. It is the study of the behavior and decision-making of entire economies.

   a. Tobit model
   b. Macroeconomics
   c. Nominal value
   d. New Trade Theory

10. _____ or government expenditure is classified by economists into three main types. Government purchases of goods and services for current use are classed as government consumption. Government purchases of goods and services intended to create future benefits, such as infrastructure investment or research spending, are classed as government investment.

    a. 100-year flood
    b. 1921 recession
    c. 130-30 fund
    d. Government spending

11. _____, 1st Baron Keynes was a renowned economist from Britain whose many ideas on economic and political theories as well as on many governments' monetary policies influenced America. He advocated a government that played an active role in the lives of people regarding business, economy, etc. In this role, the government would use fiscal measures to reduce the consequences of recessions, economic depressions and booms.

a. Adam Smith
b. Adolf Hitler
c. Adolph Fischer
d. John Maynard Keynes

12. _____ is a macroeconomic theory that argues that private sector decisions sometimes lead to inefficient macroeconomic outcomes and therefore advocates active policy responses by the public sector, including monetary policy actions by the central bank and fiscal policy actions by the government to stabilize output over the business cycle.

The theories forming the basis of _____ were first presented in The General Theory of Employment, Interest and Money, published in 1936.

a. Human capital
b. Tobit model
c. Mainstream economics
d. Keynesian theory

13. _____ is the view within monetary economics that variation in the money supply has major influences on national output in the short run and the price level over longer periods and that objectives of monetary policy are best met by targeting the growth rate of the money supply.

_____ today is mainly associated with the work of Milton Friedman, who was among the generation of economists to accept Keynesian economics and then criticize it on his own terms. Friedman and Anna Schwartz wrote an influential book, Monetary History of the United States 1867-1960, and argued that 'inflation is always and everywhere a monetary phenomenon.' Friedman advocated a central bank policy aimed at keeping the supply and demand for money at equilibrium, as measured by growth in productivity and demand.

a. Marginal revenue productivity theory of wages
b. Complexity economics
c. Historical school of economics
d. Monetarism

14. _____ is the process by which the government, central bank (ii) availability of money, and (iii) cost of money or rate of interest, in order to attain a set of objectives oriented towards the growth and stability of the economy. Monetary theory provides insight into how to craft optimal _____.

_____ is referred to as either being an expansionary policy where an expansionary policy increases the total supply of money in the economy, and a contractionary policy decreases the total money supply.

a. 1921 recession
b. Monetary policy
c. 130-30 fund
d. 100-year flood

15. _____ is a school of contemporary macroeconomics that strives to provide microeconomic foundations for Keynesian economics. It developed partly as a response to criticisms of Keynesian macroeconomics by adherents of New Classical macroeconomics.

a. Law of demand
b. Keynesian theory
c. Mainstream economics
d. New Keynesian economics

Chapter 14. Macroeconomic Models: A Summary

16. _____ Theory (or _____ Theory) is a class of macroeconomic models in which business cycle fluctuations to a large extent can be accounted for by real (in contrast to nominal) shocks. (The four primary economic fluctuations are secular (trend), business cycle, seasonal, and random.) Unlike other leading theories of the business cycle, it sees recessions and periods of economic growth as the efficient response to exogenous changes in the real economic environment.
   a. Monetary policy reaction function
   b. SIMIC
   c. Balanced-growth equilibrium
   d. Real business cycle

17. The term _____ refers to economy-wide fluctuations in production or economic activity over several months or years. These fluctuations occur around a long-term growth trend, and typically involve shifts over time between periods of relatively rapid economic growth (expansion or boom), and periods of relative stagnation or decline (contraction or recession.)

    These fluctuations are often measured using the growth rate of real gross domestic product.

   a. Consumer theory
   b. Tobit model
   c. Nominal value
   d. Business cycle

18. _____ is a class of macroeconomic models in which business cycle fluctuations to a large extent can be accounted for by real (in contrast to nominal) shocks. (The four primary economic fluctuations are secular (trend), business cycle, seasonal, and random.) Unlike other leading theories of the business cycle, it sees recessions and periods of economic growth as the efficient response to exogenous changes in the real economic environment.
   a. Real business cycle theory
   b. Consumer spending
   c. War economy
   d. Solow residual

19. _____ is a common concept in economics, and gives rise to derived concepts such as consumer debt. Generally _____ is defined by opposition to production. But the precise definition can vary because different schools of economists define production quite differently.
   a. Consumption
   b. Cash or share options
   c. Foreclosure data providers
   d. Federal Reserve Bank Notes

20. _____ is an economic model based on price, utility and quantity in a market. It predicts that in a competitive market, price will function to equalize the quantity demanded by consumers, and the quantity supplied by producers, resulting in an economic equilibrium of price and quantity. The model incorporates other factors changing equilibrium as a shift of demand and/or supply.
   a. Supply and demand
   b. Rational addiction
   c. Joint demand
   d. Deferred gratification

21. The _____ was a worldwide economic downturn starting in most places in 1929 and ending at different times in the 1930s or early 1940s for different countries. It was the largest and most important economic depression in the 20th century, and is used in the 21st century as an example of how far the world's economy can fall. The _____ originated in the United States; historians most often use as a starting date the stock market crash on October 29, 1929, known as Black Tuesday.
   a. Great Depression
   b. Jarrow March
   c. British Empire Economic Conference
   d. Wall Street Crash of 1929

Chapter 14. Macroeconomic Models: A Summary

22. _____ is an assumption used in many contemporary macroeconomic models, and also in other areas of contemporary economics and game theory and in other applications of rational choice theory.

Since most macroeconomic models today study decisions over many periods, the expectations of workers, consumers, and firms about future economic conditions are an essential part of the model. How to model these expectations has long been controversial, and it is well known that the macroeconomic predictions of the model may differ depending on the assumptions made about expectations

- a. Balanced-growth equilibrium
- c. Rational expectations
- b. Potential output
- d. Minimum wage

23. _____ was an American economist, statistician and public intellectual, and a recipient of the Nobel Memorial Prize in Economic Sciences. He is best known among scholars for his theoretical and empirical research, especially consumption analysis, monetary history and theory, and for his demonstration of the complexity of stabilization policy. A global public followed his restatement of a political philosophy that insisted on minimizing the role of government in favor of the private sector.
- a. Adolf Hitler
- c. Adolph Fischer
- b. Milton Friedman
- d. Adam Smith

114 *Chapter 14. Macroeconomic Models: A Summary*

24. A _____ is:

- Rewrite _____, in generative grammar and computer science
- Standardization, a formal and widely-accepted statement, fact, definition, or qualification
- Operation, a determinate _____ for performing a mathematical operation and obtaining a certain result (Mathematics, Logic)
    - Unary operation
    - Binary operation
- _____ of inference, a function from sets of formulae to formulae (Mathematics, Logic)
- _____ of thumb, principle with broad application that is not intended to be strictly accurate or reliable for every situation. Also often simply referred to as a _____
- Moral, an atomic element of a moral code for guiding choices in human behavior
- Heuristic, a quantized '_____' which shows a tendency or probability for successful function
- A regulation, as in sports
- A Production _____, as in computer science
- Procedural law, a _____ set governing the application of laws to cases
    - A law, which may informally be called a '_____'
    - A court ruling, a decision by a court
- In the U.S. Government, a regulation mandated by Congress, but written or expanded upon by the Executive Branch.
- Norm (sociology), an informal but widely accepted _____, concept, truth, definition, or qualification (social norms, legal norms, coding norms)
- Norm (philosophy), a kind of sentence or a reason to act, feel or believe
- 'Rulership' is the concept of governance by a government:
    - Military _____, governance by a military body
    - Monastic _____, a collection of precepts that guides the life of monks or nuns in a religious order where the superior holds the place of Christ
- Slide _____

- '_____,' a song by Ayumi Hamasaki
- '_____,' a song by rapper Nas
- '_____s,' an album by the band The Whitest Boy Alive
- _____s: Pyaar Ka Superhit Formula, a 2003 Bollywood film
- ruler, an instrument for measuring lengths
- _____, a component of an astrolabe, circumferator or similar instrument
- The _____s, a bestselling self-help book
- _____ Project (Run Up-to-date Linux Everywhere), a project that aims to use up-to-date Linux software on old PCs
- _____ engine, a software system that helps managing business _____s
- Ja _____, a hip hop artist
    - R.U.L.E., a 2005 greatest hits album by rapper Ja _____
- '_____s,' a KMFDM song

a. Procter ' Gamble					b. Technocracy
c. Demand					d. Rule

Chapter 15. Exchange Rates and the International Monetary System

1. In economics, the _____ measures the payments that flow between any individual country and all other countries. It is used to summarize all international economic transactions for that country during a specific time period, usually a year. The _____ is determined by the country's exports and imports of goods, services, and financial capital, as well as financial transfers.
   a. Gross world product
   b. Gross domestic product per barrel
   c. Skyscraper Index
   d. Balance of payments

2. _____ is money accepted for exchange of goods in an economy. The prevalence of one money over another arises, usually, when a government designates through decrees that the government shall accept only particular notes and coins in payment for taxes. Typically, money of _____ consists of stamped coins and minted paper bills.
   a. Totnes pound
   b. Security thread
   c. Local currency
   d. Currency

3. In economics, an _____ is any good or commodity, transported from one country to another country in a legitimate fashion, typically for use in trade. _____ goods or services are provided to foreign consumers by domestic producers. _____ is an important part of international trade.
   a. AD-IA Model
   b. ACEA agreement
   c. Export
   d. ACCRA Cost of Living Index

4. The term _____ refers to government debt, expenditures and revenues, or to finance (particularly financial revenue) in general.

   - _____ deficit is the budget deficit of federal or local government
   - _____ policy is the discretionary spending of governments. Contrasts with monetary policy.
   - _____ year and _____ quarter are reporting periods for firms and other agencies.

   a. Procter ' Gamble
   b. Drawdown
   c. Fiscal
   d. Bucket shop

5. In economics, _____ is the use of government spending and revenue collection to influence the economy.

   _____ can be contrasted with the other main type of economic policy, monetary policy, which attempts to stabilize the economy by controlling interest rates and the supply of money. The two main instruments of _____ are government spending and taxation.

   a. Fiscal policy
   b. Fiscalism
   c. 100-year flood
   d. Sustainable investment rule

6. A _____, sometimes called a pegged exchange rate, is a type of exchange rate regime wherein a currency's value is matched to the value of another single currency or to a basket of other currencies such as gold.

   A _____ is usually used to stabilize the value of a currency, vis-a-vis the currency it is pegged to. This facilitates trade and investments between the two countries, and is especially useful for small economies where external trade forms a large part of their GDP.

Chapter 15. Exchange Rates and the International Monetary System

a. Leading indicators
b. Monetary economics
c. Law of supply
d. Fixed exchange rate

7. In economics, an _____ is any good (e.g. a commodity) or service brought into one country from another country in a legitimate fashion, typically for use in trade. It is a good that is brought in from another country for sale. _____ goods or services are provided to domestic consumers by foreign producers. An _____ in the receiving country is an export to the sending country.

a. Import
b. Economic integration
c. Incoterms
d. Import quota

8. _____ is the process by which the government, central bank (ii) availability of money, and (iii) cost of money or rate of interest, in order to attain a set of objectives oriented towards the growth and stability of the economy. Monetary theory provides insight into how to craft optimal _____.

_____ is referred to as either being an expansionary policy where an expansionary policy increases the total supply of money in the economy, and a contractionary policy decreases the total money supply.

a. 100-year flood
b. 1921 recession
c. 130-30 fund
d. Monetary policy

9. In finance, the _____s between two currencies specifies how much one currency is worth in terms of the other. It is the value of a foreign natione;s currency in terms of the home natione;s currency. For example an _____ of 102 Japanese yen to the United States dollar means that JPY 102 is worth the same as USD 1.

a. ACCRA Cost of Living Index
b. Interbank market
c. ACEA agreement
d. Exchange rate

10. A _____ secures the proper functioning of money by regulating economic agents, transaction types, and money supply.

_____s are traditionally formed by the policy decisions of individual governments and administrated as a domestic economic issue.

The current trend, however, is to use international trade and investment to alter the policy and legislation of individual governments.

a. Financial rand
b. Netting
c. Consumer basket
d. Monetary system

11. A _____ is the transfer of wealth from one party (such as a person or company) to another. A _____ is usually made in exchange for the provision of goods, services or both, or to fulfill a legal obligation.

The simplest and oldest form of _____ is barter, the exchange of one good or service for another.

a. Soft count
b. Going concern
c. Social gravity
d. Payment

Chapter 15. Exchange Rates and the International Monetary System

12. In economics, the _____ is one of the two primary components of the balance of payments, the other being the capital account. It is the sum of the balance of trade (exports minus imports of goods and services), net factor income (such as interest and dividends) and net transfer payments (such as foreign aid.)

$$\text{Current account} = \text{Balance of trade} \\ + \text{Net factor income from abroad} \\ + \text{Net unilateral transfers from abroad}$$

The _____ balance is one of two major metrics of the nature of a country's foreign trade (the other being the net capital outflow.)

   a. Gross private domestic investment
   b. Compensation of employees
   c. National Income and Product Accounts
   d. Current account

13. In financial accounting, the _____ is one of the accounts in shareholders' equity. Sole proprietorships have a single _____ in the owner's equity. Partnerships maintain a _____ for each of the partners.
   a. Net national product
   b. Capital account
   c. Compensation of employees
   d. Current account

14. The _____ is an economic model first set forth by Robert Mundell and Marcus Fleming. The model is an extension of the IS-LM model. Whereas IS-LM deals with economy under autarky, the _____ tries to describe a small open economy.
   a. Rostovian take-off model
   b. Representative agent
   c. Harrod-Domar model
   d. Mundell-Fleming model

15. In business and accounting, _____ are everything of value that is owned by a person or company. It is a claim on the property your income of a borrower. The balance sheet of a firm records the monetary value of the _____ owned by the firm.
   a. ACCRA Cost of Living Index
   b. Amortization schedule
   c. Assets
   d. ACEA agreement

16. A _____, reserve bank, or monetary authority is the entity responsible for the monetary policy of a country or of a group of member states. It is a bank that can lend money to other banks in times of need. Its primary responsibility is to maintain the stability of the national currency and money supply, but more active duties include controlling subsidized-loan interest rates, and acting as a lender of last resort to the banking sector during times of financial crisis (private banks often being integral to the national financial system.)
   a. 130-30 fund
   b. Central bank
   c. 100-year flood
   d. 1921 recession

Chapter 15. Exchange Rates and the International Monetary System

17. The _____ is the central banking system of the United States. Created in 1913 by the enactment of the Federal Reserve Act (signed by Woodrow Wilson), it is a quasi-public and quasi-private (government entity with private components) banking system that comprises (1) the presidentially appointed Board of Governors of the _____ in Washington, D.C.; (2) the Federal Open Market Committee; (3) twelve regional Federal Reserve Banks located in major cities throughout the nation acting as fiscal agents for the U.S. Treasury, each with its own nine-member board of directors; (4) numerous other private U.S. member banks, which subscribe to required amounts of non-transferable stock in their regional Federal Reserve Banks; and (5) various advisory councils. Since February 2006, Ben Bernanke has served as the Chairman of the Board of Governors of the _____.

   a. Federal Reserve System
   b. Monetary Policy Report to the Congress
   c. Term auction facility
   d. Federal Reserve System Open Market Account

18. _____ in its classic form is defined as a company from one country making a physical investment into building a factory in another country. It is the establishment of an enterprise by a foreigner. Its definition can be extended to include investments made to acquire lasting interest in enterprises operating outside of the economy of the investor.

   a. Financial Stability Forum
   b. Non-governmental organization
   c. Federal Deposit Insurance Corporation
   d. Foreign direct investment

19. _____ are potential claims on the freely usable currencies of International Monetary Fund members. _____s have the ISO 4217 currency code XDR.

   _____s are defined in terms of a basket of major currencies used in international trade and finance.

   a. Bilateral Investment Treaty
   b. Metzler paradox
   c. Quota share
   d. Special drawing rights

20. _____ is a school of macroeconomic thought that argues that economic growth can be most effectively created using incentives for people to produce (supply) goods and services, such as adjusting income tax and capital gains tax rates, and by allowing greater flexibility by reducing regulation. Consumers will then benefit from a greater supply of goods and services at lower prices.

   The term _____ was coined by journalist Jude Wanniski in 1975, and popularized the ideas of economists Robert Mundell and Arthur Laffer.

   a. Fiscal stimulus plans
   b. Clap note
   c. Supply-side economics
   d. Commodity trading advisors

21. To _____ is to impose a financial charge or other levy upon a taxpayer by a state or the functional equivalent of a state.

   _____es are also imposed by many subnational entities. _____es consist of direct _____ or indirect _____, and may be paid in money or as its labour equivalent (often but not always unpaid.)

   a. 100-year flood
   b. 1921 recession
   c. 130-30 fund
   d. Tax

22. _____ is a concept found in moral, political, and bioethical philosophy. Within these contexts, it refers to the capacity of a rational individual to make an informed, un-coerced decision. In moral and political philosophy, _____ is often used as the basis for determining moral responsibility for one's actions.
   a. ACEA agreement
   b. ACCRA Cost of Living Index
   c. Autonomy
   d. AD-IA Model

23. _____ is a specific term used in companies' financial reporting from the company-whole point of view. Because that use excludes the effects of changing ownership interest, an economic measure of _____ is necessary for financial analysis from the shareholders' point of view

_____ is defined by the Financial Accounting Standards Board, or FASB, as e;the change in equity [net assets] of a business enterprise during a period from transactions and other events and circumstances from nonowner sources. It includes all changes in equity during a period except those resulting from investments by owners and distributions to owners.e;

_____ is the sum of net income and other items that must bypass the income statement because they have not been realized, including items like an unrealized holding gain or loss from available for sale securities and foreign currency translation gains or losses.

   a. Net national income
   b. Comprehensive income
   c. Real income
   d. Windfall gain

24. The _____ is an international organization that oversees the global financial system by following the macroeconomic policies of its member countries, in particular those with an impact on exchange rates and the balance of payments. It is an organization formed to stabilize international exchange rates and facilitate development. It also offers financial and technical assistance to its members, making it an international lender of last resort.
   a. ACEA agreement
   b. Office of Thrift Supervision
   c. ACCRA Cost of Living Index
   d. International Monetary Fund

25. The _____ is where currency trading takes place. It is where banks and other official institutions facilitate the buying and selling of foreign currencies. FX transactions typically involve one party purchasing a quantity of one currency in exchange for paying a quantity of another.
   a. Currency swap
   b. Covered interest arbitrage
   c. Foreign exchange market
   d. Floating currency

26. A _____ is a place of residence or refuge and comfort. It is usually a place in which an individual or a family can rest and be able to store personal property. Most modern-day households contain sanitary facilities and a means of preparing food.
   a. 130-30 fund
   b. Home
   c. 1921 recession
   d. 100-year flood

27. _____ is a term used to described a tendency or preference towards a particular perspective, ideology or result, especially when the tendency interferes with the ability to be impartial, unprejudiced, or objective. The term _____ed is used to describe an action, judgment, or other outcome influenced by a prejudged perspective. It is also used to refer to a person or body of people whose actions or judgments exhibit _____.

a. 130-30 fund
b. 1921 recession
c. 100-year flood
d. Bias

28. In economics, _____ is the total demand for final goods and services in the economy (Y) at a given time and price level. It is the amount of goods and services in the economy that will be purchased at all possible price levels. This is the demand for the gross domestic product of a country when inventory levels are static.
    a. Aggregate expenditure
    b. Aggregate demand
    c. Aggregation problem
    d. Aggregate supply

29. In economics, _____ is the total supply of goods and services produced by a national economy during a specific time period. It is the total amount of goods and services in the economy available at all possible price levels.
    a. Aggregate expenditure
    b. Aggregate supply
    c. Aggregation problem
    d. Aggregate demand

30. The _____ is the official currency of 16 of the 27 member states of the European Union (EU.) The states, known collectively as the Eurozone, are Austria, Belgium, Cyprus, Finland, France, Germany, Greece, Ireland, Italy, Luxembourg, Malta, the Netherlands, Portugal, Slovakia, Slovenia, and Spain. The currency is also used in a further five European countries, with and without formal agreements and is consequently used daily by some 327 million Europeans.
    a. Euro
    b. IRS Code 3401
    c. Equity capital market
    d. Import and Export Price Indices

31. In economics, _____ is the total amount of money available in an economy at a particular point in time. There are several ways to define 'money', but standard measures usually include currency in circulation and demand deposits.

    _____ data are recorded and published, usually by the government or the central bank of the country.

    a. Velocity of money
    b. Neutrality of money
    c. Veil of money
    d. Money supply

32. _____ is a voluntary transfer of resources from one country to another, given at least partly with the objective of benefiting the recipient country. It may have other functions as well: it may be given as a signal of diplomatic approval, or to strengthen a military ally, to reward a government for behaviour desired by the donor, to extend the donor's cultural influence, to provide infrastructure needed by the donor for resource extraction from the recipient country, or to gain other kinds of commercial access. Humanitarianism and altruism are, nevertheless, significant motivations for the giving of _____.
    a. ACEA agreement
    b. Aid
    c. AD-IA Model
    d. ACCRA Cost of Living Index

Chapter 15. Exchange Rates and the International Monetary System 121

33. Economics:

- _____, the desire to own something and the ability to pay for it
- _____ curve, a graphic representation of a _____ schedule
- _____ deposit, the money in checking accounts
- _____ pull theory, the theory that inflation occurs when _____ for goods and services exceeds existing supplies
- _____ schedule, a table that lists the quantity of a good a person will buy it each different price
- _____ side economics, the school of economics at believes government spending and tax cuts open economy by raising _____

a. Variability
b. Production
c. McKesson ' Robbins scandal
d. Demand

34. _____s is the social science that studies the production, distribution, and consumption of goods and services. The term _____s comes from the Ancient Greek οἰκονομία from οἶκος (oikos, 'house') + νόμος (nomos, 'custom' or 'law'), hence 'rules of the house(hold)'. Current _____ models developed out of the broader field of political economy in the late 19th century, owing to a desire to use an empirical approach more akin to the physical sciences.

a. Opportunity cost
b. Energy economics
c. Inflation
d. Economic

35. _____ is the increase in the amount of the goods and services produced by an economy over time. It is conventionally measured as the percent rate of increase in real gross domestic product, or real GDP. Growth is usually calculated in real terms, i.e. inflation-adjusted terms, in order to net out the effect of inflation on the price of the goods and services produced.

a. ACEA agreement
b. AD-IA Model
c. ACCRA Cost of Living Index
d. Economic growth

36. The _____ of monetary management established the rules for commercial and financial relations among the world's major industrial states in the mid 20th Century. The _____ was the first example of a fully negotiated monetary order intended to govern monetary relations among independent nation-states.

Preparing to rebuild the international economic system as World War II was still raging, 730 delegates from all 44 Allied nations gathered at the Mount Washington Hotel in Bretton Woods, New Hampshire, United States, for the United Nations Monetary and Financial Conference.

a. Bretton Woods system
b. 130-30 fund
c. 100-year flood
d. 1921 recession

37. _____ is the a method of technical and economic research of the systems for purpose to optimize a parity between system's consumer functions or properties and expenses to achieve those functions or properties.

Chapter 15. Exchange Rates and the International Monetary System

This methodology for continuous perfection of production, industrial technologies, organizational structures was developed by Juryj Sobolev in 1948 at the 'Perm telephone factory'

- 1948 Juryj Sobolev - the first success in application of a method analysis at the 'Perm telephone factory'.
- 1949 - the first application for the invention as result of use of the new method.

Today in economically developed countries practically each enterprise or the company use methodology of the kind of functional-cost analysis as a practice of the quality management, most full satisfying to principles of standards of series ISO 9000.

- Interest of consumer not in products itself, but the advantage which it will receive from its usage.
- The consumer aspires to reduce his expenses
- Functions needed by consumer can be executed in the various ways, and, hence, with various efficiency and expenses. Among possible alternatives of realization of functions exist such in which the parity of quality and the price is the optimal for the consumer.

The goal of _____ is achievement of the highest consumer satisfaction of production at simultaneous decrease in all kinds of industrial expenses Classical _____ has three English synonyms - Value Engineering, Value Management, Value Analysis.

   a. Function cost analysis
   c. Staple financing
   b. Willingness to pay
   d. Monopoly wage

38. The _____ is one of the world's most important central banks, responsible for monetary policy covering the 16 member States of the Eurozone. It was established by the European Union (EU) in 1998 with its headquarters in Frankfurt, Germany.

The predecessor to the _____ was the European Monetary Institute .

   a. ACEA agreement
   c. ACCRA Cost of Living Index
   b. AD-IA Model
   d. European Central Bank

39. In cases of extreme appreciation or depreciation, a central bank will normally intervene to stabilize the currency. Thus, the exchange rate regimes of floating currencies may more technically be known as a _____. A central bank might, for instance, allow a currency price to float freely between an upper and lower bound, a price 'ceiling' and 'floor'.

   a. Continuous linked settlement
   c. Foreign exchange reserves
   b. Triangular arbitrage
   d. Managed float

40. A _____ or a flexible exchange rate is a type of exchange rate regime wherein a currency's value is allowed to fluctuate according to the foreign exchange market. A currency that uses a _____ is known as a floating currency. The opposite of a _____ is a fixed exchange rate.

   a. Foreign exchange market
   c. Trade Weighted US dollar Index
   b. Floating currency
   d. Floating exchange rate

Chapter 15. Exchange Rates and the International Monetary System

41. A _____ is a monetary authority which is required to maintain a fixed exchange rate with a foreign currency. This policy objective requires the conventional objectives of a central bank to be subordinated to the exchange rate target.

The main qualities of an orthodox _____ are:

- A _____'s foreign currency reserves must be sufficient to ensure that all holders of its notes and coins (and all banks creditor of a Reserve Account at the _____) can convert them into the reserve currency (usually 110-115% of the monetary base M0.)
- A _____ maintains absolute, unlimited convertibility between its notes and coins and the currency against which they are pegged (the anchor currency), at a fixed rate of exchange, with no restrictions on current-account or capital-account transactions.
- A _____ only earns profit from interests on foreign reserves (less the expense of note-issuing), and does not engage in forward-exchange transactions. These foreign reserves exist (1) because local notes have been issued in exchange, or (2) because commercial banks must by regulation deposit a minimum reserve at the _____. (1) generates a seignorage revenue. (2) is the revenue on minimum reserves (revenue of investment activities less cost of minimum reserves remuneration)
- A _____ has no discretionary powers to effect monetary policy and does not lend to the government. Governments cannot print money, and can only tax or borrow to meet their spending commitments.
- A _____ does not act as a lender of last resort to commercial banks, and does not regulate reserve requirements.
- A _____ does not attempt to manipulate interest rates by establishing a discount rate like a central bank. The peg with the foreign currency tends to keep interest rates and inflation very closely aligned to those in the country against whose currency the peg is fixed.

The _____ in question will no longer issue fiat money but instead will only issue one unit of local currency for each unit (or decided amount) of foreign currency it has in its vault (often a hard currency such as the U.S. dollar or the euro.) The surplus on the balance of payments of that country is reflected by higher deposits local banks hold at the central bank as well as (initially) higher deposits of the (net) exporting firms at their local banks.

a. Petrodollar
c. Reserve currency
b. Currency board
d. Currency competition

42. _____ occurs when the inhabitants of a country use foreign currency in parallel to or instead of the domestic currency.

_____ can occur

- unofficially, when private agents prefer the foreign currency over the domestic currency. They hold for example deposits in the foreign currency because of a bad track record of the local currency.
- semiofficially (or officially bimonetary systems), where foreign currency is legal tender, but plays a secondary role to domestic currency
- officially, when a country ceases to issue the domestic currency and uses only foreign currency. It adopts the foreign currency as legal tender.

The term _____ is not only applied to usage of the United States dollar, but also generally to the use of any foreign currency as the national currency.

a. Currency board
c. World currency
b. Commodity money
d. Dollarization

43. From a Keynesian point of view, a _____ in the public sector is achieved when the government equates the revenues with expenditure over the business cycles. In other words, a government's budget is balanced if its income is equal to its expenditure. It is a budget in which revenues are equal to spending.

a. Budget crisis
c. Budget support
b. Budget theory
d. Balanced budget

44. _____ is a reduction in the value of a currency with respect to other monetary units. In common modern usage, it specifically implies an official lowering of the value of a country's currency within a fixed exchange rate system, by which the monetary authority formally sets a new fixed rate with respect to a foreign reference currency. In contrast, (currency) depreciation is used for the unofficial decrease in the exchange rate in a floating exchange rate system.

a. Devaluation
c. Petrodollar recycling
b. Reserve currency
d. Texas redbacks

45. _____ in economics and business is the result of an exchange and from that trade we assign a numerical monetary value to a good, service or asset. If Alice trades Bob 4 apples for an orange, the _____ of an orange is 4 apples. Inversely, the _____ of an apple is 1/4 oranges.

a. Price book
c. Premium pricing
b. Price war
d. Price

46. The _____ is the difference between the monetary value of exports and imports in an economy over a certain period of time. It is the relationship between a nation's imports and exports. A positive _____ is known as a trade surplus and consists of exporting more than is imported; a negative _____ is known as a trade deficit or, informally, a trade gap.

a. SIMIC
c. Marginal propensity to import
b. Rational expectations
d. Balance of trade

47. In economics, a _____ is a general slowdown in economic activity over a sustained period of time, or a business cycle contraction. During _____s, many macroeconomic indicators vary in a similar way. Production as measured by Gross Domestic Product (GDP), employment, investment spending, capacity utilization, household incomes and business profits all fall during _____s.

a. Leading indicators
c. Treasury View
b. Monetary economics
d. Recession

48. A _____ occurs when an entity spends more money than it takes in. The opposite of a _____ is a budget surplus. Debt is essentially an accumulated flow of deficits.

a. Budget deficit
c. Lump-sum tax
b. Funding body
d. Public Financial Management

49. In finance, _____ is the risk of losses caused by interest rate changes. The prices of most financial instruments, such as stocks and bonds move inversely with interest rates, so investors are subject to capital loss when rates rise.

In the investment world, there are two types of risk rating. One is to manifest company's credit and another to equity securities. The former is represented by the systems of Fitch Ratings, Moody's and Standard ' Poor's whereas the later by that of Comisi>ón Clasificadora de Riesgo, although the two types have some similarities to some extent.

a. Net pay
b. Seasonal industry
c. Rate risk
d. Leontief production function

50. In finance, _____ is a financial action that does not promise safety of the initial investment along with the return on the principal sum. _____ typically involves the lending of money or the purchase of assets, equity or debt but in a manner that has not been given thorough analysis or is deemed to have low margin of safety or a significant risk of the loss of the principal investment. The term, '_____,' which is formally defined as above in Graham and Dodd's 1934 text, Security Analysis, contrasts with the term 'investment,' which is a financial operation that, upon thorough analysis, promises safety of principal and a satisfactory return.

a. Hybrid market
b. Global Financial Centres Index
c. Municipal Bond Arbitrage
d. Speculation

51. _____s are payments made by a corporation to its shareholders. It is the portion of corporate profits paid out to stockholders. When a corporation earns a profit or surplus, that money can be put to two uses: it can either be re-invested in the business (called retained earnings), or it can be paid to the shareholders as a _____.

a. Dividend yield
b. Dividend
c. Dividend cover
d. Dividend puzzle

52. _____ is monetary policy that seeks to increase the size of the money supply. In most nations, monetary policy is controlled by either a central bank or a finance ministry

Neoclassical and Keynesian economics significantly differ on the effects and effectiveness of monetary policy on influencing the real economy; there is no clear consensus on how monetary policy affects real economic variables (aggregate output or income, employment.) Both economic schools accept that monetary policy affects monetary variables (price levels, interest rates.)

a. AD-IA Model
b. ACCRA Cost of Living Index
c. ACEA agreement
d. Expansionary monetary policy

53. A _____ is an event that suddenly changes the price of a commodity or service. It may be caused by a sudden increase or decrease in the supply of a particular good. This sudden change affects the equilibrium price.

a. Friedman rule
b. SIMIC
c. Supply shock
d. Demand shock

54. The _____ is an economic and political union of 27 member states, located primarily in Europe. It was established by the Treaty of Maastricht on 1 November 1993, upon the foundations of the pre-existing European Economic Community. With a population of almost 500 million, the _____ generates an estimated 30% share (US$18.4 trillion in 2008) of the nominal gross world product.

a. ACEA agreement
b. European Union
c. European Court of Justice
d. ACCRA Cost of Living Index

55. The _____ was signed by the then G6 on February 22, 1987 in Paris, France. Italy had been an invited member, but declined to finalize the agreement. The goal of the _____ was to stabilize the international currency markets and halt the continued decline of the US Dollar caused by the Plaza Accord .
a. 100-year flood
b. Plaza Agreement
c. Mellonomics
d. Louvre Accord

56. The _____ was signed on 7 February 1992 in Maastricht, the Netherlands after final negotiations on 9 December 1991 between the members of the European Community and entered into force on 1 November 1993 during the Delors Commission. It created the European Union and led to the creation of the euro. The _____ has been amended to a degree by later treaties.
a. 100-year flood
b. Treaty of Amsterdam
c. Maastricht Treaty
d. Treaties of Rome

Chapter 16. Monetary and Fiscal Policy in the Open Economy

1. _____ and Keynesian Theory) is a macroeconomic theory based on the ideas of 20th-century British economist John Maynard Keynes. _____ argues that private sector decisions sometimes lead to inefficient macroeconomic outcomes and therefore advocates active policy responses by the public sector, including monetary policy actions by the central bank and fiscal policy actions by the government to stabilize output over the business cycle.

The theories forming the basis of _____ were first presented in The General Theory of Employment, Interest and Money, published in 1936.

 a. Keynesian economics
 b. Market failure
 c. Rational choice theory
 d. Deflation

2. The _____ is an economic model first set forth by Robert Mundell and Marcus Fleming. The model is an extension of the IS-LM model. Whereas IS-LM deals with economy under autarky, the _____ tries to describe a small open economy.
 a. Harrod-Domar model
 b. Rostovian take-off model
 c. Representative agent
 d. Mundell-Fleming model

3. An autarky is an economy that is self-sufficient and does not take part in international trade, or severely limits trade with the outside world. Likewise the term refers to an ecosystem not affected by influences from the outside, which relies entirely on its own resources. In the economic meaning, it is also referred to as a _____.
 a. Transition economy
 b. Digital economy
 c. Closed economy
 d. Network Economy

4. The term _____ refers to government debt, expenditures and revenues, or to finance (particularly financial revenue) in general.

- _____ deficit is the budget deficit of federal or local government
- _____ policy is the discretionary spending of governments. Contrasts with monetary policy.
- _____ year and _____ quarter are reporting periods for firms and other agencies.

 a. Fiscal
 b. Procter ' Gamble
 c. Bucket shop
 d. Drawdown

5. In economics, _____ is the use of government spending and revenue collection to influence the economy.

_____ can be contrasted with the other main type of economic policy, monetary policy, which attempts to stabilize the economy by controlling interest rates and the supply of money. The two main instruments of _____ are government spending and taxation.

 a. 100-year flood
 b. Sustainable investment rule
 c. Fiscal policy
 d. Fiscalism

6. An _____ is an economy in which people, including businesses, can trade in goods and services with other people and businesses in the international community at large. This contrasts with a closed economy in which international trade cannot take place.

Chapter 16. Monetary and Fiscal Policy in the Open Economy

The act of selling goods or services to a foreign country is called exporting.

a. Attention work
b. Information economy
c. Open economy
d. Indicative planning

7. _____ is a fee paid on borrowed assets. It is the price paid for the use of borrowed money, or, money earned by deposited funds. Assets that are sometimes lent with _____ include money, shares, consumer goods through hire purchase, major assets such as aircraft, and even entire factories in finance lease arrangements.

a. Insolvency
b. Interest
c. Asset protection
d. Internal debt

8. An _____ is the price a borrower pays for the use of money they do not own, for instance a small company might borrow from a bank to kick start their business, and the return a lender receives for deferring the use of funds, by lending it to the borrower. _____s are normally expressed as a percentage rate over the period of one year.

_____s targets are also a vital tool of monetary policy and are used to control variables like investment, inflation, and unemployment.

a. ACCRA Cost of Living Index
b. Enterprise value
c. Interest rate
d. Arrow-Debreu model

9. _____, 1st Baron Keynes was a renowned economist from Britain whose many ideas on economic and political theories as well as on many governments' monetary policies influenced America. He advocated a government that played an active role in the lives of people regarding business, economy, etc. In this role, the government would use fiscal measures to reduce the consequences of recessions, economic depressions and booms.

a. Adolph Fischer
b. Adam Smith
c. John Maynard Keynes
d. Adolf Hitler

10. In economics, _____ is the total demand for final goods and services in the economy (Y) at a given time and price level. It is the amount of goods and services in the economy that will be purchased at all possible price levels. This is the demand for the gross domestic product of a country when inventory levels are static.

a. Aggregate demand
b. Aggregate expenditure
c. Aggregation problem
d. Aggregate supply

Chapter 16. Monetary and Fiscal Policy in the Open Economy

11. Economics:

    - _____, the desire to own something and the ability to pay for it
    - _____ curve, a graphic representation of a _____ schedule
    - _____ deposit, the money in checking accounts
    - _____ pull theory, the theory that inflation occurs when _____ for goods and services exceeds existing supplies
    - _____ schedule, a table that lists the quantity of a good a person will buy it each different price
    - _____ side economics, the school of economics at believes government spending and tax cuts open economy by raising _____

    a. Production
    b. Demand
    c. McKesson ' Robbins scandal
    d. Variability

12. _____s is the social science that studies the production, distribution, and consumption of goods and services. The term _____s comes from the Ancient Greek oá¼°κονομῖα from oá¼¶κος (oikos, 'house') + vῐΌμος (nomos, 'custom' or 'law'), hence 'rules of the house(hold)'. Current _____ models developed out of the broader field of political economy in the late 19th century, owing to a desire to use an empirical approach more akin to the physical sciences.

    a. Inflation
    b. Opportunity cost
    c. Energy economics
    d. Economic

13. The _____ is an international organization that oversees the global financial system by following the macroeconomic policies of its member countries, in particular those with an impact on exchange rates and the balance of payments. It is an organization formed to stabilize international exchange rates and facilitate development. It also offers financial and technical assistance to its members, making it an international lender of last resort.

    a. International Monetary Fund
    b. ACEA agreement
    c. Office of Thrift Supervision
    d. ACCRA Cost of Living Index

14. A _____, sometimes called a pegged exchange rate, is a type of exchange rate regime wherein a currency's value is matched to the value of another single currency or to a basket of other currencies such as gold.

    A _____ is usually used to stabilize the value of a currency, vis-a-vis the currency it is pegged to. This facilitates trade and investments between the two countries, and is especially useful for small economies where external trade forms a large part of their GDP.

    a. Fixed exchange rate
    b. Leading indicators
    c. Monetary economics
    d. Law of supply

15. Market _____ is a business, economics or investment term that refers to an asset's ability to be easily converted through an act of buying or selling without causing a significant movement in the price and with minimum loss of value. Money, or cash on hand, is the most liquid asset. An act of exchange of a less liquid asset with a more liquid asset is called liquidation.

    a. 130-30 fund
    b. 1921 recession
    c. Liquidity
    d. 100-year flood

Chapter 16. Monetary and Fiscal Policy in the Open Economy

16. The term _____ is used in macroeconomics to refer to a situation where a country's nominal interest rate has been lowered nearly to or equal to zero to avoid a recession, but the liquidity in the market created by these low interest rates does not stimulate the economy to full employment. In this situation, any further increase in the money supply will not stimulate the economy any further. This is because any further injection of liquidity will no longer lower the nominal interest rate, as the nominal interest rate cannot drop below zero.
    a. Liquidity trap
    b. Minimum wage
    c. Robertson lag
    d. Macroeconomic models

17. In finance, the _____s between two currencies specifies how much one currency is worth in terms of the other. It is the value of a foreign natione;s currency in terms of the home natione;s currency. For example an _____ of 102 Japanese yen to the United States dollar means that JPY 102 is worth the same as USD 1.
    a. ACEA agreement
    b. Exchange rate
    c. ACCRA Cost of Living Index
    d. Interbank market

18. _____ is the process by which the government, central bank (ii) availability of money, and (iii) cost of money or rate of interest, in order to attain a set of objectives oriented towards the growth and stability of the economy. Monetary theory provides insight into how to craft optimal _____.

    _____ is referred to as either being an expansionary policy where an expansionary policy increases the total supply of money in the economy, and a contractionary policy decreases the total money supply.

    a. 130-30 fund
    b. 1921 recession
    c. Monetary policy
    d. 100-year flood

19. _____ or government expenditure is classified by economists into three main types. Government purchases of goods and services for current use are classed as government consumption. Government purchases of goods and services intended to create future benefits, such as infrastructure investment or research spending, are classed as government investment.
    a. Government spending
    b. 1921 recession
    c. 130-30 fund
    d. 100-year flood

20. _____ is a common concept in economics, and gives rise to derived concepts such as consumer debt. Generally _____ is defined by opposition to production. But the precise definition can vary because different schools of economists define production quite differently.
    a. Foreclosure data providers
    b. Cash or share options
    c. Federal Reserve Bank Notes
    d. Consumption

21. The _____ is the central banking system of the United States. Created in 1913 by the enactment of the Federal Reserve Act (signed by Woodrow Wilson), it is a quasi-public and quasi-private (government entity with private components) banking system that comprises (1) the presidentially appointed Board of Governors of the _____ in Washington, D.C.; (2) the Federal Open Market Committee; (3) twelve regional Federal Reserve Banks located in major cities throughout the nation acting as fiscal agents for the U.S. Treasury, each with its own nine-member board of directors; (4) numerous other private U.S. member banks, which subscribe to required amounts of non-transferable stock in their regional Federal Reserve Banks; and (5) various advisory councils. Since February 2006, Ben Bernanke has served as the Chairman of the Board of Governors of the _____.

Chapter 16. Monetary and Fiscal Policy in the Open Economy

a. Term auction facility
b. Monetary Policy Report to the Congress
c. Federal Reserve System Open Market Account
d. Federal Reserve System

22. The _____ was a worldwide economic downturn starting in most places in 1929 and ending at different times in the 1930s or early 1940s for different countries. It was the largest and most important economic depression in the 20th century, and is used in the 21st century as an example of how far the world's economy can fall. The _____ originated in the United States; historians most often use as a starting date the stock market crash on October 29, 1929, known as Black Tuesday.
   a. Wall Street Crash of 1929
   b. Jarrow March
   c. British Empire Economic Conference
   d. Great Depression

23. A _____, reserve bank, or monetary authority is the entity responsible for the monetary policy of a country or of a group of member states. It is a bank that can lend money to other banks in times of need. Its primary responsibility is to maintain the stability of the national currency and money supply, but more active duties include controlling subsidized-loan interest rates, and acting as a lender of last resort to the banking sector during times of financial crisis (private banks often being integral to the national financial system.)
   a. 100-year flood
   b. 130-30 fund
   c. Central bank
   d. 1921 recession

24. A _____ product is a product designed for cheapness and short-term convenience rather than medium to long-term durability, with most products only intended for single use. The term is also sometimes used for products that may last several months (ex. _____ air filters) to distinguish from similar products that last indefinitely (ex.
   a. 130-30 fund
   b. 1921 recession
   c. Disposable
   d. 100-year flood

25. _____ is gross income minus income tax on that income.

Discretionary income is income after subtracting taxes and normal expenses (such as rent or mortgage, utilities, insurance, medical, transportation, property maintenance, child support, inflation, food and sundries, 'c.) to maintain a certain standard of living.

   a. Disposable personal income
   b. Disposable income
   c. Taxation as theft
   d. Stamp Act

26. In statistics, _____ indicates the strength and direction of a linear relationship between two random variables. That is in contrast with the usage of the term in colloquial speech, which denotes any relationship, not necessarily linear. In general statistical usage, _____ or co-relation refers to the departure of two random variables from independence.
   a. 130-30 fund
   b. 1921 recession
   c. Correlation
   d. 100-year flood

27. A _____ is an expression that compares quantities relative to each other. The most common examples involve two quantities, but any number of quantities can be compared. _____s are represented mathematically by separating each quantity with a colon, for example the _____ 2:3, which is read as the _____ 'two to three'.
   a. 100-year flood
   b. Ratio
   c. 130-30 fund
   d. Y-intercept

28. The _____ is the market for securities, where companies and governments can raise longterm funds. It is a market in which money is lent for periods longer than a year. The _____ includes the stock market and the bond market.
   a. Multi-family office
   b. Capital market
   c. Performance attribution
   d. Financial instrument

Chapter 17. The Money Supply and the Banking System

1. The _____ is the central banking system of the United States. Created in 1913 by the enactment of the Federal Reserve Act (signed by Woodrow Wilson), it is a quasi-public and quasi-private (government entity with private components) banking system that comprises (1) the presidentially appointed Board of Governors of the _____ in Washington, D.C.; (2) the Federal Open Market Committee; (3) twelve regional Federal Reserve Banks located in major cities throughout the nation acting as fiscal agents for the U.S. Treasury, each with its own nine-member board of directors; (4) numerous other private U.S. member banks, which subscribe to required amounts of non-transferable stock in their regional Federal Reserve Banks; and (5) various advisory councils. Since February 2006, Ben Bernanke has served as the Chairman of the Board of Governors of the _____.

   a. Term auction facility
   b. Federal Reserve System
   c. Monetary Policy Report to the Congress
   d. Federal Reserve System Open Market Account

2. In economics, _____ is the total amount of money available in an economy at a particular point in time. There are several ways to define 'money', but standard measures usually include currency in circulation and demand deposits.

   _____ data are recorded and published, usually by the government or the central bank of the country.

   a. Neutrality of money
   b. Veil of money
   c. Velocity of money
   d. Money supply

3. In statistics, _____ has two related meanings:

   - the arithmetic _____
   - the expected value of a random variable, which is also called the population _____.

   It is sometimes stated that the '_____' _____s average. This is incorrect if '_____' is taken in the specific sense of 'arithmetic _____' as there are different types of averages: the _____, median, and mode. Other simple statistical analyses use measures of spread, such as range, interquartile range, or standard deviation. For a real-valued random variable X, the _____ is the expectation of X. Note that not every probability distribution has a defined _____ (or variance); see the Cauchy distribution for an example.

   a. 1921 recession
   b. 130-30 fund
   c. 100-year flood
   d. Mean

4. _____ is the view within monetary economics that variation in the money supply has major influences on national output in the short run and the price level over longer periods and that objectives of monetary policy are best met by targeting the growth rate of the money supply.

   _____ today is mainly associated with the work of Milton Friedman, who was among the generation of economists to accept Keynesian economics and then criticize it on his own terms. Friedman and Anna Schwartz wrote an influential book, Monetary History of the United States 1867-1960, and argued that 'inflation is always and everywhere a monetary phenomenon.' Friedman advocated a central bank policy aimed at keeping the supply and demand for money at equilibrium, as measured by growth in productivity and demand.

   a. Historical school of economics
   b. Marginal revenue productivity theory of wages
   c. Complexity economics
   d. Monetarism

Chapter 17. The Money Supply and the Banking System

5. To act as a _____, a commodity, a form of money stored, and retrieved - and be predictably useful when it is so retrieved.

This is distinct from the standard of deferred payment function which requires acceptability to parties one owes a debt to and a minimum of opportunity to cheat others.

a. World currency
c. Petrodollar
b. Store of value
d. Fiat money

6. A _____ is a standard monetary unit of measurement of the market value/cost of goods, services, or assets. It is one of three well-known functions of money. It lends meaning to profits, losses, liability, or assets.

a. ACEA agreement
c. AD-IA Model
b. ACCRA Cost of Living Index
d. Unit of account

7. The _____ is the average frequency with which a unit of money is spent in a specific period of time. Velocity associates the amount of economic activity associated with a given money supply. When the period is understood, the velocity may be present as a pure number; otherwise it should be given as a pure number over time.

a. Chartalism
c. Neutrality of money
b. Money supply
d. Velocity of money

8. _____ is widely regarded as the first modern school of economic thought. It is the idea that free markets can regulate themselves. Its major developers include Adam Smith, David Ricardo, Thomas Malthus and John Stuart Mill. Sometimes the definition of _____ is expanded to include William Petty, Johann Heinrich von Thünen.

a. Tendency of the rate of profit to fall
c. Schools of economic thought
b. Marginalism
d. Classical economics

9. Economics:

- _____, the desire to own something and the ability to pay for it
- _____ curve, a graphic representation of a _____ schedule
- _____ deposit, the money in checking accounts
- _____ pull theory, the theory that inflation occurs when _____ for goods and services exceeds existing supplies
- _____ schedule, a table that lists the quantity of a good a person will buy it each different price
- _____ side economics, the school of economics at believes government spending and tax cuts open economy by raising _____

a. Variability
c. Production
b. McKesson ' Robbins scandal
d. Demand

10. _____s is the social science that studies the production, distribution, and consumption of goods and services. The term _____s comes from the Ancient Greek οἰκονομῑα from οἶκος (oikos, 'house') + νόμος (nomos, 'custom' or 'law'), hence 'rules of the house(hold)'. Current _____ models developed out of the broader field of political economy in the late 19th century, owing to a desire to use an empirical approach more akin to the physical sciences.

Chapter 17. The Money Supply and the Banking System

a. Opportunity cost
b. Energy economics
c. Inflation
d. Economic

11. _____ is the a method of technical and economic research of the systems for purpose to optimize a parity between system's consumer functions or properties and expenses to achieve those functions or properties.

This methodology for continuous perfection of production, industrial technologies, organizational structures was developed by Juryj Sobolev in 1948 at the 'Perm telephone factory'

- 1948 Juryj Sobolev - the first success in application of a method analysis at the 'Perm telephone factory' .
- 1949 - the first application for the invention as result of use of the new method.

Today in economically developed countries practically each enterprise or the company use methodology of the kind of functional-cost analysis as a practice of the quality management, most full satisfying to principles of standards of series ISO 9000.

- Interest of consumer not in products itself, but the advantage which it will receive from its usage.
- The consumer aspires to reduce his expenses
- Functions needed by consumer can be executed in the various ways, and, hence, with various efficiency and expenses. Among possible alternatives of realization of functions exist such in which the parity of quality and the price is the optimal for the consumer.

The goal of _____ is achievement of the highest consumer satisfaction of production at simultaneous decrease in all kinds of industrial expenses Classical _____ has three English synonyms - Value Engineering, Value Management, Value Analysis.

a. Staple financing
b. Willingness to pay
c. Monopoly wage
d. Function cost analysis

12. An _____ is a deposit account that allows the transfer of funds from a savings account to a checking account in order to cover a check written or to maintain a minimum balance.
a. Universal bank
b. Asset liability management
c. Automatic transfer service account
d. Anonymous internet banking

13. A consumer price index (_____) is a measure of the average price of consumer goods and services purchased by households. A consumer price index measures a price change for a constant market basket of goods and services from one period to the next within the same area (city, region, or nation.) It is a price index determined by measuring the price of a standard group of goods meant to represent the typical market basket of a typical urban consumer.
a. CPI
b. Hedonic price index
c. Cost-of-living index
d. Lipstick index

14. _____ is money accepted for exchange of goods in an economy. The prevalence of one money over another arises, usually, when a government designates through decrees that the government shall accept only particular notes and coins in payment for taxes. Typically, money of _____ consists of stamped coins and minted paper bills.

a. Currency
b. Security thread
c. Local currency
d. Totnes pound

15. _____ is a type of bank account where the money in the account is legally able to be withdrawn immediately upon demand (or 'at call'.) This type of bank account can also be referred to as a 'cheque' or 'checking' or transactional account.

This type of bank account, allowing immediate conversion of the account balance into cash or withdrawal to another account, can be contrasted with a time deposit (also known as a certificate of deposit or term deposit), where the funds are not legally available for immediate withdrawal by the depositor.

a. Clawbacks in economic development
b. Demand deposit
c. Tangible Common Equity
d. Debt rescheduling

16. The _____ is the official currency of 16 of the 27 member states of the European Union (EU.) The states, known collectively as the Eurozone, are Austria, Belgium, Cyprus, Finland, France, Germany, Greece, Ireland, Italy, Luxembourg, Malta, the Netherlands, Portugal, Slovakia, Slovenia, and Spain. The currency is also used in a further five European countries, with and without formal agreements and is consequently used daily by some 327 million Europeans.

a. Import and Export Price Indices
b. Euro
c. IRS Code 3401
d. Equity capital market

17. In finance, the _____s between two currencies specifies how much one currency is worth in terms of the other. It is the value of a foreign natione;s currency in terms of the home natione;s currency. For example an _____ of 102 Japanese yen to the United States dollar means that JPY 102 is worth the same as USD 1.

a. Interbank market
b. ACEA agreement
c. ACCRA Cost of Living Index
d. Exchange rate

18. In finance, the _____ is the global financial market for short-term borrowing and lending. It provides short-term liquidity funding for the global financial system. The _____ is where short-term obligations such as Treasury bills, commercial paper and bankers' acceptances are bought and sold.

a. Consignment stock
b. Deferred compensation
c. Money market
d. T-Model

19. In the United States, a _____ is a deposit account that pays interest, on which checks may be written.

They are structured to comply with Regulation Q, which prohibits interest on checking accounts: NOW accounts are interest-bearing, and checks may be written on them, but legally they are not interest-bearing checking accounts.

In the early 1970s, smaller banks in Massachusetts created the _____ to compete with the larger commercial banks.

a. Lombard banking
b. Daylight overdraft
c. Bought deal
d. Negotiable order of withdrawal account

Chapter 17. The Money Supply and the Banking System

20. A _____ allows a borrower to use a financial security as collateral for a cash loan at a fixed rate of interest. In a repo, the borrower agrees to sell immediately a security to a lender and also agrees to buy the same security from the lender at a fixed price at some later date. A repo is equivalent to a cash transaction combined with a forward contract.
    a. Delivery month
    b. SPI 200 futures contract
    c. Repurchase agreement
    d. Volatility arbitrage

21. A _____ is a money deposit at a banking institution that cannot be withdrawn for a certain 'term' or period of time. When the term is over it can be withdrawn or it can be held for another term. Generally speaking, the longer the term the better the yield on the money.
    a. Deposit market share
    b. Fractional-reserve banking
    c. Finance charge
    d. Time deposit

22. In economics, a _____ is a redistribution of income in the market system. These payments are considered to be nonexhaustive because they do not directly absorb resources or create output. Examples of certain _____s include welfare (financial aid), social security, and government subsidies for certain businesses (firms.)
    a. 1921 recession
    b. 100-year flood
    c. 130-30 fund
    d. Transfer payment

23. _____ are banks' holdings of deposits in accounts with their central bank (for instance the European Central Bank or the Federal Reserve, in the latter case including federal funds), plus currency that is physically held in bank vaults (vault cash.) The central banks of some nations set minimum reserve requirements. Even when no requirements are set, banks commonly wish to hold some reserves, called desired reserves, against unexpected events.
    a. Sweep account
    b. Bilateral netting
    c. Bank reserves
    d. Structuring

24. A _____ is a current account at a banking institution that allows money to be deposited and withdrawn by the account holder, with the transactions and resulting balance being recorded on the bank's books. Some banks charge a fee for this service, while others may pay the customer interest on the funds deposited.

    Although restrictions placed on access depend upon the terms and conditions of the account and the provider, the account holder retains rights to have their funds repaid on demand.

    a. Stated income loan
    b. Bank statement
    c. Deposit account
    d. Large Value Transfer System

25. _____ is a reduction in the value of a currency with respect to other monetary units. In common modern usage, it specifically implies an official lowering of the value of a country's currency within a fixed exchange rate system, by which the monetary authority formally sets a new fixed rate with respect to a foreign reference currency. In contrast, (currency) depreciation is used for the unofficial decrease in the exchange rate in a floating exchange rate system.
    a. Petrodollar recycling
    b. Devaluation
    c. Reserve currency
    d. Texas redbacks

26. A _____ is the transfer of wealth from one party (such as a person or company) to another. A _____ is usually made in exchange for the provision of goods, services or both, or to fulfill a legal obligation.

    The simplest and oldest form of _____ is barter, the exchange of one good or service for another.

Chapter 17. The Money Supply and the Banking System

a. Payment
c. Soft count
b. Going concern
d. Social gravity

27. A _____, reserve bank, or monetary authority is the entity responsible for the monetary policy of a country or of a group of member states. It is a bank that can lend money to other banks in times of need. Its primary responsibility is to maintain the stability of the national currency and money supply, but more active duties include controlling subsidized-loan interest rates, and acting as a lender of last resort to the banking sector during times of financial crisis (private banks often being integral to the national financial system.)

a. 1921 recession
c. 130-30 fund
b. Central Bank
d. 100-year flood

28. The _____ , a component of the Federal Reserve System, is charged under United States law with overseeing the nation's open market operations. It is the Federal Reserve Committee that makes key decisions about interest rates and the growth jam of the United States money supply. It is the principal organ of United States national monetary policy.

a. Primary Dealer Credit Facility
c. Federal Open Market Committee
b. Fed Funds Probability
d. Federal Reserve Transparency Act

29. _____ is the process by which the government, central bank (ii) availability of money, and (iii) cost of money or rate of interest, in order to attain a set of objectives oriented towards the growth and stability of the economy. Monetary theory provides insight into how to craft optimal _____.

_____ is referred to as either being an expansionary policy where an expansionary policy increases the total supply of money in the economy, and a contractionary policy decreases the total money supply.

a. 1921 recession
c. 100-year flood
b. 130-30 fund
d. Monetary policy

30. In economics, the _____ is the term used to refer to the environment in which bonds are bought and sold between a central bank ' its regulated banks. It is not a free market process.

- To intervene in the 'business cycle', a central bank may choose to go into the _____ and buy or sell government bonds, which is known as _____ operations to increase reserves.

a. Inside money
c. Open Market
b. ACCRA Cost of Living Index
d. Outside money

31. In financial accounting, a _____ or statement of financial position is a summary of a person's or organization's balances. Assets, liabilities and ownership equity are listed as of a specific date, such as the end of its financial year. A _____ is often described as a snapshot of a company's financial condition.

a. 1921 recession
c. 100-year flood
b. Balance sheet
d. 130-30 fund

32. The _____ is the difference between the monetary value of exports and imports in an economy over a certain period of time. It is the relationship between a nation's imports and exports. A positive _____ is known as a trade surplus and consists of exporting more than is imported; a negative _____ is known as a trade deficit or, informally, a trade gap.

Chapter 17. The Money Supply and the Banking System 139

    a. SIMIC
    b. Balance of trade
    c. Marginal propensity to import
    d. Rational expectations

33. In economics, the _____ is a term relating to the money supply, the amount of money in the economy. The _____ comprises only coins, paper money, and commercial banks' reserves with the central bank. Broader measures of the money supply include the public's bank deposits .
    a. Quantum economics
    b. Chartalism
    c. Monetary economy
    d. Monetary base

34. A security is a fungible, negotiable instrument representing financial value. _____ are broadly categorized into debt _____; equity _____, e.g., common stocks; and derivative (finance) contracts such as forwards, futures, options and swaps. The company or other entity issuing the security is called the issuer.
    a. Securities
    b. Red herring prospectus
    c. Pass-Through Certificates
    d. Settlement risk

35. Discounting is a financial mechanism in which a debtor obtains the right to delay payments to a creditor, for a defined period of time, in exchange for a charge or fee. Essentially, the party that owes money in the present purchases the right to delay the payment until some future date. The _____, or charge, is simply the difference between the original amount owed in the present and the amount that has to be paid in the future to settle the debt.
    a. Certified Risk Manager
    b. Reinsurance
    c. Reliability theory
    d. Discount

36. The _____ is an interest rate a central bank charges depository institutions that borrow reserves from it.

The term _____ has two meanings:

- the same as interest rate; the term 'discount' does not refer to the meaning of the word, but to the purpose of using the quantity, such as computations of present value, e.g. net present value or discounted cash flow

- the annual effective _____, which is the annual interest divided by the capital including that interest; this rate is lower than the interest rate; it corresponds to using the value after a year as the nominal value, and seeing the initial value as the nominal value minus a discount; it is used for Treasury Bills and similar financial instruments

The annual effective _____ is the annual interest divided by the capital including that interest, which is the interest rate divided by 100% plus the interest rate. It is the annual discount factor to be applied to the future cash flow, to find the discount, subtracted from a future value to find the value one year earlier.

For example, suppose there is a government bond that sells for $95 and pays $100 in a year's time.

    a. Johansen test
    b. Discount rate
    c. Stochastic volatility
    d. Perpetuity

37. In business and accounting, _____ are everything of value that is owned by a person or company. It is a claim on the property your income of a borrower. The balance sheet of a firm records the monetary value of the _____ owned by the firm.

Chapter 17. The Money Supply and the Banking System

a. ACEA agreement
b. ACCRA Cost of Living Index
c. Amortization schedule
d. Assets

38.

A _____ is a type of financial intermediary and a type of bank. Commercial banking is also known as business banking. It is a bank that provides checking accounts, savings accounts, and money market accounts and that accepts time deposits.

a. Commercial bank
b. Bought deal
c. Daylight overdraft
d. Lombard banking

39. A _____ is an expression that compares quantities relative to each other. The most common examples involve two quantities, but any number of quantities can be compared. _____s are represented mathematically by separating each quantity with a colon, for example the _____ 2:3, which is read as the _____ 'two to three'.

a. Ratio
b. Y-intercept
c. 130-30 fund
d. 100-year flood

40. The reserve requirement (or required _____) is a bank regulation that sets the minimum reserves each bank must hold to customer deposits and notes. It would normally be in the form of fiat currency stored in a bank vault (vault cash), or with a central bank.

The _____ is sometimes used as a tool in the monetary policy, influencing the country's economy, borrowing, and interest rates.

a. Dividend unit
b. First player wins
c. Reserve ratio
d. Bank-State-Branch

41. The accounting equation relates assets, _____, and owner's equity:

Assets = _____ + Owner's Equity

The accounting equation is the mathematical structure of the balance sheet.

The Australian Accounting Research Foundation defines _____ as: 'future sacrifice of economic benefits that the entity is presently obliged to make to other entities as a result of past transactions and other past events.'

Probably the most accepted accounting definition of liability is the one used by the International Accounting Standards Board (IASB.) The following is a quotation from IFRS Framework:

A liability is a present obligation of the enterprise arising from past events, the settlement of which is expected to result in an outflow from the enterprise of resources embodying economic benefits

-

Chapter 17. The Money Supply and the Banking System

Regulations as to the recognition of _____ are different all over the world, but are roughly similar to those of the IASB.

a. Competition law theory
b. Coase theorem
c. Community property
d. Liabilities

42. The most common mechanism used to measure this increase in the money supply is typically called the _____. It calculates the maximum amount of money that an initial deposit can be expanded to with a given reserve ratio - such a factor is called a multiplier.

The _____, m, is the inverse of the reserve requirement, R:

$$m = \frac{1}{R}$$

This formula stems from the fact that the sum of the 'amount loaned out' column above can be expressed mathematically as a geometric series with a common ratio of 1 − R.

a. Fixed-income arbitrage
b. Flow to Equity-Approach
c. Kibbutz volunteers
d. Money multiplier

43. _____s are accounts maintained by retail financial institutions that pay interest but can not be used directly as money (for example, by writing a cheque.) These accounts let customers set aside a portion of their liquid assets while earning a monetary return.

_____s are offered by commercial banks, savings and loan associations, credit unions, building societies and mutual savings banks.

a. Lombard Club
b. Fractional-reserve banking
c. Fair Finance Watch
d. Savings account

44. The _____ is a bank regulation that sets the minimum reserves each bank must hold to customer deposits and notes. It would normally be in the form of fiat currency stored in a bank vault (vault cash), or with a central bank.

The reserve ratio is sometimes used as a tool in the monetary policy, influencing the country's economy, borrowing, and interest rates.

a. Private money
b. Reserve requirement
c. Fractional-reserve banking
d. Probability of default

45. _____ is the increase in the amount of the goods and services produced by an economy over time. It is conventionally measured as the percent rate of increase in real gross domestic product, or real GDP. Growth is usually calculated in real terms, i.e. inflation-adjusted terms, in order to net out the effect of inflation on the price of the goods and services produced.

a. ACCRA Cost of Living Index
b. ACEA agreement
c. AD-IA Model
d. Economic growth

46. In economics, a _____ is a table that lists the quantity of a good a person will buy it each different price See Demand curve.
   a. Demand schedule
   b. Federal Reserve districts
   c. Free contract
   d. Rational irrationality

47. _____ and Keynesian Theory) is a macroeconomic theory based on the ideas of 20th-century British economist John Maynard Keynes. _____ argues that private sector decisions sometimes lead to inefficient macroeconomic outcomes and therefore advocates active policy responses by the public sector, including monetary policy actions by the central bank and fiscal policy actions by the government to stabilize output over the business cycle.

The theories forming the basis of _____ were first presented in The General Theory of Employment, Interest and Money, published in 1936.

   a. Keynesian economics
   b. Deflation
   c. Market failure
   d. Rational choice theory

48. _____ is a fee paid on borrowed assets. It is the price paid for the use of borrowed money , or, money earned by deposited funds . Assets that are sometimes lent with _____ include money, shares, consumer goods through hire purchase, major assets such as aircraft, and even entire factories in finance lease arrangements.
   a. Insolvency
   b. Asset protection
   c. Interest
   d. Internal debt

49. An _____ is the price a borrower pays for the use of money they do not own, for instance a small company might borrow from a bank to kick start their business, and the return a lender receives for deferring the use of funds, by lending it to the borrower. _____s are normally expressed as a percentage rate over the period of one year.

_____s targets are also a vital tool of monetary policy and are used to control variables like investment, inflation, and unemployment.

   a. Interest rate
   b. ACCRA Cost of Living Index
   c. Enterprise value
   d. Arrow-Debreu model

50. The _____ was a worldwide economic downturn starting in most places in 1929 and ending at different times in the 1930s or early 1940s for different countries. It was the largest and most important economic depression in the 20th century, and is used in the 21st century as an example of how far the world's economy can fall. The _____ originated in the United States; historians most often use as a starting date the stock market crash on October 29, 1929, known as Black Tuesday.
   a. Jarrow March
   b. Great Depression
   c. British Empire Economic Conference
   d. Wall Street Crash of 1929

Chapter 18. Monetary Policy

1. A _____, reserve bank, or monetary authority is the entity responsible for the monetary policy of a country or of a group of member states. It is a bank that can lend money to other banks in times of need. Its primary responsibility is to maintain the stability of the national currency and money supply, but more active duties include controlling subsidized-loan interest rates, and acting as a lender of last resort to the banking sector during times of financial crisis (private banks often being integral to the national financial system.)

    a. 130-30 fund
    b. 100-year flood
    c. Central Bank
    d. 1921 recession

2. The _____ , a component of the Federal Reserve System, is charged under United States law with overseeing the nation's open market operations. It is the Federal Reserve Committee that makes key decisions about interest rates and the growth jam of the United States money supply. It is the principal organ of United States national monetary policy.

    a. Primary Dealer Credit Facility
    b. Federal Reserve Transparency Act
    c. Fed Funds Probability
    d. Federal Open Market Committee

3. The _____ is the central banking system of the United States. Created in 1913 by the enactment of the Federal Reserve Act (signed by Woodrow Wilson), it is a quasi-public and quasi-private (government entity with private components) banking system that comprises (1) the presidentially appointed Board of Governors of the _____ in Washington, D.C.; (2) the Federal Open Market Committee; (3) twelve regional Federal Reserve Banks located in major cities throughout the nation acting as fiscal agents for the U.S. Treasury, each with its own nine-member board of directors; (4) numerous other private U.S. member banks, which subscribe to required amounts of non-transferable stock in their regional Federal Reserve Banks; and (5) various advisory councils. Since February 2006, Ben Bernanke has served as the Chairman of the Board of Governors of the _____.

    a. Federal Reserve System Open Market Account
    b. Monetary Policy Report to the Congress
    c. Term auction facility
    d. Federal Reserve System

4. _____ and Keynesian Theory) is a macroeconomic theory based on the ideas of 20th-century British economist John Maynard Keynes. _____ argues that private sector decisions sometimes lead to inefficient macroeconomic outcomes and therefore advocates active policy responses by the public sector, including monetary policy actions by the central bank and fiscal policy actions by the government to stabilize output over the business cycle.

    The theories forming the basis of _____ were first presented in The General Theory of Employment, Interest and Money, published in 1936.

    a. Rational choice theory
    b. Deflation
    c. Market failure
    d. Keynesian economics

5. _____ is the process by which the government, central bank (ii) availability of money, and (iii) cost of money or rate of interest, in order to attain a set of objectives oriented towards the growth and stability of the economy. Monetary theory provides insight into how to craft optimal _____.

    _____ is referred to as either being an expansionary policy where an expansionary policy increases the total supply of money in the economy, and a contractionary policy decreases the total money supply.

    a. 1921 recession
    b. 130-30 fund
    c. 100-year flood
    d. Monetary policy

Chapter 18. Monetary Policy

6. In economics, the _____ is the term used to refer to the environment in which bonds are bought and sold between a central bank ' its regulated banks. It is not a free market process.

- To intervene in the 'business cycle', a central bank may choose to go into the _____ and buy or sell government bonds, which is known as _____ operations to increase reserves.

   a. Open Market
   b. ACCRA Cost of Living Index
   c. Outside money
   d. Inside money

7. In financial accounting, a _____ or statement of financial position is a summary of a person's or organization's balances. Assets, liabilities and ownership equity are listed as of a specific date, such as the end of its financial year. A _____ is often described as a snapshot of a company's financial condition.

   a. 1921 recession
   b. 130-30 fund
   c. Balance sheet
   d. 100-year flood

8. _____ is an American economist and was the Chairman of the Federal Reserve of the United States from 1987 to 2006. He currently works as a private advisor and providing consulting for firms through his company, Greenspan Associates LLC.

First appointed Federal Reserve chairman by President Ronald Reagan in August 1987, he was reappointed at successive four-year intervals until retiring on January 31, 2006 after the second-longest tenure in the position.

   a. Adam Smith
   b. Adolph Fischer
   c. Alan Greenspan
   d. Adolf Hitler

9. In economics, the _____ measures the payments that flow between any individual country and all other countries. It is used to summarize all international economic transactions for that country during a specific time period, usually a year. The _____ is determined by the country's exports and imports of goods, services, and financial capital, as well as financial transfers.

   a. Balance of payments
   b. Gross domestic product per barrel
   c. Gross world product
   d. Skyscraper Index

10. _____s is the social science that studies the production, distribution, and consumption of goods and services. The term _____s comes from the Ancient Greek oá¼°κονομῖα from oá¼¶κος (oikos, 'house') + vĺŒμος (nomos, 'custom' or 'law'), hence 'rules of the house(hold)'. Current _____ models developed out of the broader field of political economy in the late 19th century, owing to a desire to use an empirical approach more akin to the physical sciences.

   a. Energy economics
   b. Inflation
   c. Opportunity cost
   d. Economic

11. A _____ is the transfer of wealth from one party (such as a person or company) to another. A _____ is usually made in exchange for the provision of goods, services or both, or to fulfill a legal obligation.

The simplest and oldest form of _____ is barter, the exchange of one good or service for another.

Chapter 18. Monetary Policy

    a. Going concern
    c. Payment
    b. Social gravity
    d. Soft count

12. _____, 1st Baron Keynes was a renowned economist from Britain whose many ideas on economic and political theories as well as on many governments' monetary policies influenced America. He advocated a government that played an active role in the lives of people regarding business, economy, etc. In this role, the government would use fiscal measures to reduce the consequences of recessions, economic depressions and booms.
    a. Adam Smith
    c. Adolph Fischer
    b. Adolf Hitler
    d. John Maynard Keynes

13. In economics, _____ is the total amount of money available in an economy at a particular point in time. There are several ways to define 'money', but standard measures usually include currency in circulation and demand deposits.

_____ data are recorded and published, usually by the government or the central bank of the country.

    a. Neutrality of money
    c. Velocity of money
    b. Money supply
    d. Veil of money

14. In economics, _____ is a rise in the general level of prices of goods and services in an economy over a period of time. When the general price level rises, each unit of currency buys fewer goods and services; consequently, _____ is also a decline in the real value of money--a loss of purchasing power in the medium of exchange which is also the monetary unit of account in the economy. A chief measure of general price-level _____ is the general _____ rate, which is the percentage change in a general price index (normally the Consumer Price Index) over time.
    a. Economic
    c. Energy economics
    b. Opportunity cost
    d. Inflation

15. _____ is a fee paid on borrowed assets. It is the price paid for the use of borrowed money, or, money earned by deposited funds. Assets that are sometimes lent with _____ include money, shares, consumer goods through hire purchase, major assets such as aircraft, and even entire factories in finance lease arrangements.
    a. Insolvency
    c. Asset protection
    b. Internal debt
    d. Interest

16. An _____ is the price a borrower pays for the use of money they do not own, for instance a small company might borrow from a bank to kick start their business, and the return a lender receives for deferring the use of funds, by lending it to the borrower. _____s are normally expressed as a percentage rate over the period of one year.

_____s targets are also a vital tool of monetary policy and are used to control variables like investment, inflation, and unemployment.

    a. Enterprise value
    c. ACCRA Cost of Living Index
    b. Arrow-Debreu model
    d. Interest rate

17. Market _____ is a business, economics or investment term that refers to an asset's ability to be easily converted through an act of buying or selling without causing a significant movement in the price and with minimum loss of value. Money, or cash on hand, is the most liquid asset. An act of exchange of a less liquid asset with a more liquid asset is called liquidation.

Chapter 18. Monetary Policy

a. 100-year flood
b. 1921 recession
c. 130-30 fund
d. Liquidity

18. The term _____ is used in macroeconomics to refer to a situation where a country's nominal interest rate has been lowered nearly to or equal to zero to avoid a recession, but the liquidity in the market created by these low interest rates does not stimulate the economy to full employment. In this situation, any further increase in the money supply will not stimulate the economy any further. This is because any further injection of liquidity will no longer lower the nominal interest rate, as the nominal interest rate cannot drop below zero.
   a. Minimum wage
   b. Liquidity trap
   c. Robertson lag
   d. Macroeconomic models

19. In finance, the _____s between two currencies specifies how much one currency is worth in terms of the other. It is the value of a foreign natione;s currency in terms of the home natione;s currency. For example an _____ of 102 Japanese yen to the United States dollar means that JPY 102 is worth the same as USD 1.
   a. ACCRA Cost of Living Index
   b. Interbank market
   c. Exchange rate
   d. ACEA agreement

20. The _____ was a worldwide economic downturn starting in most places in 1929 and ending at different times in the 1930s or early 1940s for different countries. It was the largest and most important economic depression in the 20th century, and is used in the 21st century as an example of how far the world's economy can fall. The _____ originated in the United States; historians most often use as a starting date the stock market crash on October 29, 1929, known as Black Tuesday.
   a. Wall Street Crash of 1929
   b. British Empire Economic Conference
   c. Jarrow March
   d. Great Depression

21. In economics, _____ is the total demand for final goods and services in the economy (Y) at a given time and price level. It is the amount of goods and services in the economy that will be purchased at all possible price levels. This is the demand for the gross domestic product of a country when inventory levels are static.
   a. Aggregate supply
   b. Aggregate expenditure
   c. Aggregation problem
   d. Aggregate demand

22. Economics:

   - _____,the desire to own something and the ability to pay for it
   - _____ curve,a graphic representation of a _____ schedule
   - _____ deposit, the money in checking accounts
   - _____ pull theory,the theory that inflation occurs when _____ for goods and services exceeds existing supplies
   - _____ schedule,a table that lists the quantity of a good a person will buy it each different price
   - _____ side economics,the school of economics at believes government spending and tax cuts open economy by raising _____

a. Variability
b. Production
c. McKesson ' Robbins scandal
d. Demand

Chapter 18. Monetary Policy

23. In economics, _____ is the ratio of the percent change in one variable to the percent change in another variable. It is a tool for measuring the responsiveness of a function to changes in parameters in a relative way. Commonly analyzed are _____ of substitution, price and wealth.
   a. ACCRA Cost of Living Index
   b. Elasticity
   c. ACEA agreement
   d. Elasticity of demand

24. A _____ product is a product designed for cheapness and short-term convenience rather than medium to long-term durability, with most products only intended for single use. The term is also sometimes used for products that may last several months (ex. _____ air filters) to distinguish from similar products that last indefinitely (ex.
   a. 130-30 fund
   b. 1921 recession
   c. 100-year flood
   d. Disposable

25. _____ is gross income minus income tax on that income.

Discretionary income is income after subtracting taxes and normal expenses (such as rent or mortgage, utilities, insurance, medical, transportation, property maintenance, child support, inflation, food and sundries, 'c.) to maintain a certain standard of living.

   a. Disposable income
   b. Disposable personal income
   c. Taxation as theft
   d. Stamp Act

26. In the United States, _____ are overnight borrowings by banks to maintain their bank reserves at the Federal Reserve. Banks keep reserves at Federal Reserve Banks to meet their reserve requirements and to clear financial transactions. Transactions in the _____ market enable depository institutions with reserve balances in excess of reserve requirements to lend reserves to institutions with reserve deficiencies.
   a. Federal Reserve Transparency Act
   b. Federal funds rate
   c. Term auction facility
   d. Federal funds

27. In the United States, the _____ is the interest rate at which private depository institutions (mostly banks) lend balances (federal funds) at the Federal Reserve to other depository institutions, usually overnight. It is the interest rate banks charge each other for loans. Changing the target rate is one way the Chairman of the Federal Reserve can influence the supply of money in the U.S. economy..
   a. Federal banking
   b. Monetary Policy Report to the Congress
   c. Term auction facility
   d. Federal funds rate

28. In economics, the _____ is a historical inverse relation between the rate of unemployment and the rate of inflation in an economy. Stated simply, the lower the unemployment in an economy, the higher the rate of increase in nominal wages in the economy. Rate of Change of Wages against Unemployment, United Kingdom 1913-1948 from Phillips (1958)

William Phillips, a New Zealand born economist, wrote a paper in 1958 titled The Relationship between Unemployment and the Rate of Change of Money Wages in the United Kingdom 1861-1957, which was published in the quarterly journal Economica.

   a. Demand curve
   b. Phillips curve
   c. Cost curve
   d. Lorenz curve

29. In economics, a _____ is a monetary-policy rule that stipulates how much the central bank would or should change the nominal interest rate in response to divergences of actual inflation rates from target inflation rates and of actual Gross Domestic Product (GDP) from potential GDP. It was first proposed by the by U.S. economist John B. Taylor in 1993. The rule can be written as follows:

$$i_t = \pi_t + r_t^* + a_\pi(\pi_t - \pi_t^*) + a_y(y_t - \bar{y}_t).$$

In this equation, i_t is the target short-term nominal interest rate (e.g. the federal funds rate in the US), π_t is the rate of inflation as measured by the GDP deflator, π_t^* is the desired rate of inflation, r_t^* is the assumed equilibrium real interest rate, y_t is the logarithm of real GDP, and $\bar{y}_t$ is the logarithm of potential output, as determined by a linear trend.

a. Fed Funds Probability
b. Federal Reserve Banks
c. Term Securities Lending Facility
d. Taylor rule

Chapter 18. Monetary Policy   149

30. A _____ is:

- Rewrite _____, in generative grammar and computer science
- Standardization, a formal and widely-accepted statement, fact, definition, or qualification
- Operation, a determinate _____ for performing a mathematical operation and obtaining a certain result (Mathematics, Logic)
    - Unary operation
    - Binary operation
- _____ of inference, a function from sets of formulae to formulae (Mathematics, Logic)
- _____ of thumb, principle with broad application that is not intended to be strictly accurate or reliable for every situation. Also often simply referred to as a _____
- Moral, an atomic element of a moral code for guiding choices in human behavior
- Heuristic, a quantized '_____' which shows a tendency or probability for successful function
- A regulation, as in sports
- A Production _____, as in computer science
- Procedural law, a _____ set governing the application of laws to cases
    - A law, which may informally be called a '_____'
    - A court ruling, a decision by a court
- In the U.S. Government, a regulation mandated by Congress, but written or expanded upon by the Executive Branch.
- Norm (sociology), an informal but widely accepted _____, concept, truth, definition, or qualification (social norms, legal norms, coding norms)
- Norm (philosophy), a kind of sentence or a reason to act, feel or believe
- 'Rulership' is the concept of governance by a government:
    - Military _____, governance by a military body
    - Monastic _____, a collection of precepts that guides the life of monks or nuns in a religious order where the superior holds the place of Christ
- Slide _____

- '_____,' a song by Ayumi Hamasaki
- '_____,' a song by rapper Nas
- '_____s,' an album by the band The Whitest Boy Alive
- _____s: Pyaar Ka Superhit Formula, a 2003 Bollywood film
- ruler, an instrument for measuring lengths
- _____, a component of an astrolabe, circumferator or similar instrument
- The _____s, a bestselling self-help book
- _____ Project (Run Up-to-date Linux Everywhere), a project that aims to use up-to-date Linux software on old PCs
- _____ engine, a software system that helps managing business _____s
- Ja _____, a hip hop artist
    - R.U.L.E., a 2005 greatest hits album by rapper Ja _____
- '_____s,' a KMFDM song

a. Technocracy   b. Demand
c. Procter ' Gamble   d. Rule

Chapter 18. Monetary Policy

31. The _____ is one of the world's most important central banks, responsible for monetary policy covering the 16 member States of the Eurozone. It was established by the European Union (EU) in 1998 with its headquarters in Frankfurt, Germany.

The predecessor to the _____ was the European Monetary Institute.

   a. ACCRA Cost of Living Index   b. European Central Bank
   c. AD-IA Model   d. ACEA agreement

32. In economics, _____ describes a situation where a decision-maker's preferences change over time, such that what is preferred at one point in time is inconsistent with what is preferred at another point in time. It is often easiest to think about preferences over time in this context by thinking of decision-makers as being made up of many different 'selves', with each self representing the decision-maker at a different point in time. So, for example, there is my today self, my tomorrow self, my next Tuesday self, my year from now self, etc.

   a. Bondareva-Shapley theorem   b. Graph continuous
   c. Dynamic inconsistency   d. Cheap talk

33. A _____ or a flexible exchange rate is a type of exchange rate regime wherein a currency's value is allowed to fluctuate according to the foreign exchange market. A currency that uses a _____ is known as a floating currency. The opposite of a _____ is a fixed exchange rate.

   a. Foreign exchange market   b. Floating currency
   c. Trade Weighted US dollar Index   d. Floating exchange rate

34. _____ is an economic policy in which a central bank estimates and makes public a projected, or 'target,' inflation rate and then attempts to steer actual inflation towards the target through the use of interest rate changes and other monetary tools.

Because interest rates and the inflation rate tend to be inversely related, the likely moves of the central bank to raise or lower interest rates become more transparent under the policy of _____. Examples:

- if inflation appears to be above the target, the bank is likely to raise interest rates. This usually (but not always) has the effect over time of cooling the economy and bringing down inflation.

- if inflation appears to be below the target, the bank is likely to lower interest rates. This usually (again, not always) has the effect over time of accelerating the economy and raising inflation.

   a. Employment Cost Index   b. Incomes policies
   c. Inflation swap   d. Inflation targeting

35. _____ is a decrease in the rate of inflation. This phase of the business cycle, in which retailers can no longer pass on higher prices to their customers, often occurs during a recession. In contrast, deflation occurs when prices are actually dropping.

   a. Mundell-Tobin effect   b. Reflation
   c. Stealth inflation   d. Disinflation

Chapter 19. Fiscal Stabilization Policy

1. The term _____ refers to government debt, expenditures and revenues, or to finance (particularly financial revenue) in general.

   - _____ deficit is the budget deficit of federal or local government
   - _____ policy is the discretionary spending of governments. Contrasts with monetary policy.
   - _____ year and _____ quarter are reporting periods for firms and other agencies.

   a. Drawdown
   c. Bucket shop
   b. Procter ' Gamble
   d. Fiscal

2. In economics, _____ is the use of government spending and revenue collection to influence the economy.

   _____ can be contrasted with the other main type of economic policy, monetary policy, which attempts to stabilize the economy by controlling interest rates and the supply of money. The two main instruments of _____ are government spending and taxation.

   a. 100-year flood
   c. Fiscal policy
   b. Sustainable investment rule
   d. Fiscalism

3. A _____ is a package or set of measures introduced to stabilise a financial system or economy. The term can refer to policies in two distinct sets of circumstances: business cycle stabilization and crisis stabilization.

   Stabilization can refer to correcting the normal behavior of the business cycle.

   a. Volunteers for Economic Growth Alliance
   c. Capacity Development
   b. New International Economic Order
   d. Stabilization policy

4. In economics, _____ is inflation that is very high or 'out of control', a condition in which prices increase rapidly as a currency loses its value. Definitions used by the media vary from a cumulative inflation rate over three years approaching 100% to 'inflation exceeding 50% a month.' In informal usage the term is often applied to much lower rates. As a rule of thumb, normal inflation is reported per year, but _____ is often reported for much shorter intervals, often per month.
   a. 130-30 fund
   c. 1921 recession
   b. 100-year flood
   d. Hyperinflation

5. _____ and Keynesian Theory) is a macroeconomic theory based on the ideas of 20th-century British economist John Maynard Keynes. _____ argues that private sector decisions sometimes lead to inefficient macroeconomic outcomes and therefore advocates active policy responses by the public sector, including monetary policy actions by the central bank and fiscal policy actions by the government to stabilize output over the business cycle.

   The theories forming the basis of _____ were first presented in The General Theory of Employment, Interest and Money, published in 1936.

   a. Market failure
   c. Rational choice theory
   b. Deflation
   d. Keynesian economics

Chapter 19. Fiscal Stabilization Policy

6. The _____ is an expected return that the provider of capital plans to earn on their investment.

Capital (money) used for funding a business should earn returns for the capital providers who risk their capital. For an investment to be worthwhile, the expected return on capital must be greater than the _____.

   a. Capital intensive
   b. Cost of capital
   c. Modigliani-Miller theorem
   d. Capital expenditure

7. In microeconomics, _____ is quite simply the conversion of inputs into outputs. It is an economic process that uses resources to create a good or service that is suitable for exchange. This can include manufacturing, storing, shipping, and packaging.
   a. Red Guards
   b. MET
   c. Solved
   d. Production

8. In economics, a _____ is a function that specifies the output of a firm, an industry, or an entire economy for all combinations of inputs. A meta-_____ compares the practice of the existing entities converting inputs X into output y to determine the most efficient practice _____ of the existing entities, whether the most efficient feasible practice production or the most efficient actual practice production. In either case, the maximum output of a technologically-determined production process is a mathematical function of input factors of production.
   a. Post-Fordism
   b. Constant elasticity of substitution
   c. Short-run
   d. Production function

9. In economics, _____ is the process by which a firm determines the price and output level that returns the greatest profit. There are several approaches to this problem. The total revenue--total cost method relies on the fact that profit equals revenue minus cost, and the marginal revenue--marginal cost method is based on the fact that total profit in a perfectly competitive market reaches its maximum point where marginal revenue equals marginal cost.
   a. Normal profit
   b. Profit maximization
   c. 100-year flood
   d. Profit margin

10. From a Keynesian point of view, a _____ in the public sector is achieved when the government equates the revenues with expenditure over the business cycles. In other words, a government's budget is balanced if its income is equal to its expenditure. It is a budget in which revenues are equal to spending.
    a. Budget support
    b. Balanced budget
    c. Budget theory
    d. Budget crisis

11. _____ or government expenditure is classified by economists into three main types. Government purchases of goods and services for current use are classed as government consumption. Government purchases of goods and services intended to create future benefits, such as infrastructure investment or research spending, are classed as government investment.
    a. 1921 recession
    b. 130-30 fund
    c. Government spending
    d. 100-year flood

12. In economics, _____ is the total demand for final goods and services in the economy (Y) at a given time and price level. It is the amount of goods and services in the economy that will be purchased at all possible price levels. This is the demand for the gross domestic product of a country when inventory levels are static.

Chapter 19. Fiscal Stabilization Policy

a. Aggregation problem
b. Aggregate supply
c. Aggregate demand
d. Aggregate expenditure

13. Economics:

- _____, the desire to own something and the ability to pay for it
- _____ curve, a graphic representation of a _____ schedule
- _____ deposit, the money in checking accounts
- _____ pull theory, the theory that inflation occurs when _____ for goods and services exceeds existing supplies
- _____ schedule, a table that lists the quantity of a good a person will buy it each different price
- _____ side economics, the school of economics at believes government spending and tax cuts open economy by raising _____

a. Demand
b. Variability
c. Production
d. McKesson ' Robbins scandal

14. _____ is a common concept in economics, and gives rise to derived concepts such as consumer debt. Generally _____ is defined by opposition to production. But the precise definition can vary because different schools of economists define production quite differently.

a. Consumption
b. Cash or share options
c. Foreclosure data providers
d. Federal Reserve Bank Notes

15. _____ is an assumption used in many contemporary macroeconomic models, and also in other areas of contemporary economics and game theory and in other applications of rational choice theory.

Since most macroeconomic models today study decisions over many periods, the expectations of workers, consumers, and firms about future economic conditions are an essential part of the model. How to model these expectations has long been controversial, and it is well known that the macroeconomic predictions of the model may differ depending on the assumptions made about expectations

a. Minimum wage
b. Rational expectations
c. Potential output
d. Balanced-growth equilibrium

16. In economics, a _____ is a general slowdown in economic activity over a sustained period of time, or a business cycle contraction. During _____s, many macroeconomic indicators vary in a similar way. Production as measured by Gross Domestic Product (GDP), employment, investment spending, capacity utilization, household incomes and business profits all fall during _____s.

a. Treasury View
b. Leading indicators
c. Monetary economics
d. Recession

17. A _____ occurs when an entity spends more money than it takes in. The opposite of a _____ is a budget surplus. Debt is essentially an accumulated flow of deficits.

a. Lump-sum tax
b. Funding body
c. Public Financial Management
d. Budget deficit

18. The _____ is the official currency of 16 of the 27 member states of the European Union (EU.) The states, known collectively as the Eurozone, are Austria, Belgium, Cyprus, Finland, France, Germany, Greece, Ireland, Italy, Luxembourg, Malta, the Netherlands, Portugal, Slovakia, Slovenia, and Spain. The currency is also used in a further five European countries, with and without formal agreements and is consequently used daily by some 327 million Europeans.

a. Import and Export Price Indices
b. IRS Code 3401
c. Equity capital market
d. Euro

19. A _____ is an object whose consumption increases the utility of the consumer, for which the quantity demanded exceeds the quantity supplied at zero price. _____s are usually modeled as having diminishing marginal utility. The first individual purchase has high utility; the second has less.

a. Composite good
b. Merit good
c. Pie method
d. Good

20. In economics, economic output is divided into physical goods and intangible services. Consumption of _____ is assumed to produce utility. It is often used when referring to a _____ Tax.

a. Private good
b. Goods and services
c. Manufactured goods
d. Composite good

21. _____ is a school of macroeconomic thought that argues that economic growth can be most effectively created using incentives for people to produce (supply) goods and services, such as adjusting income tax and capital gains tax rates, and by allowing greater flexibility by reducing regulation. Consumers will then benefit from a greater supply of goods and services at lower prices.

The term _____ was coined by journalist Jude Wanniski in 1975, and popularized the ideas of economists Robert Mundell and Arthur Laffer.

a. Clap note
b. Commodity trading advisors
c. Fiscal stimulus plans
d. Supply-side economics

22. In economics, the _____ measures the payments that flow between any individual country and all other countries. It is used to summarize all international economic transactions for that country during a specific time period, usually a year. The _____ is determined by the country's exports and imports of goods, services, and financial capital, as well as financial transfers.

a. Gross domestic product per barrel
b. Balance of payments
c. Gross world product
d. Skyscraper Index

23. A _____ is the transfer of wealth from one party (such as a person or company) to another. A _____ is usually made in exchange for the provision of goods, services or both, or to fulfill a legal obligation.

The simplest and oldest form of _____ is barter, the exchange of one good or service for another.

Chapter 19. Fiscal Stabilization Policy

a. Going concern
b. Soft count
c. Social gravity
d. Payment

24. To _____ is to impose a financial charge or other levy upon a taxpayer by a state or the functional equivalent of a state.

_____es are also imposed by many subnational entities. _____es consist of direct _____ or indirect _____, and may be paid in money or as its labour equivalent (often but not always unpaid.)

a. 130-30 fund
b. 1921 recession
c. 100-year flood
d. Tax

25. The _____ or gross domestic income (GDI), a basic measure of an economy's economic performance, is the market value of all final goods and services produced within the borders of a nation in a year. _____ can be defined in three ways, all of which are conceptually identical. First, it is equal to the total expenditures for all final goods and services produced within the country in a stipulated period of time (usually a 365-day year.)

a. Countercyclical
b. Monopolistic competition
c. Gross domestic product
d. Market structure

26. _____, 1st Baron Keynes was a renowned economist from Britain whose many ideas on economic and political theories as well as on many governments' monetary policies influenced America. He advocated a government that played an active role in the lives of people regarding business, economy, etc. In this role, the government would use fiscal measures to reduce the consequences of recessions, economic depressions and booms.

a. Adam Smith
b. Adolf Hitler
c. Adolph Fischer
d. John Maynard Keynes

27. _____ is the view within monetary economics that variation in the money supply has major influences on national output in the short run and the price level over longer periods and that objectives of monetary policy are best met by targeting the growth rate of the money supply.

_____ today is mainly associated with the work of Milton Friedman, who was among the generation of economists to accept Keynesian economics and then criticize it on his own terms. Friedman and Anna Schwartz wrote an influential book, Monetary History of the United States 1867-1960, and argued that 'inflation is always and everywhere a monetary phenomenon.' Friedman advocated a central bank policy aimed at keeping the supply and demand for money at equilibrium, as measured by growth in productivity and demand.

a. Historical school of economics
b. Marginal revenue productivity theory of wages
c. Complexity economics
d. Monetarism

28. _____ is the process by which the government, central bank (ii) availability of money, and (iii) cost of money or rate of interest, in order to attain a set of objectives oriented towards the growth and stability of the economy. Monetary theory provides insight into how to craft optimal _____.

_____ is referred to as either being an expansionary policy where an expansionary policy increases the total supply of money in the economy, and a contractionary policy decreases the total money supply.

a. 130-30 fund
b. 100-year flood
c. 1921 recession
d. Monetary policy

29. _____ is a school of contemporary macroeconomics that strives to provide microeconomic foundations for Keynesian economics. It developed partly as a response to criticisms of Keynesian macroeconomics by adherents of New Classical macroeconomics.
   a. Keynesian theory
   b. Law of demand
   c. New Keynesian economics
   d. Mainstream economics

30. _____ is widely regarded as the first modern school of economic thought. It is the idea that free markets can regulate themselves. Its major developers include Adam Smith, David Ricardo, Thomas Malthus and John Stuart Mill. Sometimes the definition of _____ is expanded to include William Petty, Johann Heinrich von Thünen.
   a. Marginalism
   b. Tendency of the rate of profit to fall
   c. Schools of economic thought
   d. Classical economics

31. _____s is the social science that studies the production, distribution, and consumption of goods and services. The term _____s comes from the Ancient Greek οἰκονομῐ́α from οἶκος (oikos, 'house') + νόμος (nomos, 'custom' or 'law'), hence 'rules of the house(hold)'. Current _____ models developed out of the broader field of political economy in the late 19th century, owing to a desire to use an empirical approach more akin to the physical sciences.
   a. Opportunity cost
   b. Inflation
   c. Economic
   d. Energy economics

32. An _____, in economics, is the amount by which the real Gross domestic product exceeds potential GDP. The real GDP is also known as GDP 'adjusted for inflation', 'constant prices' GDP or 'constant dollar' GDP, because it measures the aggregate output in a country's income accounts in a given year, expressed in base-year prices. On the other hand, the potential GDP is the quantity of real GDP when a country's economy is at full-employment.
   a. Inflationary gap
   b. ACCRA Cost of Living Index
   c. ACEA agreement
   d. AD-IA Model

33. An _____ is a tax levied on the financial income of people, corporations, or other legal entities. Various _____ systems exist, with varying degrees of tax incidence. Income taxation can be progressive, proportional, or regressive.
   a. AD-IA Model
   b. ACEA agreement
   c. ACCRA Cost of Living Index
   d. Income tax

34. _____ is the government's approach to taxation, both from the practical and normative side of the question.

Policymakers debate the nature of the tax structure they plan to implement (i.e., how progressive or regressive) and how they might affect individuals and businesses (i.e., tax incidence.)

The reason for such focus is economic efficiency as advisor to the Stuart King of England Richard Petty had noted that the government does not want to kill the goose that lays the golden egg.

   a. Partnership taxation
   b. Tax policy
   c. Commuter tax
   d. Tax-allocation district

35. The _____ was a worldwide economic downturn starting in most places in 1929 and ending at different times in the 1930s or early 1940s for different countries. It was the largest and most important economic depression in the 20th century, and is used in the 21st century as an example of how far the world's economy can fall. The _____ originated in the United States; historians most often use as a starting date the stock market crash on October 29, 1929, known as Black Tuesday.
   a. Wall Street Crash of 1929
   b. British Empire Economic Conference
   c. Great Depression
   d. Jarrow March

36. _____ was the 31st President of the United States (1929-1933.) Besides his political career, Hoover was a professional mining engineer and author. As the United States Secretary of Commerce in the 1920s under Presidents Warren Harding and Calvin Coolidge, he promoted government intervention under the rubric 'economic modernization'.
   a. Adam Smith
   b. Adolf Hitler
   c. Adolph Fischer
   d. Herbert Hoover

158 Chapter 19. Fiscal Stabilization Policy

37. A _____ is:

- Rewrite _____, in generative grammar and computer science
- Standardization, a formal and widely-accepted statement, fact, definition, or qualification
- Operation, a determinate _____ for performing a mathematical operation and obtaining a certain result (Mathematics, Logic)
    - Unary operation
    - Binary operation
- _____ of inference, a function from sets of formulae to formulae (Mathematics, Logic)
- _____ of thumb, principle with broad application that is not intended to be strictly accurate or reliable for every situation. Also often simply referred to as a _____
- Moral, an atomic element of a moral code for guiding choices in human behavior
- Heuristic, a quantized '_____' which shows a tendency or probability for successful function
- A regulation, as in sports
- A Production _____, as in computer science
- Procedural law, a _____ set governing the application of laws to cases
    - A law, which may informally be called a '_____'
    - A court ruling, a decision by a court
- In the U.S. Government, a regulation mandated by Congress, but written or expanded upon by the Executive Branch.
- Norm (sociology), an informal but widely accepted _____, concept, truth, definition, or qualification (social norms, legal norms, coding norms)
- Norm (philosophy), a kind of sentence or a reason to act, feel or believe
- 'Rulership' is the concept of governance by a government:
    - Military _____, governance by a military body
    - Monastic _____, a collection of precepts that guides the life of monks or nuns in a religious order where the superior holds the place of Christ
- Slide _____

- '_____,' a song by Ayumi Hamasaki
- '_____,' a song by rapper Nas
- '_____s,' an album by the band The Whitest Boy Alive
- _____s: Pyaar Ka Superhit Formula, a 2003 Bollywood film
- ruler, an instrument for measuring lengths
- _____, a component of an astrolabe, circumferator or similar instrument
- The _____s, a bestselling self-help book
- _____ Project (Run Up-to-date Linux Everywhere), a project that aims to use up-to-date Linux software on old PCs
- _____ engine, a software system that helps managing business _____s
- Ja _____, a hip hop artist
    - R.U.L.E., a 2005 greatest hits album by rapper Ja _____
- '_____s,' a KMFDM song

a. Procter ' Gamble
b. Technocracy
c. Rule
d. Demand

38. _____ forms part of the public sector deficit. _____ differs from cyclical deficit in that it exists even when the economy is at its potential.

_____ issues can only be addressed by explicit and direct government policies: reducing spending (including entitlements), increasing the tax base, and/or increasing tax rates.

a. Sovereign credit
c. Structural deficit
b. Minimum Municipal Obligation
d. Tax increment financing

Chapter 20. Policies to Promote Economic Growth

1. In economics, _____ is the total demand for final goods and services in the economy (Y) at a given time and price level. It is the amount of goods and services in the economy that will be purchased at all possible price levels. This is the demand for the gross domestic product of a country when inventory levels are static.
   a. Aggregate supply
   b. Aggregate expenditure
   c. Aggregation problem
   d. Aggregate demand

2. In economics, _____ is the total supply of goods and services produced by a national economy during a specific time period. It is the total amount of goods and services in the economy available at all possible price levels.
   a. Aggregate demand
   b. Aggregation problem
   c. Aggregate expenditure
   d. Aggregate supply

3. _____ or government expenditure is classified by economists into three main types. Government purchases of goods and services for current use are classed as government consumption. Government purchases of goods and services intended to create future benefits, such as infrastructure investment or research spending, are classed as government investment.
   a. 100-year flood
   b. Government spending
   c. 1921 recession
   d. 130-30 fund

4. _____, 1st Baron Keynes was a renowned economist from Britain whose many ideas on economic and political theories as well as on many governments' monetary policies influenced America. He advocated a government that played an active role in the lives of people regarding business, economy, etc. In this role, the government would use fiscal measures to reduce the consequences of recessions, economic depressions and booms.
   a. Adam Smith
   b. Adolph Fischer
   c. Adolf Hitler
   d. John Maynard Keynes

5. _____ and Keynesian Theory) is a macroeconomic theory based on the ideas of 20th-century British economist John Maynard Keynes. _____ argues that private sector decisions sometimes lead to inefficient macroeconomic outcomes and therefore advocates active policy responses by the public sector, including monetary policy actions by the central bank and fiscal policy actions by the government to stabilize output over the business cycle.

   The theories forming the basis of _____ were first presented in The General Theory of Employment, Interest and Money, published in 1936.

   a. Keynesian economics
   b. Rational choice theory
   c. Market failure
   d. Deflation

6. _____ is the view within monetary economics that variation in the money supply has major influences on national output in the short run and the price level over longer periods and that objectives of monetary policy are best met by targeting the growth rate of the money supply.

   _____ today is mainly associated with the work of Milton Friedman, who was among the generation of economists to accept Keynesian economics and then criticize it on his own terms. Friedman and Anna Schwartz wrote an influential book, Monetary History of the United States 1867-1960, and argued that 'inflation is always and everywhere a monetary phenomenon.' Friedman advocated a central bank policy aimed at keeping the supply and demand for money at equilibrium, as measured by growth in productivity and demand.

Chapter 20. Policies to Promote Economic Growth

a. Complexity economics
b. Historical school of economics
c. Monetarism
d. Marginal revenue productivity theory of wages

7. _____ is the process by which the government, central bank (ii) availability of money, and (iii) cost of money or rate of interest, in order to attain a set of objectives oriented towards the growth and stability of the economy. Monetary theory provides insight into how to craft optimal _____.

_____ is referred to as either being an expansionary policy where an expansionary policy increases the total supply of money in the economy, and a contractionary policy decreases the total money supply.

a. 130-30 fund
b. Monetary policy
c. 1921 recession
d. 100-year flood

8. _____ is a school of contemporary macroeconomics that strives to provide microeconomic foundations for Keynesian economics. It developed partly as a response to criticisms of Keynesian macroeconomics by adherents of New Classical macroeconomics.

a. Law of demand
b. New Keynesian economics
c. Mainstream economics
d. Keynesian theory

9. _____ Theory (or _____ Theory) is a class of macroeconomic models in which business cycle fluctuations to a large extent can be accounted for by real (in contrast to nominal) shocks. (The four primary economic fluctuations are secular (trend), business cycle, seasonal, and random.) Unlike other leading theories of the business cycle, it sees recessions and periods of economic growth as the efficient response to exogenous changes in the real economic environment.

a. Monetary policy reaction function
b. Balanced-growth equilibrium
c. SIMIC
d. Real business cycle

10. The term _____ refers to economy-wide fluctuations in production or economic activity over several months or years. These fluctuations occur around a long-term growth trend, and typically involve shifts over time between periods of relatively rapid economic growth (expansion or boom), and periods of relative stagnation or decline (contraction or recession.)

These fluctuations are often measured using the growth rate of real gross domestic product.

a. Tobit model
b. Consumer theory
c. Nominal value
d. Business cycle

11. _____ is widely regarded as the first modern school of economic thought. It is the idea that free markets can regulate themselves.Its major developers include Adam Smith, David Ricardo, Thomas Malthus and John Stuart Mill. Sometimes the definition of _____ is expanded to include William Petty, Johann Heinrich von Thünen.

a. Schools of economic thought
b. Tendency of the rate of profit to fall
c. Marginalism
d. Classical economics

Chapter 20. Policies to Promote Economic Growth

12. Economics:

    - _____, the desire to own something and the ability to pay for it
    - _____ curve, a graphic representation of a _____ schedule
    - _____ deposit, the money in checking accounts
    - _____ pull theory, the theory that inflation occurs when _____ for goods and services exceeds existing supplies
    - _____ schedule, a table that lists the quantity of a good a person will buy it each different price
    - _____ side economics, the school of economics at believes government spending and tax cuts open economy by raising _____

    a. McKesson ' Robbins scandal
    b. Production
    c. Demand
    d. Variability

13. _____s is the social science that studies the production, distribution, and consumption of goods and services. The term _____s comes from the Ancient Greek oá¼°κονομῖα from oá¼¶κος (oikos, 'house') + vĺŒμος (nomos, 'custom' or 'law'), hence 'rules of the house(hold)'. Current _____ models developed out of the broader field of political economy in the late 19th century, owing to a desire to use an empirical approach more akin to the physical sciences.

    a. Economic
    b. Opportunity cost
    c. Energy economics
    d. Inflation

14. _____ is the increase in the amount of the goods and services produced by an economy over time. It is conventionally measured as the percent rate of increase in real gross domestic product, or real GDP. Growth is usually calculated in real terms, i.e. inflation-adjusted terms, in order to net out the effect of inflation on the price of the goods and services produced.

    a. Economic growth
    b. AD-IA Model
    c. ACCRA Cost of Living Index
    d. ACEA agreement

15. _____ is a branch of economics that deals with the performance, structure, and behavior of a national or regional economy as a whole. Along with microeconomics, _____ is one of the two most general fields in economics. It is the study of the behavior and decision-making of entire economies.

    a. Macroeconomics
    b. New Trade Theory
    c. Tobit model
    d. Nominal value

16. In microeconomics, _____ is quite simply the conversion of inputs into outputs. It is an economic process that uses resources to create a good or service that is suitable for exchange. This can include manufacturing, storing, shipping, and packaging.

    a. Red Guards
    b. Solved
    c. MET
    d. Production

17. In economics, a _____ is a function that specifies the output of a firm, an industry, or an entire economy for all combinations of inputs. A meta-_____ compares the practice of the existing entities converting inputs X into output y to determine the most efficient practice _____ of the existing entities, whether the most efficient feasible practice production or the most efficient actual practice production. In either case, the maximum output of a technologically-determined production process is a mathematical function of input factors of production.

Chapter 20. Policies to Promote Economic Growth

a. Post-Fordism
b. Constant elasticity of substitution
c. Short-run
d. Production function

18. _____ is a common concept in economics, and gives rise to derived concepts such as consumer debt. Generally _____ is defined by opposition to production. But the precise definition can vary because different schools of economists define production quite differently.
   a. Consumption
   b. Federal Reserve Bank Notes
   c. Foreclosure data providers
   d. Cash or share options

19. _____ is an economic model based on price, utility and quantity in a market. It predicts that in a competitive market, price will function to equalize the quantity demanded by consumers, and the quantity supplied by producers, resulting in an economic equilibrium of price and quantity. The model incorporates other factors changing equilibrium as a shift of demand and/or supply.
   a. Joint demand
   b. Deferred gratification
   c. Rational addiction
   d. Supply and demand

20. _____ is a school of macroeconomic thought that argues that economic growth can be most effectively created using incentives for people to produce (supply) goods and services, such as adjusting income tax and capital gains tax rates, and by allowing greater flexibility by reducing regulation. Consumers will then benefit from a greater supply of goods and services at lower prices.

   The term _____ was coined by journalist Jude Wanniski in 1975, and popularized the ideas of economists Robert Mundell and Arthur Laffer.
   a. Clap note
   b. Fiscal stimulus plans
   c. Commodity trading advisors
   d. Supply-side economics

21. In labor economics, the _____ hypothesis argues that wages, at least in some markets, are determined by more than simply supply and demand. Specifically, it points to the incentive for managers to pay their employees more than the market-clearing wage in order to increase their productivity or efficiency. This increased labor productivity pays for the relatively higher wages.
   a. Efficiency wage
   b. Earnings calls
   c. Exogenous growth model
   d. Inflatable rats

22. The _____ or gross domestic income (GDI), a basic measure of an economy's economic performance, is the market value of all final goods and services produced within the borders of a nation in a year. _____ can be defined in three ways, all of which are conceptually identical. First, it is equal to the total expenditures for all final goods and services produced within the country in a stipulated period of time (usually a 365-day year.)
   a. Gross domestic product
   b. Countercyclical
   c. Monopolistic competition
   d. Market structure

23. The supply of labor is the number of total hours that workers wish to work at a given real wage rate.

   _____ curves are derived from the 'labor-leisure' trade-off. More hours worked earn higher incomes but necessitate a cut in the amount of leisure that workers enjoy.

a. Creative capitalism
b. Late capitalism
c. Labor supply
d. Human trafficking

24. _____ in economics refers to metrics and measures of output from production processes, per unit of input. Labor _____, for example, is typically measured as a ratio of output per labor-hour, an input. _____ may be conceived of as a metrics of the technical or engineering efficiency of production.
   a. Production-possibility frontier
   b. Productivity
   c. Piece work
   d. Fordism

25. In economics, the _____ measures the payments that flow between any individual country and all other countries. It is used to summarize all international economic transactions for that country during a specific time period, usually a year. The _____ is determined by the country's exports and imports of goods, services, and financial capital, as well as financial transfers.
   a. Skyscraper Index
   b. Gross world product
   c. Balance of payments
   d. Gross domestic product per barrel

26. A _____ is the transfer of wealth from one party (such as a person or company) to another. A _____ is usually made in exchange for the provision of goods, services or both, or to fulfill a legal obligation.

The simplest and oldest form of _____ is barter, the exchange of one good or service for another.

   a. Soft count
   b. Payment
   c. Social gravity
   d. Going concern

27. In economics, _____ is the total amount of money available in an economy at a particular point in time. There are several ways to define 'money', but standard measures usually include currency in circulation and demand deposits.

_____ data are recorded and published, usually by the government or the central bank of the country.

   a. Veil of money
   b. Money supply
   c. Velocity of money
   d. Neutrality of money

28. In finance, a _____ is a debt security, in which the authorized issuer owes the holders a debt and, depending on the terms of the _____, is obliged to pay interest (the coupon) and/or to repay the principal at a later date, termed maturity. A _____ is a formal contract to repay borrowed money with interest at fixed intervals.

Thus a _____ is like a loan: the issuer is the borrower (debtor), the holder is the lender (creditor), and the coupon is the interest.

   a. Prize Bond
   b. Bond
   c. Zero-coupon
   d. Callable

29. _____ is a fee paid on borrowed assets. It is the price paid for the use of borrowed money , or, money earned by deposited funds . Assets that are sometimes lent with _____ include money, shares, consumer goods through hire purchase, major assets such as aircraft, and even entire factories in finance lease arrangements.

a. Interest
b. Internal debt
c. Asset protection
d. Insolvency

30. An _____ is a tax levied on the financial income of people, corporations, or other legal entities. Various _____ systems exist, with varying degrees of tax incidence. Income taxation can be progressive, proportional, or regressive.

a. ACCRA Cost of Living Index
b. AD-IA Model
c. ACEA agreement
d. Income tax

31. In economics, the _____ is a historical inverse relation between the rate of unemployment and the rate of inflation in an economy. Stated simply, the lower the unemployment in an economy, the higher the rate of increase in nominal wages in the economy. Rate of Change of Wages against Unemployment, United Kingdom 1913-1948 from Phillips (1958)

William Phillips, a New Zealand born economist, wrote a paper in 1958 titled The Relationship between Unemployment and the Rate of Change of Money Wages in the United Kingdom 1861-1957, which was published in the quarterly journal Economica.

a. Demand curve
b. Lorenz curve
c. Phillips curve
d. Cost curve

32. To _____ is to impose a financial charge or other levy upon a taxpayer by a state or the functional equivalent of a state.

_____es are also imposed by many subnational entities. _____es consist of direct _____ or indirect _____, and may be paid in money or as its labour equivalent (often but not always unpaid.)

a. 130-30 fund
b. 100-year flood
c. 1921 recession
d. Tax

33. A _____ is a reduction in taxes. Economic stimulus via _____s, along with interest rate intervention and deficit spending, are one of the central tenets of Keynesian economics.

The immediate effects of a _____ are, generally, a decrease in the real income of the government and an increase in the real income of those whose tax rate has been lowered.

a. Direct taxes
b. Popiwek
c. Withholding tax
d. Tax cut

34. The term _____s refers to wages that have been adjusted for inflation. This term is used in contrast to nominal wages or unadjusted wages.

The use of adjusted figures is in undertaking some form of economic analysis.

a. Federal Wage System
b. Profit sharing
c. Living wage
d. Real wage

35. In economics, _____ is a rise in the general level of prices of goods and services in an economy over a period of time. When the general price level rises, each unit of currency buys fewer goods and services; consequently, _____ is also a decline in the real value of money--a loss of purchasing power in the medium of exchange which is also the monetary unit of account in the economy. A chief measure of general price-level _____ is the general _____ rate, which is the percentage change in a general price index (normally the Consumer Price Index) over time.
   a. Energy economics
   b. Economic
   c. Inflation
   d. Opportunity cost

36. _____ is a class of macroeconomic models in which business cycle fluctuations to a large extent can be accounted for by real (in contrast to nominal) shocks. (The four primary economic fluctuations are secular (trend), business cycle, seasonal, and random.) Unlike other leading theories of the business cycle, it sees recessions and periods of economic growth as the efficient response to exogenous changes in the real economic environment.
   a. Consumer spending
   b. Solow residual
   c. War economy
   d. Real business cycle theory

37. In economics, the _____ is used to illustrate the idea that increases in the rate of taxation do not necessarily increase tax revenue. (For instance, whereas a 0% income tax rate will generate no revenue, neither will a 100% rate, as citizens will have no incentive to make money.) Increasing taxes beyond the peak of the curve point will decrease tax revenue.
   a. 1921 recession
   b. 100-year flood
   c. 130-30 fund
   d. Laffer curve

38. To tax is to impose a financial charge or other levy upon a taxpayer by a state or the functional equivalent of a state. _____ are also imposed by many subnational entities. _____ consist of direct tax or indirect tax, and may be paid in money or as its labour equivalent (often but not always unpaid.)

   a. 1921 recession
   b. Taxes
   c. 100-year flood
   d. 130-30 fund

39. From a Keynesian point of view, a _____ in the public sector is achieved when the government equates the revenues with expenditure over the business cycles. In other words, a government's budget is balanced if its income is equal to its expenditure. It is a budget in which revenues are equal to spending.
   a. Budget crisis
   b. Budget theory
   c. Balanced budget
   d. Budget support

40. In a company, _____ is the sum of all financial records of salaries, wages, bonuses and deductions.

A paycheck, is traditionally a paper document issued by an employer to pay an employee for services rendered. While most commonly used in the United States, recently the physical paycheck has been increasingly replaced by electronic direct deposit to bank accounts.

   a. Payroll
   b. Total Expense Ratio
   c. 100-year flood
   d. Tax expense

Chapter 20. Policies to Promote Economic Growth

41. The _____ is the current method of accelerated asset depreciation required by the United States income tax code. Under _____, all assets are divided into classes which dictate the number of years over which an asset's cost will be recovered.

Prior to the Accelerated Cost Recovery System (ACRS), most capital purchases were depreciated using a straight line technique, that allowed for the depreciation of the asset over its useful life.

a. 130-30 fund
c. 100-year flood
b. 1921 recession
d. Modified Accelerated Cost Recovery System

42. _____ refers to the economic policies promoted by United States President Ronald Reagan during the 1980s. The four pillars of Reagan's economic policy were to:

1. reduce the growth of government spending,
2. reduce income and capital gains marginal tax rates,
3. reduce government regulation of the economy,
4. control the money supply to reduce inflation.

In attempting to cut back on domestic spending while lowering taxes, Reagan's approach was a departure from his immediate predecessors.

Reagan became president during a period of high inflation and unemployment (commonly referred to as stagflation), which had largely abated by the time he left office eight years later.

Prior to the Reagan Administration was a roughly ten year period of economic stagnation and inflation, known as stagflation.

a. Business sector
c. Happiness economics
b. Social savings
d. Reaganomics

43. _____ is the process of changing the way taxes are collected or managed by the government.

_____ers have different goals. Some seek to reduce the level of taxation of all people by the government.

a. Special-purpose local-option sales tax
c. Tax Reform
b. Tax break
d. Nil-rate band

44. The term _____ refers to government debt, expenditures and revenues, or to finance (particularly financial revenue) in general.

- _____ deficit is the budget deficit of federal or local government
- _____ policy is the discretionary spending of governments. Contrasts with monetary policy.
- _____ year and _____ quarter are reporting periods for firms and other agencies.

a. Fiscal
b. Drawdown
c. Procter ' Gamble
d. Bucket shop

45. In economics, _____ is the use of government spending and revenue collection to influence the economy.

_____ can be contrasted with the other main type of economic policy, monetary policy, which attempts to stabilize the economy by controlling interest rates and the supply of money. The two main instruments of _____ are government spending and taxation.

a. 100-year flood
b. Fiscalism
c. Sustainable investment rule
d. Fiscal policy

Chapter 21. Consumption and Investment

1. _____ or government expenditure is classified by economists into three main types. Government purchases of goods and services for current use are classed as government consumption. Government purchases of goods and services intended to create future benefits, such as infrastructure investment or research spending, are classed as government investment.
   - a. 100-year flood
   - b. Government spending
   - c. 130-30 fund
   - d. 1921 recession

2. The _____ is 'the basic residential unit in which economic production, consumption, inheritance, child rearing, and shelter are organized and carried out'; [the _____] 'may or may not be synonymous with family'.

   The _____ is the basic unit of analysis in many social, microeconomic and government models. The term refers to all individuals who live in the same dwelling.

   - a. Family economics
   - b. 130-30 fund
   - c. Household
   - d. 100-year flood

3. _____, 1st Baron Keynes was a renowned economist from Britain whose many ideas on economic and political theories as well as on many governments' monetary policies influenced America. He advocated a government that played an active role in the lives of people regarding business, economy, etc. In this role, the government would use fiscal measures to reduce the consequences of recessions, economic depressions and booms.
   - a. John Maynard Keynes
   - b. Adolph Fischer
   - c. Adolf Hitler
   - d. Adam Smith

4. _____ and Keynesian Theory) is a macroeconomic theory based on the ideas of 20th-century British economist John Maynard Keynes. _____ argues that private sector decisions sometimes lead to inefficient macroeconomic outcomes and therefore advocates active policy responses by the public sector, including monetary policy actions by the central bank and fiscal policy actions by the government to stabilize output over the business cycle.

   The theories forming the basis of _____ were first presented in The General Theory of Employment, Interest and Money, published in 1936.

   - a. Rational choice theory
   - b. Deflation
   - c. Market failure
   - d. Keynesian economics

5. _____ is the view within monetary economics that variation in the money supply has major influences on national output in the short run and the price level over longer periods and that objectives of monetary policy are best met by targeting the growth rate of the money supply.

   _____ today is mainly associated with the work of Milton Friedman, who was among the generation of economists to accept Keynesian economics and then criticize it on his own terms. Friedman and Anna Schwartz wrote an influential book, Monetary History of the United States 1867-1960, and argued that 'inflation is always and everywhere a monetary phenomenon.' Friedman advocated a central bank policy aimed at keeping the supply and demand for money at equilibrium, as measured by growth in productivity and demand.

   - a. Marginal revenue productivity theory of wages
   - b. Historical school of economics
   - c. Complexity economics
   - d. Monetarism

Chapter 21. Consumption and Investment

6. _____ is the process by which the government, central bank (ii) availability of money, and (iii) cost of money or rate of interest, in order to attain a set of objectives oriented towards the growth and stability of the economy. Monetary theory provides insight into how to craft optimal _____.

_____ is referred to as either being an expansionary policy where an expansionary policy increases the total supply of money in the economy, and a contractionary policy decreases the total money supply.

- a. 100-year flood
- b. 1921 recession
- c. 130-30 fund
- d. Monetary policy

7. _____ is a school of contemporary macroeconomics that strives to provide microeconomic foundations for Keynesian economics. It developed partly as a response to criticisms of Keynesian macroeconomics by adherents of New Classical macroeconomics.
- a. Keynesian theory
- b. Mainstream economics
- c. Law of demand
- d. New Keynesian economics

8. In economics, _____ is the total demand for final goods and services in the economy (Y) at a given time and price level. It is the amount of goods and services in the economy that will be purchased at all possible price levels. This is the demand for the gross domestic product of a country when inventory levels are static.
- a. Aggregation problem
- b. Aggregate expenditure
- c. Aggregate supply
- d. Aggregate demand

9. _____ is widely regarded as the first modern school of economic thought. It is the idea that free markets can regulate themselves.Its major developers include Adam Smith, David Ricardo, Thomas Malthus and John Stuart Mill. Sometimes the definition of _____ is expanded to include William Petty, Johann Heinrich von Thünen.
- a. Tendency of the rate of profit to fall
- b. Schools of economic thought
- c. Marginalism
- d. Classical economics

10. _____ is a common concept in economics, and gives rise to derived concepts such as consumer debt. Generally _____ is defined by opposition to production. But the precise definition can vary because different schools of economists define production quite differently.
- a. Foreclosure data providers
- b. Consumption
- c. Federal Reserve Bank Notes
- d. Cash or share options

11. In economics, the _____ is a single mathematical function used to express consumer spending. It was developed by John Maynard Keynes and detailed most famously in his book The General Theory of Employment, Interest, and Money. The function is used to calculate the amount of total consumption in an economy.
- a. Liquidity preference
- b. DAD-SAS model
- c. Procyclical
- d. Consumption function

Chapter 21. Consumption and Investment

12. Economics:

    - _____, the desire to own something and the ability to pay for it
    - _____ curve, a graphic representation of a _____ schedule
    - _____ deposit, the money in checking accounts
    - _____ pull theory, the theory that inflation occurs when _____ for goods and services exceeds existing supplies
    - _____ schedule, a table that lists the quantity of a good a person will buy it each different price
    - _____ side economics, the school of economics at believes government spending and tax cuts open economy by raising _____

    a. McKesson ' Robbins scandal
    c. Variability
    b. Production
    d. Demand

13. _____s is the social science that studies the production, distribution, and consumption of goods and services. The term _____s comes from the Ancient Greek oἰκονομία from oἶκος (oikos, 'house') + νόμος (nomos, 'custom' or 'law'), hence 'rules of the house(hold)'. Current _____ models developed out of the broader field of political economy in the late 19th century, owing to a desire to use an empirical approach more akin to the physical sciences.

    a. Energy economics
    c. Inflation
    b. Economic
    d. Opportunity cost

14. _____ is the percentage of income spent. To find the percentage of income spent, one needs to divide consumption by income, or $APC = \dfrac{C}{Y}$. In an economy in which each individual consumer saves lots of money, there is a tendency of people losing their jobs because demand for goods and services will be low.

    a. Equity ratio
    c. Average propensity to consume
    b. Inventory turnover
    d. Operating leverage

15. The _____ is an economics term that refers to the proportion of income which is saved, usually expressed for household savings as a percentage of total household disposable income. The ratio differs considerably over time and between countries. The savings ratio can be affected by: the proportion of older people, as they have less motivation and capability to save; the rate of inflation, as expectations of rising prices encourage can encourage people to spend now rather than later

    a. Unearned income
    c. Independent income
    b. Aggregate income
    d. Average propensity to save

16. In economic models, the _____ time frame assumes no fixed factors of production. Firms can enter or leave the marketplace, and the cost (and availability) of land, labor, raw materials, and capital goods can be assumed to vary. In contrast, in the short-run time frame, certain factors are assumed to be fixed, because there is not sufficient time for them to change.

    a. Productivity world
    c. Price/performance ratio
    b. Diseconomies of scale
    d. Long-run

17. A variety of measures of _____ and output are used in economics to estimate total economic activity in a country or region, including gross domestic product (GDP), gross national product (GNP), and net _____.

There are three main ways of calculating these numbers; the output approach, the income approach and the expenditure approach. In theory, the three must yield the same, because total expenditures on goods and services must equal the total income paid to the producers (Gnational income), and that must also equal the total value of the output of goods and services (GNP.)

a. GNI per capita
b. Volume index
c. Gross world product
d. National income

18. The _____ was a worldwide economic downturn starting in most places in 1929 and ending at different times in the 1930s or early 1940s for different countries. It was the largest and most important economic depression in the 20th century, and is used in the 21st century as an example of how far the world's economy can fall. The _____ originated in the United States; historians most often use as a starting date the stock market crash on October 29, 1929, known as Black Tuesday.

a. Jarrow March
b. Great Depression
c. Wall Street Crash of 1929
d. British Empire Economic Conference

19. The _____ is an economic concept analysing individual consumption patterns. It was developed by the economists Irving Fisher, Roy Harrod, Alberto Ando and Franco Modigliani.

Unlike the Keynesian consumption function, which assumes consumption is entirely based on current income, _____ assumes that individuals consume a constant percentage of the present value of their life income.

a. Guns versus butter model
b. Mundell-Fleming model
c. Big Push Model
d. Life cycle hypothesis

20. The _____ is a theory of consumption that was developed by the American economist Milton Friedman. In its simplest form, the hypothesis states that the choices made by consumers regarding their consumption patterns are determined not by current income but by their longer-term income expectations. The key conclusion of this theory is that transitory, short-term changes in income have little effect on consumer spending behavior.

a. Washington Consensus
b. Balanced-growth equilibrium
c. Natural rate of unemployment
d. Permanent income hypothesis

21. _____ is the point where a person stops employment completely. A person may also semi-retire and keep some sort of _____ job, out of choice rather than necessity. This usually happens upon reaching a determined age, when physical conditions don't allow the person to work any more (by illness or accident), or even for personal choice (usually in the presence of an adequate pension or personal savings.)

a. 100-year flood
b. Termination of employment
c. Retirement
d. Layoff

22. In economics, the term _____ of income or _____ refers to a simple economic model which describes the reciprocal circulation of income between producers and consumers. In the _____ model, the inter-dependent entities of producer and consumer are referred to as 'firms' and 'households' respectively and provide each other with factors in order to facilitate the flow of income. Firms provide consumers with goods and services in exchange for consumer expenditure and 'factors of production' from households.

a. 100-year flood
b. Circular flow
c. 1921 recession
d. 130-30 fund

23. _____ is a specific term used in companies' financial reporting from the company-whole point of view. Because that use excludes the effects of changing ownership interest, an economic measure of _____ is necessary for financial analysis from the shareholders' point of view

_____ is defined by the Financial Accounting Standards Board, or FASB, as e;the change in equity [net assets] of a business enterprise during a period from transactions and other events and circumstances from nonowner sources. It includes all changes in equity during a period except those resulting from investments by owners and distributions to owners.e;

_____ is the sum of net income and other items that must bypass the income statement because they have not been realized, including items like an unrealized holding gain or loss from available for sale securities and foreign currency translation gains or losses.

a. Comprehensive income
b. Real income
c. Windfall gain
d. Net national income

24. In economics, the concept of the _____ refers to the decision-making time frame of a firm in which at least one factor of production is fixed. Costs which are fixed in the _____ have no impact on a firms decisions. For example a firm can raise output by increasing the amount of labour through overtime.
a. Product Pipeline
b. Hicks-neutral technical change
c. Productivity model
d. Short-run

25. The term _____ refers to government debt, expenditures and revenues, or to finance (particularly financial revenue) in general.

- _____ deficit is the budget deficit of federal or local government
- _____ policy is the discretionary spending of governments. Contrasts with monetary policy.
- _____ year and _____ quarter are reporting periods for firms and other agencies.

a. Bucket shop
b. Fiscal
c. Drawdown
d. Procter ' Gamble

26. In economics, _____ is the use of government spending and revenue collection to influence the economy.

_____ can be contrasted with the other main type of economic policy, monetary policy, which attempts to stabilize the economy by controlling interest rates and the supply of money. The two main instruments of _____ are government spending and taxation.

a. Fiscal policy
b. Fiscalism
c. 100-year flood
d. Sustainable investment rule

27. Market _____ is a business, economics or investment term that refers to an asset's ability to be easily converted through an act of buying or selling without causing a significant movement in the price and with minimum loss of value. Money, or cash on hand, is the most liquid asset. An act of exchange of a less liquid asset with a more liquid asset is called liquidation.
   a. Liquidity
   b. 130-30 fund
   c. 1921 recession
   d. 100-year flood

28. The term _____ is used in macroeconomics to refer to a situation where a country's nominal interest rate has been lowered nearly to or equal to zero to avoid a recession, but the liquidity in the market created by these low interest rates does not stimulate the economy to full employment. In this situation, any further increase in the money supply will not stimulate the economy any further. This is because any further injection of liquidity will no longer lower the nominal interest rate, as the nominal interest rate cannot drop below zero.
   a. Liquidity trap
   b. Macroeconomic models
   c. Robertson lag
   d. Minimum wage

29. _____ was an American economist, statistician and public intellectual, and a recipient of the Nobel Memorial Prize in Economic Sciences. He is best known among scholars for his theoretical and empirical research, especially consumption analysis, monetary history and theory, and for his demonstration of the complexity of stabilization policy. A global public followed his restatement of a political philosophy that insisted on minimizing the role of government in favor of the private sector.
   a. Adolf Hitler
   b. Adam Smith
   c. Adolph Fischer
   d. Milton Friedman

Chapter 21. Consumption and Investment 175

30. A _____ is:

- Rewrite _____, in generative grammar and computer science
- Standardization, a formal and widely-accepted statement, fact, definition, or qualification
- Operation, a determinate _____ for performing a mathematical operation and obtaining a certain result (Mathematics, Logic)
    - Unary operation
    - Binary operation
- _____ of inference, a function from sets of formulae to formulae (Mathematics, Logic)
- _____ of thumb, principle with broad application that is not intended to be strictly accurate or reliable for every situation. Also often simply referred to as a _____
- Moral, an atomic element of a moral code for guiding choices in human behavior
- Heuristic, a quantized '_____' which shows a tendency or probability for successful function
- A regulation, as in sports
- A Production _____, as in computer science
- Procedural law, a _____ set governing the application of laws to cases
    - A law, which may informally be called a '_____'
    - A court ruling, a decision by a court
- In the U.S. Government, a regulation mandated by Congress, but written or expanded upon by the Executive Branch.
- Norm (sociology), an informal but widely accepted _____, concept, truth, definition, or qualification (social norms, legal norms, coding norms)
- Norm (philosophy), a kind of sentence or a reason to act, feel or believe
- 'Rulership' is the concept of governance by a government:
    - Military _____, governance by a military body
    - Monastic _____, a collection of precepts that guides the life of monks or nuns in a religious order where the superior holds the place of Christ
- Slide _____

- '_____,' a song by Ayumi Hamasaki
- '_____,' a song by rapper Nas
- '_____s,' an album by the band The Whitest Boy Alive
- _____s: Pyaar Ka Superhit Formula, a 2003 Bollywood film
- ruler, an instrument for measuring lengths
- _____, a component of an astrolabe, circumferator or similar instrument
- The _____s, a bestselling self-help book
- _____ Project (Run Up-to-date Linux Everywhere), a project that aims to use up-to-date Linux software on old PCs
- _____ engine, a software system that helps managing business _____s
- Ja _____, a hip hop artist
    - R.U.L.E., a 2005 greatest hits album by rapper Ja _____
- '_____s,' a KMFDM song

a. Demand
b. Technocracy
c. Procter ' Gamble
d. Rule

Chapter 21. Consumption and Investment

31. _____ is an assumption used in many contemporary macroeconomic models, and also in other areas of contemporary economics and game theory and in other applications of rational choice theory.

Since most macroeconomic models today study decisions over many periods, the expectations of workers, consumers, and firms about future economic conditions are an essential part of the model. How to model these expectations has long been controversial, and it is well known that the macroeconomic predictions of the model may differ depending on the assumptions made about expectations

    a. Potential output
    b. Minimum wage
    c. Balanced-growth equilibrium
    d. Rational expectations

32. The _____ or gross domestic income (GDI), a basic measure of an economy's economic performance, is the market value of all final goods and services produced within the borders of a nation in a year. _____ can be defined in three ways, all of which are conceptually identical. First, it is equal to the total expenditures for all final goods and services produced within the country in a stipulated period of time (usually a 365-day year.)

    a. Market structure
    b. Monopolistic competition
    c. Countercyclical
    d. Gross domestic product

33. An _____, in economics, is the amount by which the real Gross domestic product exceeds potential GDP. The real GDP is also known as GDP 'adjusted for inflation', 'constant prices' GDP or 'constant dollar' GDP, because it measures the aggregate output in a country's income accounts in a given year, expressed in base-year prices. On the other hand, the potential GDP is the quantity of real GDP when a country's economy is at full-employment.

    a. AD-IA Model
    b. Inflationary gap
    c. ACCRA Cost of Living Index
    d. ACEA agreement

34. _____ in economics refers to investment in fixed capital, i.e. tangible capital goods (real means of production or residential buildings), or to the replacement of depreciated capital goods.

Thus, _____ is investment in physical assets such as machinery, land, buildings, installations, vehicles, or technology. Normally, a company balance sheet will state both the amount of expenditure on fixed assets during the quarter or year, and the total value of the stock of fixed assets owned.

    a. Depreciation
    b. Historical cost
    c. Deferred financing costs
    d. Fixed investment

35. The _____ is an expected return that the provider of capital plans to earn on their investment.

Capital (money) used for funding a business should earn returns for the capital providers who risk their capital. For an investment to be worthwhile, the expected return on capital must be greater than the _____.

    a. Capital expenditure
    b. Capital intensive
    c. Modigliani-Miller theorem
    d. Cost of capital

Chapter 21. Consumption and Investment

36. In economics, _____ is inflation that is very high or 'out of control', a condition in which prices increase rapidly as a currency loses its value. Definitions used by the media vary from a cumulative inflation rate over three years approaching 100% to 'inflation exceeding 50% a month.' In informal usage the term is often applied to much lower rates. As a rule of thumb, normal inflation is reported per year, but _____ is often reported for much shorter intervals, often per month.
   a. Hyperinflation
   b. 1921 recession
   c. 100-year flood
   d. 130-30 fund

37. A _____ refers to any type debt instrument, such as a loan, bond, mortgage that does not have a fixed rate of interest over the life of the instrument. Such debt typically uses an index or other base rate for establishing the interest rate for each relevant period. One of the most common rates to use as the basis for applying interest rates is the London Inter-bank Offered Rate, or LIBOR
   a. Disposal tax effect
   b. Floating interest rate
   c. Moneylender
   d. Money market

38. To _____ is to impose a financial charge or other levy upon a taxpayer by a state or the functional equivalent of a state.

_____es are also imposed by many subnational entities. _____es consist of direct _____ or indirect _____, and may be paid in money or as its labour equivalent (often but not always unpaid.)

   a. Tax
   b. 130-30 fund
   c. 100-year flood
   d. 1921 recession

39. The term _____ describes two different concepts:

   - The first is a recognition of partial payment already made towards taxes due.
   - The second is a state benefit paid to workers through the tax system, which has the effect of increasing (rather than reducing) net income.

Within the Australian, Canadian, United Kingdom, and United States tax systems, a _____ is a recognition of partial payment already made towards taxes due. A similar concept exists (fr:Avoir fiscal) in the French tax system. This situation arises, for example, when standard rate tax has been deducted at source , but the tax-payer is subject to further taxation at a higher rate. It also applies in dividend imputation systems.

   a. 100-year flood
   b. 130-30 fund
   c. 1921 recession
   d. Tax credit

Chapter 22. Money Demand

1. _____ and Keynesian Theory) is a macroeconomic theory based on the ideas of 20th-century British economist John Maynard Keynes. _____ argues that private sector decisions sometimes lead to inefficient macroeconomic outcomes and therefore advocates active policy responses by the public sector, including monetary policy actions by the central bank and fiscal policy actions by the government to stabilize output over the business cycle.

The theories forming the basis of _____ were first presented in The General Theory of Employment, Interest and Money, published in 1936.

   a. Deflation
   c. Market failure
   b. Rational choice theory
   d. Keynesian economics

2. To act as a _____, a commodity, a form of money stored, and retrieved - and be predictably useful when it is so retrieved.

This is distinct from the standard of deferred payment function which requires acceptability to parties one owes a debt to and a minimum of opportunity to cheat others.

   a. Fiat money
   c. World currency
   b. Petrodollar
   d. Store of value

3. Economics:

   - _____, the desire to own something and the ability to pay for it
   - _____ curve, a graphic representation of a _____ schedule
   - _____ deposit, the money in checking accounts
   - _____ pull theory, the theory that inflation occurs when _____ for goods and services exceeds existing supplies
   - _____ schedule, a table that lists the quantity of a good a person will buy it each different price
   - _____ side economics, the school of economics at believes government spending and tax cuts open economy by raising _____

   a. Production
   c. Demand
   b. McKesson ' Robbins scandal
   d. Variability

4. _____ is the a method of technical and economic research of the systems for purpose to optimize a parity between system's consumer functions or properties and expenses to achieve those functions or properties.

This methodology for continuous perfection of production, industrial technologies, organizational structures was developed by Juryj Sobolev in 1948 at the 'Perm telephone factory'

   - 1948 Juryj Sobolev - the first success in application of a method analysis at the 'Perm telephone factory'.
   - 1949 - the first application for the invention as result of use of the new method.

Chapter 22. Money Demand

Today in economically developed countries practically each enterprise or the company use methodology of the kind of functional-cost analysis as a practice of the quality management, most full satisfying to principles of standards of series ISO 9000.

- Interest of consumer not in products itself, but the advantage which it will receive from its usage.
- The consumer aspires to reduce his expenses
- Functions needed by consumer can be executed in the various ways, and, hence, with various efficiency and expenses. Among possible alternatives of realization of functions exist such in which the parity of quality and the price is the optimal for the consumer.

The goal of _____ is achievement of the highest consumer satisfaction of production at simultaneous decrease in all kinds of industrial expenses Classical _____ has three English synonyms - Value Engineering, Value Management, Value Analysis.

   a. Function cost analysis   b. Willingness to pay
   c. Staple financing   d. Monopoly wage

5. _____, 1st Baron Keynes was a renowned economist from Britain whose many ideas on economic and political theories as well as on many governments' monetary policies influenced America. He advocated a government that played an active role in the lives of people regarding business, economy, etc. In this role, the government would use fiscal measures to reduce the consequences of recessions, economic depressions and booms.

   a. Adolf Hitler   b. Adam Smith
   c. Adolph Fischer   d. John Maynard Keynes

6. _____ is the demand for financial assets, such as securities, money or foreign currency that is not dictated by real transactions such as trade, or financing.

The need for cash to take advantage of investment opportunities that may arise.

In economic theory, specifically Keynesian economics, _____ is one of the determinants of demand for money (and credit), the others being transactions demand and precautionary demand.

   a. Spending multiplier   b. Multiplier effect
   c. Keynesian Revolution   d. Speculative demand

7. _____ is the demand for financial assets, e.g., securities, money or foreign currency. It is used for purposes of business transactions and personal consumption.

The need to accommodate a firm's expected cash transactions.

   a. Spending multiplier   b. Multiplier effect
   c. Keynesian cross   d. Transactions demand

8. The _____ is the desired holding of money balances in the form of cash or bank deposits.

Chapter 22. Money Demand

Money is dominated as store of value by interest bearing assets. However, money is necessary to carry out transactions, or in other words, it provides liquidity.

a. Conglomerate merger
b. Borrowing base
c. Market neutral
d. Demand for money

9. _____ is the view within monetary economics that variation in the money supply has major influences on national output in the short run and the price level over longer periods and that objectives of monetary policy are best met by targeting the growth rate of the money supply.

_____ today is mainly associated with the work of Milton Friedman, who was among the generation of economists to accept Keynesian economics and then criticize it on his own terms. Friedman and Anna Schwartz wrote an influential book, Monetary History of the United States 1867-1960, and argued that 'inflation is always and everywhere a monetary phenomenon.' Friedman advocated a central bank policy aimed at keeping the supply and demand for money at equilibrium, as measured by growth in productivity and demand.

a. Historical school of economics
b. Monetarism
c. Complexity economics
d. Marginal revenue productivity theory of wages

10. The _____ is the average frequency with which a unit of money is spent in a specific period of time. Velocity associates the amount of economic activity associated with a given money supply. When the period is understood, the velocity may be present as a pure number; otherwise it should be given as a pure number over time.

a. Neutrality of money
b. Chartalism
c. Money supply
d. Velocity of money

11. _____ is widely regarded as the first modern school of economic thought. It is the idea that free markets can regulate themselves. Its major developers include Adam Smith, David Ricardo, Thomas Malthus and John Stuart Mill. Sometimes the definition of _____ is expanded to include William Petty, Johann Heinrich von Thünen.

a. Marginalism
b. Schools of economic thought
c. Tendency of the rate of profit to fall
d. Classical economics

12. _____s is the social science that studies the production, distribution, and consumption of goods and services. The term _____s comes from the Ancient Greek οἰκονομῖα from οἶκος (oikos, 'house') + νόμος (nomos, 'custom' or 'law'), hence 'rules of the house(hold)'. Current _____ models developed out of the broader field of political economy in the late 19th century, owing to a desire to use an empirical approach more akin to the physical sciences.

a. Inflation
b. Opportunity cost
c. Energy economics
d. Economic

13. In microeconomics, _____ is the extra revenue that an additional unit of product will bring. It is the additional income from selling one more unit of a good; sometimes equal to price. It can also be described as the change in total revenue/change in number of units sold.

a. Reservation price
b. Marginal revenue
c. Market demand schedule
d. Long term

14. In finance, a _____ is a debt security, in which the authorized issuer owes the holders a debt and, depending on the terms of the _____, is obliged to pay interest (the coupon) and/or to repay the principal at a later date, termed maturity. A _____ is a formal contract to repay borrowed money with interest at fixed intervals.

Thus a _____ is like a loan: the issuer is the borrower (debtor), the holder is the lender (creditor), and the coupon is the interest.

  a. Zero-coupon   b. Callable
  c. Prize Bond   d. Bond

15. The _____ is a financial market where participants buy and sell debt securities, usually in the form of bonds. As of 2006, the size of the international _____ is an estimated $44.9 trillion, of which the size of the outstanding U.S. _____ debt was $25.2 trillion.

Nearly all of the $923 billion average daily trading volume in the U.S. _____ takes place between broker-dealers and large institutions in a decentralized, over-the-counter market.

  a. 100-year flood   b. Pool factor
  c. 130-30 fund   d. Bond market

16. The _____ is the central banking system of the United States. Created in 1913 by the enactment of the Federal Reserve Act (signed by Woodrow Wilson), it is a quasi-public and quasi-private (government entity with private components) banking system that comprises (1) the presidentially appointed Board of Governors of the _____ in Washington, D.C.; (2) the Federal Open Market Committee; (3) twelve regional Federal Reserve Banks located in major cities throughout the nation acting as fiscal agents for the U.S. Treasury, each with its own nine-member board of directors; (4) numerous other private U.S. member banks, which subscribe to required amounts of non-transferable stock in their regional Federal Reserve Banks; and (5) various advisory councils. Since February 2006, Ben Bernanke has served as the Chairman of the Board of Governors of the _____.

  a. Term auction facility   b. Federal Reserve System Open Market Account
  c. Monetary Policy Report to the Congress   d. Federal Reserve System

17. _____ is a concept in economics, finance, and psychology related to the behaviour of consumers and investors under uncertainty. _____ is the reluctance of a person to accept a bargain with an uncertain payoff rather than another bargain with a more certain, but possibly lower, expected payoff. For example, a risk-averse investor might choose to put his or her money into a bank account with a low but guaranteed interest rate, rather than into a stock that is likely to have high returns, but also has a chance of becoming worthless.

  a. Compound annual growth rate   b. Risk theory
  c. Reinsurance   d. Risk aversion

18. In finance, the _____s between two currencies specifies how much one currency is worth in terms of the other. It is the value of a foreign natione;s currency in terms of the home natione;s currency. For example an _____ of 102 Japanese yen to the United States dollar means that JPY 102 is worth the same as USD 1.

  a. Interbank market   b. Exchange rate
  c. ACEA agreement   d. ACCRA Cost of Living Index

19. In business and accounting, _____ are everything of value that is owned by a person or company. It is a claim on the property your income of a borrower. The balance sheet of a firm records the monetary value of the _____ owned by the firm.

  a. Amortization schedule
  b. Assets
  c. ACEA agreement
  d. ACCRA Cost of Living Index

20. _____ is a fee paid on borrowed assets. It is the price paid for the use of borrowed money , or, money earned by deposited funds . Assets that are sometimes lent with _____ include money, shares, consumer goods through hire purchase, major assets such as aircraft, and even entire factories in finance lease arrangements.

  a. Insolvency
  b. Asset protection
  c. Interest
  d. Internal debt

21. An _____ is the price a borrower pays for the use of money they do not own, for instance a small company might borrow from a bank to kick start their business, and the return a lender receives for deferring the use of funds, by lending it to the borrower. _____s are normally expressed as a percentage rate over the period of one year.

_____s targets are also a vital tool of monetary policy and are used to control variables like investment, inflation, and unemployment.

  a. Arrow-Debreu model
  b. ACCRA Cost of Living Index
  c. Enterprise value
  d. Interest rate

22. _____ refers to the computer-based systems used to perform financial transactions electronically.

The term is used for a number of different concepts:

- Cardholder-initiated transactions, where a cardholder makes use of a payment card
- Direct deposit payroll payments for a business to its employees, possibly via a payroll services company
- Direct debit payments from customer to business, where the transaction is initiated by the business with customer permission
- Electronic bill payment in online banking, which may be delivered by _____ or paper check
- Transactions involving stored value of electronic money, possibly in a private currency
- Wire transfer via an international banking network (generally carries a higher fee)
- Electronic Benefit Transfer

Electronic funds transferPOS (short for _____ at Point of Sale) is an Australian and New Zealand electronic processing system for credit cards, debit cards and charge cards.

European banks and card companies also sometimes reference 'Electronic funds transferPOS' as the system used for processing card transactions through terminals on points of sale, though the system is not the trademarked Australian/New Zealand variant.

Credit cards

_____ may be initiated by a cardholder when a payment card such as a credit card or debit card is used.

Chapter 22. Money Demand

a. Electronic Payments Network
c. Issuing bank
b. Electronic funds transfer
d. Interbank network

23. In finance, the _____ is the global financial market for short-term borrowing and lending. It provides short-term liquidity funding for the global financial system. The _____ is where short-term obligations such as Treasury bills, commercial paper and bankers' acceptances are bought and sold.

a. T-Model
b. Deferred compensation
c. Consignment stock
d. Money market

24. A _____ is an account set up at a bank or other financial institution where the funds are automatically managed between a primary cash account and secondary investment accounts.

In banking, _____s are primarily used as a legal workaround to the prohibition on paying interest on business checking accounts. In this system, the funds are described as being 'swept overnight' into an investment vehicle of some kind.

a. Bank reserves
b. Sweep account
c. Sweep investment
d. Routing transit number

25. _____ are banks' holdings of deposits in accounts with their central bank (for instance the European Central Bank or the Federal Reserve, in the latter case including federal funds), plus currency that is physically held in bank vaults (vault cash.) The central banks of some nations set minimum reserve requirements. Even when no requirements are set, banks commonly wish to hold some reserves, called desired reserves, against unexpected events.

a. Bilateral netting
b. Structuring
c. Sweep account
d. Bank reserves

26. A _____ is a professionally managed type of collective investment scheme that pools money from many investors and invests it in stocks, bonds, short-term money market instruments, and/or other securities. The _____ will have a fund manager that trades the pooled money on a regular basis. As of early 2008, the worldwide value of all _____s totals more than $26 trillion.

a. Dark pools of liquidity
b. Self-invested personal pension
c. Participating policy
d. Mutual fund

Chapter 1

1. d	2. a	3. b	4. a	5. d	6. d	7. b	8. a	9. d	10. b
11. d	12. b	13. b	14. b	15. d	16. d	17. d	18. c	19. d	20. b
21. b	22. a	23. d	24. c	25. d	26. c	27. d	28. d	29. d	30. a
31. d	32. b	33. c	34. d	35. b	36. d	37. b	38. c	39. d	

Chapter 2

1. c	2. b	3. d	4. d	5. a	6. c	7. b	8. d	9. d	10. d
11. b	12. a	13. d	14. d	15. a	16. d	17. a	18. d	19. c	20. a
21. d	22. d	23. d	24. d	25. d	26. a	27. d	28. c	29. b	30. c
31. c	32. d	33. c	34. b	35. d	36. d	37. c	38. c	39. b	40. d
41. a	42. a	43. c	44. b	45. a	46. a	47. b	48. d	49. d	50. c
51. c	52. c	53. b	54. a	55. d	56. d	57. d	58. d	59. d	60. c
61. d	62. d	63. d	64. b						

Chapter 3

1. d	2. d	3. d	4. d	5. a	6. b	7. b	8. d	9. d	10. b
11. d	12. a	13. d	14. c	15. a	16. b	17. a	18. d	19. a	20. c
21. b	22. d	23. d	24. c	25. b	26. c	27. d	28. b	29. d	30. a
31. b	32. b	33. a	34. c	35. d	36. a	37. b	38. c	39. d	40. a
41. d	42. b	43. a	44. a	45. b	46. d	47. d	48. d	49. d	50. a

Chapter 4

1. a	2. d	3. a	4. d	5. d	6. d	7. d	8. d	9. d	10. a
11. d	12. d	13. c	14. d	15. d	16. a	17. b	18. d	19. b	20. a
21. a	22. d	23. d	24. c	25. d	26. c	27. d	28. d	29. d	30. d
31. b	32. b	33. d	34. d	35. d	36. d	37. a	38. c	39. c	40. c
41. a	42. d	43. c	44. b	45. b	46. d	47. a	48. d	49. a	50. d
51. c	52. d	53. d							

Chapter 5

1. d	2. c	3. b	4. d	5. d	6. a	7. d	8. d	9. b	10. d
11. b	12. d	13. d	14. d	15. b	16. c	17. d	18. d	19. d	20. d
21. a	22. d	23. d	24. c	25. d	26. a	27. a	28. a	29. d	30. d

Chapter 6

1. d	2. b	3. d	4. c	5. c	6. d	7. d	8. d	9. d	10. a
11. d	12. a	13. c	14. d	15. d	16. a	17. b	18. a	19. a	20. d
21. c	22. d	23. d	24. d	25. b	26. a	27. d	28. d	29. a	30. d
31. d	32. c	33. c	34. c	35. d	36. d	37. a	38. b	39. b	40. d
41. b	42. c	43. d	44. b	45. d	46. b	47. d	48. d	49. b	50. c
51. d									

ANSWER KEY

Chapter 7
1. d 2. c 3. a 4. b 5. b 6. b 7. d 8. d 9. c 10. d
11. a 12. b 13. c 14. d 15. b 16. d 17. b 18. d 19. d 20. c
21. c 22. d 23. c 24. a 25. a 26. c 27. d 28. d 29. a 30. c
31. d 32. d 33. b 34. c 35. c 36. d 37. b 38. a 39. d 40. b
41. a 42. b 43. c

Chapter 8
1. c 2. b 3. c 4. d 5. d 6. d 7. b 8. d 9. b 10. c
11. d 12. d 13. b 14. c 15. d 16. a 17. d 18. a 19. d 20. a
21. d 22. b 23. d 24. d 25. d 26. d 27. d 28. d

Chapter 9
1. d 2. b 3. d 4. d 5. a 6. b 7. d 8. d 9. b 10. d
11. c 12. d 13. d 14. b 15. d 16. d 17. a 18. a 19. b 20. d
21. d 22. d 23. a 24. c 25. d 26. d 27. d 28. d 29. b 30. b
31. d 32. a 33. a 34. d 35. d 36. b 37. d 38. b 39. c 40. a
41. a 42. a 43. d 44. c 45. a 46. a 47. d 48. a 49. d 50. d
51. d 52. a 53. d 54. a

Chapter 10
1. d 2. b 3. d 4. d 5. b 6. d 7. a 8. d 9. c 10. d
11. d 12. a 13. d 14. b 15. d 16. c 17. c 18. a 19. d 20. a
21. d 22. d 23. d 24. d 25. d 26. d 27. a 28. d 29. d 30. d
31. b 32. a 33. a 34. c

Chapter 11
1. d 2. d 3. b 4. a 5. d 6. d 7. d 8. d 9. d 10. d
11. b 12. a 13. d 14. d 15. d 16. c 17. d 18. d 19. a 20. d
21. d 22. d 23. d 24. d 25. d 26. c 27. d 28. a 29. c 30. c
31. b 32. d

Chapter 12
1. d 2. d 3. c 4. a 5. b 6. c 7. b 8. a 9. c 10. d
11. d 12. d 13. d 14. b 15. c 16. a 17. c 18. a 19. d 20. c
21. a 22. d 23. b 24. d 25. d 26. d 27. d 28. a

Chapter 13
1. d 2. d 3. d 4. d 5. d 6. c 7. c 8. a 9. a 10. c
11. b 12. d 13. d 14. d 15. d 16. b 17. c 18. d 19. d 20. b
21. c 22. c 23. a 24. d 25. b 26. d 27. d 28. d 29. b 30. d

Chapter 14

1. d	2. a	3. d	4. d	5. b	6. d	7. b	8. c	9. b	10. d
11. d	12. d	13. d	14. b	15. d	16. d	17. d	18. a	19. a	20. a
21. a	22. c	23. b	24. d						

Chapter 15

1. d	2. d	3. c	4. c	5. a	6. d	7. a	8. d	9. d	10. d
11. d	12. d	13. b	14. d	15. c	16. b	17. a	18. d	19. d	20. c
21. d	22. c	23. b	24. d	25. c	26. b	27. d	28. b	29. b	30. a
31. d	32. b	33. d	34. d	35. d	36. a	37. a	38. d	39. d	40. d
41. b	42. d	43. d	44. a	45. d	46. d	47. d	48. a	49. c	50. d
51. b	52. d	53. c	54. b	55. d	56. c				

Chapter 16

1. a	2. d	3. c	4. a	5. c	6. c	7. b	8. c	9. c	10. a
11. b	12. d	13. a	14. a	15. c	16. a	17. b	18. c	19. a	20. d
21. d	22. c	23. c	24. c	25. b	26. c	27. b	28. b		

Chapter 17

1. b	2. d	3. d	4. d	5. b	6. d	7. d	8. d	9. d	10. d
11. d	12. c	13. a	14. a	15. b	16. b	17. d	18. c	19. d	20. c
21. d	22. d	23. c	24. c	25. b	26. a	27. b	28. c	29. d	30. c
31. b	32. b	33. d	34. a	35. d	36. b	37. d	38. a	39. a	40. c
41. d	42. d	43. d	44. b	45. d	46. a	47. a	48. c	49. a	50. b

Chapter 18

1. c	2. d	3. d	4. d	5. d	6. a	7. c	8. c	9. a	10. d
11. c	12. d	13. b	14. d	15. d	16. d	17. d	18. b	19. c	20. d
21. d	22. d	23. b	24. d	25. a	26. d	27. d	28. b	29. d	30. d
31. b	32. c	33. d	34. d	35. d					

Chapter 19

1. d	2. c	3. d	4. d	5. d	6. b	7. d	8. d	9. b	10. b
11. c	12. c	13. a	14. a	15. b	16. d	17. d	18. d	19. d	20. b
21. d	22. b	23. d	24. d	25. c	26. d	27. d	28. d	29. c	30. d
31. c	32. a	33. d	34. b	35. c	36. d	37. c	38. c		

Chapter 20

1. d	2. d	3. b	4. d	5. a	6. c	7. b	8. b	9. d	10. d
11. d	12. c	13. a	14. a	15. a	16. d	17. d	18. a	19. d	20. d
21. a	22. a	23. c	24. b	25. c	26. b	27. b	28. b	29. a	30. d
31. c	32. d	33. d	34. d	35. c	36. d	37. d	38. b	39. c	40. a
41. d	42. d	43. c	44. a	45. d					

ANSWER KEY

Chapter 21

1. b	2. c	3. a	4. d	5. d	6. d	7. d	8. d	9. d	10. b
11. d	12. d	13. b	14. c	15. d	16. d	17. d	18. b	19. d	20. d
21. c	22. b	23. a	24. d	25. b	26. a	27. a	28. a	29. d	30. d
31. d	32. d	33. b	34. d	35. d	36. a	37. b	38. a	39. d	

Chapter 22

1. d	2. d	3. c	4. a	5. d	6. d	7. d	8. d	9. b	10. d
11. d	12. d	13. b	14. d	15. d	16. d	17. d	18. b	19. b	20. c
21. d	22. b	23. d	24. b	25. d	26. d				

www.ingramcontent.com/pod-product-compliance
Lightning Source LLC
Chambersburg PA
CBHW082147230426
43672CB00015B/2862